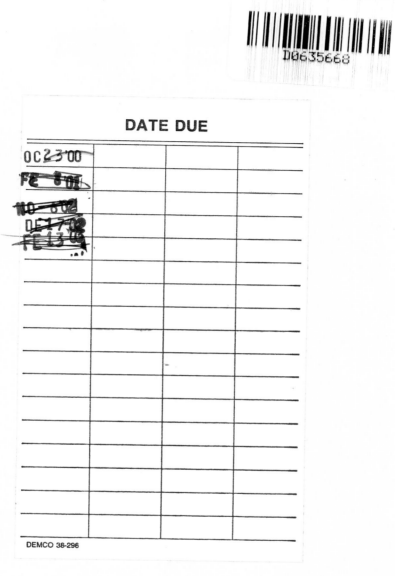

DATE DUE

OC 23 '00			
FE 8 01			
NO 8 02			
DE 17 02			
FE 13 03			

DEMCO 38-296

ALSO BY WILLIAM KNOEDELSEDER

Stiffed: A True Story of MCA, the Music Business,

and the Mafia

IN

EDDIE'S

NAME

IN

EDDIE'S

NAME

One Family's

Triumph

over Tragedy

BRYN FREEDMAN

WILLIAM KNOEDELSEDER

ff

FABER AND FABER, INC.

FARRAR, STRAUS AND GIROUX · New York

Faber, Inc.
r, Straus and Giroux
19 Union Square West, New York 10003

Copyright © 1999 by Bryn Freedman and William Knoedelseder
All rights reserved
Distributed in Canada by Penguin Books Canada Limited
Printed in the United States of America
Designed by Abby Kagan
First edition, 1999

Library of Congress Cataloging-in-Publication Data
Freedman, Bryn.
    *In Eddie's name : one family's triumph over tragedy / Bryn
Freedman, William Knoedelseder. — 1st ed.*
        p.   cm.
    ISBN 0-571-19924-0 (alk. paper)
        *1. Juvenile homicide—Pennsylvania—Philadelphia—Case studies.
2. Murder victims' families—Pennsylvania—Philadelphia—Case
studies.   3. Polec, Edward William, 1978-1994.   I. Knoedelseder,
William, 1947-   .   II. Title.*
    HV9067.H6F68   1999
    364.15′23′0974811—dc21   *99-34886*

DEDICATION

To our parents—
Bob and Mary Freedman and Evelyn Freedman,
and Bill and Lorraine Knoedelseder
—who taught us how to love.

And to our children—Matt, Colin, and Halle—who are teaching us why.

In memory of Deb Hebert

IN

EDDIE'S

NAME

I

The evening of November 11, 1994, was crisp and clear in Philadelphia. Winter was in the wind, but the annual onslaught of ice and snow was still at least a month away.

In the quiet middle-class neighborhood of Fox Chase, John and Kathy Polec sat in their living room, working their way through a pepperoni pizza and watching *Picket Fences* on TV. They didn't notice when police sirens wailed in the distance. It was 10:30 on a Friday night and they knew where their children were: nineteen-year-old Kristie was away at college, and sixteen-year-old Eddie and fourteen-year-old Billy were no more than six blocks away, hanging with their pals either at McDonald's or at the Rec, the Fox Chase Recreation Center. As always, the boys would be heading home soon, on foot, in time for their eleven o'clock curfew.

"I decided to take the job," John said. "I told them at the office today that I'll be leaving at the end of the year."

Kathy smiled. John worked a 70-hour week at three different computer programming jobs, one of them a two-hour daily commute from Fox Chase. The new job wouldn't bring in any more money, but it would eliminate the drive. So John would have ten more hours a week to spend with the family, time to shoot pool in the basement with the boys or to work with her around the house. It wasn't exactly hitting the lottery, but Kathy believed their life was about to get better.

At 10:50 p.m. the phone rang. It was Father George Strausser from St. Cecilia's, where all the Polec kids had gone to grade school.

"How ya doin, Father?" Kathy bubbled. "John and I were just—"

The priest cut her off. "Kathy, there's been an accident here at the church and . . . uh . . . it's Eddie. You and John should come right away."

Kathy went cold. "What do you mean? What kind of accident? Is he all right?"

Father Strausser hesitated for what seemed an eternity. "Just come," he said.

Heart pounding, Kathy ran to grab a coat, shouting over her shoulder to John, "Eddie's been in some kind of accident at the church."

John was up from the couch. "I'll go; you stay here." He figured Eddie and some of his buddies had broken a church window with a soccer ball. Worst case, they'd been caught with a couple of cans of beer as well. But Kathy was already halfway out of the house when he caught up with her. She was sure Eddie had been hit by a car.

St. Cecilia's was less than half a mile away. They drove straight down Solly Avenue, past rows of modest, red-brick duplexes with white trim, all exactly like their own. Except for the late-model cars parked at the curb, the street looked just as it had when John and Kathy were kids. That was the main reason they'd moved to Fox Chase a dozen years before. It reminded them of the neighborhood in nearby Olney where they had both grown up. Like the rest of the city, Olney had changed over the years. But Fox Chase seemed frozen in time. Bordered on two sides by the deer-filled woods of Pennypack Park, it had somehow survived as a small pocket of early sixties innocence, a scene straight out of the TV show *Happy Days*. Drugs were not a serious problem. There hadn't been a murder in nearly two decades. An occasional fistfight over a girl was what passed for teenage violence.

John turned left onto Ridgeway Street and came to a stop at the corner where Kathy worked part-time as a crossing guard. It was the perfect job. She'd always been home when the kids came in from school, and from her post just seventy-five yards from the playground, she'd watched over them during recess as well.

John hung a right, then a quick left into the rear entrance of the school grounds. That's when they saw the flashing lights. At least five police cars and an ambulance were parked in a semicircle around the front steps of the church, where a small crowd was gathered. John gunned the car across the parking lot and lurched to a stop fifteen feet from the ambulance.

As they jumped out of the car, Billy came running up. His fists were clenched, his arms were rigid at his sides, and his face was drained of color.

"A bunch of kids jumped him," he said, his voice breaking. "They hit him with a baseball bat."

John ran to where police were holding people back. He saw paramedics lifting a limp form onto a gurney. There was blood on the ground, lots of it. A patrolman blocked his way. "I'm his father," John shouted. "I'm sorry, sir, but I can't let you through," the cop said. "They need room to work."

John turned and saw Kathy pushing her way through the crowd toward him, flanked by Father Strausser and Sister Judith, one of the nuns from St. Cecilia's. "They won't let us near him," he said. Kathy stood on her tiptoes to see over all the shoulders. She recognized one of the cops from the neighborhood and was trying to get his attention when she heard him say to another officer, "Oh God, that's not the mother, is it?" She started to shake uncontrollably.

John moved through the crowd to the ambulance. He opened the door. Eddie lay on his back, eyes closed, with a pink rubber brace around his neck. The paramedic who was hunched over him wheeled around and shouted, "Get out of here." John drew back as if he'd been slapped, and the door slammed in his face.

Father Strausser herded the three of them—John, Kathy, and Billy—back to their car. "They're taking him to Einstein Hospital," he said. "To the trauma unit there. You follow them; I'll meet you."

The ambulance flew out of St. Cecilia's with the Polecs right behind. Barreling through Cheltenham, John fell a few lengths back and another car got between them. "Go around them, John," Kathy pleaded. "I need to see Eddie!" It was the first time he'd heard her speak since they'd left the house.

No sooner had he passed the car than the ambulance slowed to the speed limit and the siren fell silent. "Why aren't they going faster?" Kathy asked, panic rising in her voice. "Why are they slowing down?"

John didn't respond, because he feared the answer. If they'd lost Eddie, there would be no more reason to rush. "Please, God, don't let this happen," he prayed. "Please don't let this happen." Suddenly the ambulance speeded up and the siren came back on. The rest of the way to the hospital, John prayed to the driver, "Please keep that ambulance going; don't slow down."

At the hospital, the ambulance roared up to the emergency room, while a uniformed guard diverted the Polecs to a parking spot by the lobby entrance. They bolted through the glass doors. "Is he still alive?" were the first words out of John's mouth when he reached the desk. The receptionists had no information yet. The family was escorted to a small waiting room. Behind the double doors they could hear pandemonium in the ER—people running, shouting, rolling equipment across the floor. John paced; Kathy sat dazed, playing back the events of the early evening, when she had last seen Eddie.

She was going out Christmas shopping and there wasn't much food in the house. So she gave the boys $5 for McDonald's and dropped them off on her way—Billy at the Rec, Eddie at a friend's house. As Eddie got out of the car, she told him what she always told him: "I love you, please be careful." He responded as he always did: "I love you, too, and I always am." Then that immense smile. What had happened? What went wrong?

She looked over at Billy, slumped in a chair, looking lost and bewildered. He seemed to sense her unspoken question. "There was a fight, Mom, but Eddie didn't have anything to do with it. I don't know why they went after him."

"Who are 'they'?" she sobbed. "Where did they come from?"

Billy honestly didn't know. His mind was on instant replay, too, trying to figure out how a normal Friday night had turned into such a nightmare.

When his mom dropped him off at the Rec it was early, a little after 6:00 p.m., and nobody was around yet. So he cut across the railroad tracks to McDonald's. On any given weekend night, somewhere between the Rec, McD's, Pizza Hut next door, and Stoxy's Steaks across the street, you could find pretty much every kid in Fox Chase under the age of eighteen. And sure enough, he ran into some old pals from St. Cecilia's, wolfing down Big Macs in a booth by the window. Something was up, they told him. There had been an incident in the parking lot last Friday. A carload of girls from another neighborhood. Some kid from Fox Chase had tossed a cup of Coke through their window. It landed right in the driver's lap. Now that same car was back, a red Plymouth Duster, same girl driving but with a bunch of guys, too. They were swerving at kids on the street, shouting stuff like "Better watch your ass; you're gonna get it."

Billy was heading back to the Rec when a small white car full of kids cut him off in the McDonald's parking lot. The back door flew open and some guy he'd never seen before screamed at him, "You f—ing pussy! Tell the Rec we'll be back at ten o'clock to kick their asses." As the car sped away, Billy scrambled through the hole in the back fence of McDonald's, crossed over the railroad tracks, and slipped into the safety of the Rec.

The Rec wasn't a building; it was a park—four square blocks of baseball diamonds, soccer fields, and basketball and tennis courts where Fox Chase kids gathered to play, hang out, make out, smoke cigarettes, and sometimes drink beer. With lots of trees and no roads, the Rec was a teenage safe haven—police cars couldn't patrol it and approaching adults could be spotted hundreds of yards away, allowing plenty of time to ditch whatever you were doing and run like hell. Kathy and some of the other parents regularly patrolled the Rec themselves on foot, trying to keep the mischief to a minimum. Some of them had grown up in Fox Chase and knew what went on, because they'd done it when they were teenagers. Still, there'd never been a serious incident at the Rec that anyone could recall.

Billy met up with Eddie and a group of the older boys near the main ball diamond. They'd paid a twenty-one-year-old "runner" to pick up a half keg at the beer distributor down the street. Eddie and Mark Hanson fronted the keg money. They'd make back their investment plus a nice profit, selling cups for $4 apiece, refills free. Problem was, they had no cups and no more money to buy them. So Billy was pressed into service. "Just go get 'em," Eddie said. "I'll pay you back later, I promise."

Billy protested, but went anyway, even though he knew Eddie wouldn't let him drink a drop of the beer. "You're too young," he'd say. "It wouldn't be right." Billy idolized his big brother. Not because he was a football star, an A-student, or a campus stud. Eddie was none of those. But he had a way with people that was awesome. Eddie was a magnet for fun, always at the center of a social whirl, on the phone, planning, organizing, getting a group together to do something, the bigger the group the better. Tonight was typical. Eddie wasn't even much of a beer drinker; he couldn't be, what with their mom making them blow in her face every time they came home. But for Eddie, it wasn't the beer that mattered, it was the jokes and the laughter and the good time had by all. As far as Billy could tell, his brother didn't have a serious bone in his body, or a bad one either. He had as many girl friends as guys, and he could charm the pants off any parent. He'd even got Grandpa to laugh about it last year when he shaved his head shiny as a cue ball. "Eddie could talk to a brick wall and get the wall to talk back," their dad always said.

The keg had arrived by the time he got back with the cups. It was heavy, so they all took turns lugging it down to the lower field, the farthest point in the park from prying eyes. When a cop car cruised by and flashed its spotlight across the field, they rolled the keg into a culvert and dove for cover. When the danger passed, they resumed their trek to the traditional keg site, in the clump of trees behind the kickboard on the soccer field overlooking Ferndale Avenue. Kids wandered in from all directions—boys and girls, fourteen-year-olds to eighteen-year-olds. There was no sex or age segregation in Fox Chase; younger siblings and their friends were always welcome, so long as they didn't "sip the suds." Eddie sold his cups and held court, cracking up everyone, including himself, with his trademark bad jokes poorly told. Billy suspected his brother sometimes blew the punch lines on purpose because everyone had come to expect it. Hearing Eddie screw it up was funnier than the joke itself.

Billy mentioned his run-in with the white car. Others said they'd had similar encounters and heard warnings about a ten o'clock "showdown." But nobody knew what it was all about or took it very seriously. When the beer started running out around 9:30, people began drifting toward McDonald's, drawn as much by custom as by curiosity. It was a weekend ritual to touch base back at the fast-food hub, grab a bite, and maybe call your parents from the pay phones in front of Stoxy's to say you were okay and on your way home.

When Billy got back to McDonald's, the place was buzzing. There'd been more sightings of cars full of kids that nobody knew, more taunts, more threats of impending retribution. Some kids from the neighborhood had retaliated by throwing rocks at the red car. But they hit the wrong car, and a woman suddenly burst into McD's yelling about her broken window and demanding a phone to call the cops. Time to split! Kids bailed out of the booths and made for the hole in the back fence. They heard a squeal of tires, but it wasn't the police arriving, it was "them," several carloads worth. Doors flew open and kids jumped out, some with bats in their hands. Billy scrambled up onto the tracks and turned to see them pouring through the fence behind him. He ran across the parking lot of McGarrity's Body Shop to Rockwell Avenue, opposite the Rec playground. Looking back again, he saw Bill Oehler surrounded in McGarrity's lot, getting kicked and punched by half a dozen pursuers. John Atkinson rounded the corner of the building, running for his life, arms hugging his head to cushion the blows from the bats. Atkinson went down, and Billy winced as he watched someone stand over him and whack him hard with a bat. He heard shouts from the Rec and saw a group of Fox Chase kids charging to the rescue. He joined in, but by the time they reached their comrades, the invaders had disappeared through the fence. Bill Oehler seemed okay, but John Atkinson was definitely messed up—he couldn't see straight and wasn't making much sense.

They regrouped on Ridgeway Street, midway between the play-ground and St. Cecilia's Church. There was a lot of excited chatter: "Who were those guys? What are they so pissed off about?" News of the fight was spreading like a Malibu brushfire. Eddie trotted up from the tracks, relieved to find Billy unharmed. Eddie's girlfriend, Bernadette Dietrich, came running down the street with her friend Maryann Redlinger. He quieted her fears with a hug and a kiss on the forehead, and told how the retreating mob had blown right by him without stop-ping. Within minutes the crowd had grown to about twenty and the incident seemed destined to become just a colorful piece of neigh-borhood lore. Then a local kid named Ha Pham drove up to report that he'd just seen the intruders getting into their cars at McDonald's. He thought he recognized a few of them as street toughs from his old neighborhood in Feltonville. "If it's them," he said, "you don't want to be around when they come back."

Having seen more than enough excitement for one night, the crowd quickly dispersed. A handful of kids climbed into Ha's car; an-other group guided John Atkinson through the back yards to his house several blocks away. Others struck out across the tennis courts. Bernadette and Maryann went to visit Maryann's grandparents, who lived just across the street and a few doors down. Billy, Eddie, Keith Flannigan, and Sean Gara started up the block toward St. Cecilia's, bound for home half an hour ahead of curfew. They were fifty yards from the church when they heard a shout from somewhere in the Rec: "Here they come!" They turned to see a procession of headlights rounding the corner by the playground—two, three, four, five cars. The caravan slowed for a moment, then roared up the street, coming right at them.

"Shit, let's go!" Keith hollered. The four of them crossed Rhawn Street at full tilt and tore across the parking lot between the church and the convent. But there was no way to outrun the cars. Sean kept running straight ahead, but Billy, Eddie, and Keith veered right toward the tree in front of the rectory, where they stopped for a few seconds as the cars pulled past them to cut off their escape. Then, with the cars facing in the wrong direction and people piling out, they sprinted back the way they had come. Now it was a foot race. They fanned out across the parking lot, with Eddie closest to the church. Crossing back over Rhawn Street, Billy heard contact behind him. Keith had been tackled and was now squared off against his attacker in the middle of the street. Billy grabbed him by the hood of his sweatshirt. "C'mon, man, there's too many of 'em."

Maryann's grandparents lived three doors down from the corner. The boys bounded up the porch steps and pounded on the door. Maryann let them in and slammed the door behind them. Billy collapsed on the couch, heaving. When he caught his breath, he looked around and saw that his brother wasn't in the room. "Eddie's still out there," he said, leaping to his feet. "I gotta go back for him."

Keith blocked the door. "Are you crazy?" he said. "Eddie probably ran around the corner of the church, hopped a couple of fences, and is home by now." Everyone, even Bernadette, agreed he shouldn't go. Billy gave in. "Yeah, I guess you're right," he said. "I'm sure he got away. Everybody always gets away."

They went to the window and saw neighbors on the sidewalk, looking up toward the church, moving that way. A police car pulled up by the church entrance, where a handful of people were gathered. This time Billy charged out the door. As he ran toward the church, he heard a girl crying, "Oh God, somebody please help." A policeman was talking into his car radio: "This is 0–3. Rescue in progress. We have a young male down, going in and out of consciousness." When Billy reached the patrol car, Brian Watson suddenly stepped in front of him and grabbed him by the shoulders. "Bill, come on over here with me and sit down," he said, pulling him to the side. "Get off me," Billy screamed. "Let go!" He shoved Brian out of the way, took three steps, and froze. There was Sharon Donahue sitting on the pavement, sobbing, cradling his brother's head in her lap. Eddie's eyes were open, the left one gyrating crazily. Blood was everywhere.

The doors to the ER opened and a young doctor approached hesitantly, looking as if she wanted to be anyplace in the world but there.

"You'll be able to see your son soon," she said to John and Kathy. "But not for very long, because we have to get him upstairs for a CAT scan."

"How is he?" John asked, for all of them.

"He's alive. He's lucky we had the people we did on duty tonight, because he coded twice."

"Coded?"

"Cardiac arrest—his heart stopped. Our biggest concern right now is the pressure on his brain, caused by the swelling. We have to relieve that, and we'll know more after we see the pictures."

The doctor handed Kathy a bag containing Eddie's personal effects—wristwatch, wallet, and pocket change. Kathy collapsed back into the chair, her heart beating so fast she thought it might explode in her chest. Eddie's clothes had been cut off in the ER. She sat looking at his jeans and shirt in her lap. All she could see was blood.

Kathy closed her eyes. This couldn't be happening. It was what she had feared most, from the moment the doctors placed Eddie in her arms in the delivery room. Sweetness and gentleness just poured out of his eyes. Not like Kristie, who arrived like a prancing thoroughbred, announcing to the world, "Here I am, and you're in a run for your money with me." As a baby, Eddie was so placid and even-tempered that Kathy once took him to the doctor thinking something must be wrong.

Growing up, Eddie couldn't hold a grudge for ten minutes; he was utterly incapable of sustaining anger. When he made the soccer team at age ten, the coach lauded his natural talent but lamented his lack of competitive edge. Instead of teeing off on his opponents, taking them out of plays, Eddie would chat up the visitors on the field. "Is it this humid where you live? Do you have cows there?" Eddie's problem, the coach said, was that he was more interested in people than in winning. "Please watch out for your brother," Kathy always told Kristie and Billy. "He's a lamb and the world is full of wolves."

After about an hour, the young doctor appeared again and took them into the ER. Eddie looked better than John had expected. He was unconscious and his head was swaddled in thick bandages, but the only visible sign of damage was a two-inch-wide bruise running like a railroad track down his left cheek, the imprint of a bat. Kathy leaned over the bed and pressed her head to his chest. "You're a strong boy, Eddie, you're gonna be all right," she whispered. She looked up at John. "He *is* gonna be all right, isn't he?" All John could say was "We gotta hope, Kath."

As Eddie was being wheeled to the intensive care unit, John was directed to the admissions desk to fill out all the necessary insurance forms. It was there he noticed the crowd—between seventy-five and one hundred Fox Chase kids and their parents jamming the entrance to the ER, so that nobody could move, with more people arriving every minute. He couldn't believe it. He asked the security guard if they could all be moved into a waiting room. "I've been trying to do that for an hour, sir," the guard replied. "I'd appreciate your help."

It wasn't in John's nature to step to the foreground and speak for his family. That was the role Kathy always played. She was the outgoing one who kept up most of their social contacts. Eddie was much more her child in that way. People who knew the Polecs invariably felt they knew John the least. He was the quiet one standing just behind his effervescent wife, offering a shy smile and a little wave. But Kathy wasn't here now and these people needed talking to. They were in pain, too, John thought. And they didn't come just because some kid they knew got hurt; they had come because it was Eddie.

So for the first of what would be countless times, John spoke to a crowd gathered in Eddie's name. "Kathy, Kristie, Billy, and I appreciate your coming down here like this at this hour," he said. "Ed's in very serious condition right now. But I promise that I will come back here whenever there's any development, to keep you informed about everything."

Three young girls were standing off to the side, arms wrapped around one another, tears running down their faces. John wasn't as good as Kathy at keeping track of the kids who hung around their house. "Is one of you Bernadette?" he asked. The petite blonde with big brown eyes stepped forward. Now he remembered. Eddie always talked about "Bern's eyes." He took her by the hand. "Why don't you come upstairs with us," he said.

In the fourth-floor ICU, Eddie looked worse than before, in part because of all the equipment—intravenous tubes feeding into both his arms, a ventilator plugging his mouth like some sort of scuba gear, monitors beeping digital readouts of his heart rate and other vital functions. Only a small swatch of the boy they knew remained visible, from his nose to his forehead. "His brain is swelling and we can't get the pressure down," the young doctor said. "It's getting worse."

Then a hospital administrator appeared. There was a new anti-swelling drug available, she told John. "It's experimental, meaning it hasn't been approved by the FDA yet, so we'd need your consent to administer it." John quickly signed the form she handed him, then began reading the small print. It said the drug was part of a national study in which half the patients would be given the drug and half would be given a placebo. "You mean there's no guarantee Eddie will even get the drug?" he asked. "That's correct," the woman replied.

"I don't understand how anyone could withhold this drug if they thought it might help a patient who could die without it," he said. She was sorry, the woman replied, but that's how the experiment worked and she couldn't do anything about it. John ripped up the paper and handed it back to her. He sat for a while in the waiting room, fuming, then sought out the woman and asked her for another form to sign. "I guess half a chance is better than no chance at all."

Sometime later, another woman appeared with a notepad and pen in hand. She needed to ask some questions about Eddie: What kind of person was he? What were his likes and dislikes? "Your son has suffered a lot of damage," she explained. "It's going to be very hard for him to get back to normal. We'd like to get some idea tonight what normal is for him, so we'll know what we're shooting for."

Buried somewhere in that brutal assessment was a bit of good news, John thought. At least they were talking about the future, about the possibility that Eddie might survive the night. More good news arrived just before dawn. "The swelling has stabilized," the doctor reported. "It's not getting any worse. We've induced a coma and he'll likely remain in this state for some time. It could be days or weeks."

John exhaled for what seemed like the first time since he saw the ambulance in front of St. Cecilia's. He'd been trying all night to contact Kristie at the College of St. Francis de Sales in Allentown, but her answering machine kept picking up. He was afraid she'd hear about Eddie on the radio or from a friend who read it in *The Philadelphia Inquirer*. Allentown was an hour's drive. If he went now, he'd be there before she woke up.

The doctor said something else that was heartening. Even though Eddie couldn't respond to them, he could probably hear what was going on, "so it's good for you to keep talking to him." Billy had found something in Eddie's wallet, a quote from the Bible typed on a tiny strip of fortune-cookie paper. He started repeating it to Eddie like a mantra: "Humble yourself at the face of the Lord and he will lift you up."

Before heading to Allentown, John stopped by the house to pick up some books Kathy wanted to read to Eddie, two of his favorites from childhood—Rudyard Kipling's *Rikki-Tikki-Tavi* and *The White Seal,* the story of a baby seal who flees with his family from hunters who would club him to death for his pelt. Eddie still kept them in his room, sharing shelf space with his Pearl Jam CDs. Before leaving the house, John called Kristie again and this time left a brief message.

Kristie opened her eyes at 7:30 a.m. for no reason she could figure. Her alarm clock wasn't set to go off for another three hours. The red light on her answering machine was flashing. She rolled out of bed and pushed the replay button. "Hi, Kristie, it's your dad. Eddie's been hurt and he's in the hospital. Mom and Billy are with him and I'm on my way to get you, so just stay there."

She stood stock-still, trying to comprehend the message. If Eddie had a broken arm or leg, her father wouldn't be coming to get her. So it had to be serious. She dialed Mary Ellen Douglass, her mom's best friend, who lived up the street from them. Mary Ellen was evasive. Eddie had been "jumped by some kids," she said, "but your father will tell you the rest."

"Tell me what?" Kristie screamed into the receiver. "Is Eddie dead?" No, he was alive, Mary Ellen assured her, but that was all she could say. "Your father will fill you in on everything when he gets there."

For the next ten minutes Kristie careened around her room like a pinball in play, throwing on her clothes, trying not to throw up, and talking to herself: "If Eddie's not dead, then he must be dying or Mary Ellen wouldn't have acted like that. But Dad wouldn't leave him if he was dying, so he must be okay." She was almost out the door when she remembered Eddie's Christmas present, a red flannel shirt she'd bought for him just the other day. It was all wrapped and ready to go on her closet shelf.

She was sitting on the curb with the present in her lap when John arrived twenty minutes later. "Let's go back up to your room and I'll tell you what's going on," he said. "No," she said, getting into the front seat. "I want to go to the hospital right now. You can tell me on the way."

She'd never seen her dad look so awful—dark circles around his eyes, like a raccoon, his face pale and pinched with pain. "It doesn't look good," he sighed. "We don't know if he's going to make it, but there's a chance." She began to pray out loud: "Please, God, let him live." But John interrupted. "No, don't pray that he lives; pray that he lives *normally.*"

Nothing her dad told her in the car prepared Kristie for what she saw when she entered the ICU. Eddie's face was now discolored and swollen beyond recognition. Blood soaked through the bandages around his head, and more was draining from a tube in his mouth. Milky liquid dripped from his ear. A metal shunt protruded from his forehead, inserted by the doctors to relieve the pressure on his brain. The ventilator was forcing his chest to rise and fall in exaggerated, mechanical bursts. "Hi, Eddie, I brought your Christmas present" was all she managed to get out as a greeting. She laid the package on the bed, picked up his hand, and squeezed it. "Wake up, Eddie," she repeated again and again. "Please come back."

But Eddie was never coming back. The doctors knew that now. The CAT scan, MRIs, and X-rays showed some of the worst "blunt-force trauma" they'd ever seen. Every bone in his left cheek was crushed. His skull was shattered like an eggshell, fractured in seven places. His brain had actually rotated on its stem from the force of the blows. The cerebellum was destroyed, unable to keep his heart beating.

The doctor in charge pulled John out into the hallway and gave him the grim prognosis: they could keep Eddie "technically alive" with machines and drugs until everyone had a chance to see him, but there was no possibility of recovery. And even though Eddie was brain-dead, he could still feel, the doctor said. "We're pretty certain that your son is in pain."

John slumped against the wall, speared by the thought of Eddie in some unfathomable form of agony while a machine forced air in and out of his lungs and drugs revved his heart. "You have to stop it," he said. "Stop everything. It's not right to keep him breathing just for our benefit."

He asked for a few minutes to tell the others, but when he went back into the ICU he didn't have to say much. Kathy was still bent over Eddie's bed with her head pressed to his chest, eyes closed, hearing nothing but the crazy beating of his struggling heart. The others in the room—Billy and Kristie, Kathy's two brothers and their wives, Father Strausser and Bernadette—could tell from the look on John's face that it was all over. He stood by the bed and touched his wife's arm. "They can't keep him alive any longer, Kath. They have to turn off the machines." She didn't respond. Nobody moved except to wipe away tears. They stood transfixed as a doctor came and flipped a switch on the monitors. All the blinking lights and graphs went dark. Then two nurses pulled the IVs out of Eddie's arms, removed the breathing tube from his mouth, and shut off the ventilator. His chest rose and fell one final time. "I'm so sorry," one of the nurses said as she left.

Kristie looked at the clock on the wall. It was 10:30 a.m. The alarm in her dorm room would go off any second. She closed her eyes and waited, praying she would hear it and awake from this horrible nightmare. Instead, her Uncle Jerry, the cop, put his arm around her shoulder and whispered in her ear, "We're gonna get the bastards that did this."

Cut off from the stimulating drugs, Eddie's heart gradually stopped. Kathy felt it happen, and when it did her heart seemed to fail as well. Her knees buckled and she slumped to the floor. John caught her and half-carried her to the waiting room, where Father Strausser found a wheelchair. Everyone followed them out of the ICU, so John went back into the room alone. He stared for a moment at the form on the bed, wondering if his son was still in there. Nobody knew the exact moment the spirit departed. "Switch with me, Eddie," he said. "You be me and I'll be you. Because it isn't fair what happened. You shouldn't be the one dead. It should be me. I'm not old, but I've lived. I've married and had a family. You deserve that, too, and you didn't do anything to deserve this. So whaddya say?"

His monologue was interrupted by a hospital orderly apparently coming to take the body away. "Oh, I'm sorry," the young man said. "I can come back later. We can leave him here as long as you want, in case anyone else wants to see him."

"It's all right," John said. "I'm finished. You can take him now. I don't want him on display."

On the way out of the hospital, they passed through the waiting crowd from Fox Chase. They didn't have to say a thing.

Back at the house, John lifted Kathy out of the car and carried her up the basement stairs to the couch in the living room. The place was soon filled with people—neighbors, friends from the old neighborhood whom they hadn't seen in years, nuns and priests from St. Cecilia's, Eddie's teachers from Cardinal Dougherty High School, and many of his friends. Everyone, it seemed, brought some sort of dish. "You gotta eat," they kept saying. Billy eventually retreated to his room, where he wrote Eddie a letter. "You are my hero, and I miss you," it began. John went out into the back yard by himself. It was a beautiful, sunny Saturday afternoon, and Eddie was dead. He could not reconcile the two.

It was after midnight before everyone left. What was left of the Polec family fell asleep huddled together in the living room—Kathy on the couch, John in the green chair next to her, Kristie and Billy on the floor curled up under blankets at their feet. Eddie was gone, and they knew that their lives had been changed forever. But they couldn't foresee how strong a force he would remain in their lives, or how great a change was coming.

2

Kathy sat bolt upright in the dark with a stabbing pain migrating across her abdomen. The sheets were soaked.

"Wake up, John," she said, shaking him gently. "I'm in labor."

He rose groggily to one elbow. "Are you sure?"

She rolled her eyes. It's not a pain a woman mistakes for something else, not if she's already been through childbirth. Plus, she had the sheets to prove it.

"My water broke while I was sleeping," she said. "We have to go to the hospital now."

He was out of bed in an instant, hurrying on his clothes. It was 3:00 a.m. She hated getting him up, because he looked so tired from shoveling snow. Sixteen inches of it had fallen in eight hours the day before, wet and heavy stuff that packed into ice. As soon as it had started, John moved their car around the corner, facing downhill on Second Street. The red '74 Mustang II was terrible in the snow and he wanted to make sure they didn't get stuck on their little side street. All day long he'd kept digging the car out. When the snow reached six inches, he trudged a mile and a half to her parents' house to borrow a set of tire chains. He couldn't drive there for fear of losing the parking space.

As Kathy readied herself for the hospital, John got two-year-old Kristie up and zipped her into her pink snowsuit. The plan was for him to drive the toddler over to Kathy's folks, then come back and pick her up. But the minute he walked out onto the front porch he knew they were in trouble. A snowplow had just moved down Second Street—he could see its blinking lights receding in the darkness—and had buried the Mustang up to its windows. He'd be an hour digging it out again.

"This isn't good, John," Kathy grunted through another contraction. "The baby is coming."

They had reason to believe this would be a problem childbirth. Tests at three and six months had indicated the baby was in breach position. Alarmed, but not panicked, John called the community ambulance service.

"You're in luck," the dispatcher reassured him. "Our night driver lives just a couple of blocks from you and the vehicle is parked right in front of his house. He should be there in a few minutes."

Thirty minutes passed and no ambulance arrived. Kathy's contractions were coming practically on top of one another. John called again. "You won't believe it," the dispatcher said. "A snowplow went down Second Street and buried the ambulance. They're almost done digging it out. Tell her to hang on and they'll be there shortly."

It was another fifteen minutes before there was a knock at the door. Two paramedics, flushed with exertion, stood on the porch, stamping snow off their boots. They couldn't get the ambulance onto the side street because of the snowbank created by the plow. And they couldn't use the gurney either, because the drifts were too deep. Kathy was going to have to walk the hundred yards to the vehicle. And there wasn't enough room for all of them in the back. Kristie and John would have to stay behind.

So Kathy went alone, bent double with pain and sinking up to her knees in the snow. Inside the ambulance, the paramedics propped her up on the gurney, and she watched out the window as John and Kristie waved goodbye from the front porch. He looked sad, she thought, and so young. Today was his twenty-fourth birthday.

She remembered the day he'd first shown up on her radar screen. Sixth-period lunch at Cardinal Dougherty High School. Her pal Karen was falling for a boy named Sam, and she wanted to find a date for another boy who'd also asked her out. "So do you want to meet this guy John?" Karen asked. "He's really nice." Kathy laughed. "Sure," she said, "I'll take whichever one you don't want."

He called a few days later and asked her to the movies. Their first date was on March 19, 1971—the feast of St. Joseph. He was seventeen and told funny jokes. She was sixteen and had to be home by eleven o'clock. They went to see Love Story and both of them cried. He asked if he could kiss her good night on her doorstep. Immediately afterward he asked her to his senior prom, which was two and a half months away.

When John introduced Kathy to his mother, Mrs. Polec instantly recognized her as the youngster whose Easter-basket ducklings used to follow her all over the neighborhood. "You're the little duck girl," she said. John and Kathy went out every weekend—movies, miniature golf, bowling. They just seemed to fit together.

They started talking about getting married toward the end of her senior year, but they knew they had to wait for John to get his degree in Business Administration from Drexel University. So she took a job as a legal secretary, lived at home with her parents, and saved her money while she and John endured two more years of good-night kisses and raging hormones.

There'd been an ice storm on their wedding day, too. A neighbor had carried Kathy from the house to the car for the ride to the church so her dress wouldn't drag in the melting slush. John had decorated the Mustang with red and blue crepe-paper flowers that bled together and turned into balls of mush when they got wet. The ceremony took place at her parish church, Incarnation, with a full Mass and fifty people in attendance. The reception was held at a little restaurant called The Shack, on Roosevelt Boulevard. She remembered the owner, Nick, laughing when they first approached him about having it there. "Nobody gets married in January," he boomed. "But you two look like babies and I love you, so I'll take care of it. A sit-down dinner with chicken, and I'll give you a good deal." They had a dj who played rock 'n' roll oldies and one particularly gooey Bobby Vinton song over and over again. She and John had danced till they nearly dropped.

They spent their wedding night in the little second-floor apartment they'd rented overlooking the ball fields of the Fox Chase Rec Center. The next morning they walked up the steps to St. Cecilia's and went to Mass. Then they flew to Disney World for their honeymoon, catching the last flight out of Philly before the airport was closed on account of the weather. Kathy came down with a cold in Florida and couldn't swim the whole time. It was on the second or third night there, they figure, that she got pregnant with Kristie.

"Don't push! Don't push!" the paramedic practically shouted as he coached Kathy through another contraction. It was hard not to. But she knew that one good push and the baby would be born right there in the ambulance. At the hospital the paramedics hustled her through the ER entrance. Her obstetrician, Dr. Vincent McPeak, was waiting just inside the doors. He conducted his examination trotting alongside the gurney as it rattled down the corridor to the delivery room. She was 100 percent di-

lated and fully effaced. "You're gonna be fine, Kathy," *he said.* "We're almost there, try not to push."

*As she watched the ceiling tiles tick past, Kathy thought about the
baby. She was hoping for another girl, but every relative and girl friend
who'd patted her tummy predicted it would be a boy. So she and John
hadn't even discussed girls' names, and they disagreed on boy names. She
liked Matthew Steven, but John wanted Edward William, after his father
and hers. Between contractions she decided that because it was John's
birthday and he couldn't be with her for the birth, he should get his wish.*

*In the delivery room the doctors, nurses, and attendants performed
with the precision of a Marine rifle team. Everyone locked into position.
As another contraction roiled up, someone grabbed her hand.* "Okay,
Kathy, get ready. Now! Push, push, push!"

*Edward William Polec was born at 4:47 a.m., January 21, 1978.
Weighing 8 pounds, 10 ounces, he entered the world fanny first, shooting
out of the birth canal* "like a football," *in the words of Dr. McPeak, who
made the reception.*

3

Detective Tom Perks had a bad feeling about the day ahead. Five coffees
into his shift, he was sitting at the "up man's" desk when Captain John
Appledorn walked into the squad room. The head of Homicide rarely
made an appearance on Sunday, but at 10:00 a.m. on November 13, he
was in and giving orders.

"Two Squad's got the Polec job," he told Perks. "You're up." Perks
nodded. He'd figured this was coming. Yesterday he'd seen some of the
paperwork, and the story was all over KYW Radio. A Fox Chase

teenager beaten with bats, and on the steps of his family's church, for chrissakes. Earlier the kid was critical; now he was dead.

"Christ," Perks said under his breath. With twenty-seven years on the job and six of those in Homicide, he knew this case would be a bitch. What he had here was "a murder in the middle of a riot," which meant multiple suspects and lots of witnesses to interview. Getting the "doers" would take every man on the squad, maybe more. And the media was already on this like white on rice. That always made it worse.

Perks looked around the squad room. Gray November light strained through the dirty windows. The place was a dump, with battered metal desks and industrial gray-green walls that looked as if they'd needed a paint job since the late eighties. The Homicide Division was on the first floor of Philadelphia Police Headquarters, called the Roundhouse, a four-story circular building on the corner of Eighth and Race Streets. It was just a few blocks from the tree-lined parks and graceful brick buildings that made up Independence Mall, home to the Liberty Bell and the nation's first state house. That was where Thomas Jefferson and John Adams had made friends and laws, and where members of the Continental Congress argued, drank, and ultimately signed the Declaration of Independence. But the Roundhouse had little in common with its historic neighbors. The building was a blasphemy of architectural experimentation, famous for nothing but its cheap materials and wasted space. Still, Tom Perks loved it here, loved the guys in his squad—Art Mee, Dominick Mangone, Bill Danks, Frank Jastrzembski, and Manny Santiago—the five best cops Homicide had to offer, he thought, all smart, hardworking, and funny as hell.

Perks knew the guys wouldn't be too thrilled to get the Polec case. And by rights, it shouldn't be their job. After all, the kid was beaten Friday night, when Three Squad was up. But something about this case stuck in Perks's craw. Part of it was the almost medieval brutality of the murder. Baseball bats were once a weapon of choice in Philadelphia, but there hadn't been anything like this in years. Then there was the fact that the dead kid was a former altar boy and a senior at Cardinal Dougherty High. And he was murdered on church property. Perks was a Catholic and, in his own way, a man of faith. But it wasn't so much the Catholic thing. He'd feel the same if it was a Jewish kid killed on the steps of his synagogue. It was more the feeling that nothing was sacred anymore. The more he thought about it, the more he steamed. By God, he thought, this cannot be tolerated.

He threaded a blank form into the thirty-year-old Remington in front of him and typed the case number on the top of the page— "H-94-366," indicating that Eddie Polec was the 366th homicide victim in the city of Philadelphia in 1994. Eventually there would be hundreds of forms, boxes of evidence, diagrams, charts, and photographs in this case. But for now there were only a few cold facts on a single sheet of paper.

> On Friday 11/11/94, 7th District personnel responded to a radio call of "fight on the highway" at 500 Rhawn Street. Upon arrival on the scene, they observed the body of a white male later identified as Edward Polec, who was bleeding from the head. The victim was taken to AEMC by Medic Number 12, where he was admitted listed in critical condition. On Saturday 11/12/94, the victim was pronounced dead at 10:24 a.m. by Dr. Tojino. A post mortem examination was conducted by Dr. Hood at the Office of the Medical Examiner and the cause of death was determined to be multiple trauma to the head and the manner of death a homicide.

Perks slipped the report into a file folder and watched as a batch of Fox Chase teenagers and their parents were escorted into the main squad room, then taken one by one to the small interview cubicles. They were clearly shaken; some appeared to be still in shock. The girls especially were emotional, breaking down in tears frequently as they tried to reconstruct for detectives the events of Friday night. Each one named six or seven other potential witnesses, but their descriptions of the attackers were all over the map. "Mostly white guys," said one. "Six or seven black and Puerto Rican guys," said another. "A mix of black, Asian, and Hispanic males and white females," said a third.

By early Sunday afternoon it was clear to Perks that the people who had killed Eddie Polec were strangers to him and his friends. Still, the Fox Chase kids seemed nervous about something. The detectives knew there'd been beer at the Rec before the fight—a case or a keg, depending on whom you talked to. And it quickly became evident that the kids actually believed the cops might lock people up for underage drinking or throwing rocks. The detectives tried to explain that the Homicide Division wasn't in the business of running down minor teenage infractions, but the teenagers had trouble making the distinction. In their world, getting caught drinking beer was a huge deal; their parents would kill them. They were basically good kids, Perks thought, but terribly naïve. Here he was trying to catch a bunch of killers and they were worrying about getting grounded.

As the day wore on, Two Squad began following up a lead from Northeast detectives that at least some of the attackers might have attended Abington High School. The detectives knew they had to move fast, before the kids talked too much among themselves, heard too much from the media, or lawyered up.

The Abington group was not at all what Perks expected. Abington is just across the city line from Fox Chase in Montgomery County, where row houses give way to gated estates and country clubs and where it's not unusual for teens to have new cars, cell phones, and beepers. But despite their affluent, suburban upbringing, many of these kids seemed much tougher than the Fox Chase crowd, a whole lot more street smart and far less intimidated by the police. Some of the girls in particular grated on Perks—they snapped gum, wore too much makeup, talked too loud, and, he thought, lied through their teeth. Not one of the boys expressed any sympathy for the victim, and while they talked like witnesses, they acted more like suspects. Whatever happened on Friday night, the Fox Chase kids had been way over their heads mixing it up with this crew.

By late afternoon Perks was no closer to an arrest than he'd been when he walked in that morning. He needed some air. "Yo, Art," he called across the squad room, "let's take a ride."

Art Mee was Two Squad's resident tease, a self-described "shit disturber" who prided himself on his ability to irritate his colleagues anywhere, anyplace, anytime. "Gimme the keys," he said to Perks. "I wanna get there in one piece."

As Mee headed the brown Chrysler north on 1-95, he could see that Perks had that glassy-eyed, faraway look he always got in the middle of a complicated investigation. Trying to shake his friend out of the doldrums, Mee started scat-singing his favorite Coltrane riff. "Jesus, will you shut up," Perks responded, right on cue. "The day's goin' bad enough already."

At forty-eight, Perks was the senior member of Two Squad, but only by a couple of months. Still, he was considered the grandfather of the group, an old-fashioned 1950s kind of cop—unflappable, methodical, and utterly relentless. He'd been married for twenty-four years and had three children, two boys and a girl—just like the Polecs. His daughter was a registered nurse at Albert Einstein Medical Center, where Eddie had died.

Mee had his own emotional connections to the case. He also had two boys and a girl. His cousin John was a cop who worked with Kathy's brother Jerry in the Seventh District. His brother Michael was "Mr. Mee, the music teacher," at St. Cecilia's, where he'd taught Kristie Polec the clarinet. His mother lived just up the street from the Fox Chase McDonald's.

The two men drove in silence through the Northeast section of the city. This was the heart of hardworking Philly, where most of the city's Irish- and Italian-descended cops and firefighters lived. It was a place where unions were still strong, Democrats still dominated, and people talked in terms of parishes, not towns.

They stopped the car in front of a modest two-story brick house on Rhawn Street, the home of Annette and John Atkinson, whose seventeen-year-old son, John Jr., had very nearly become a second murder victim Friday night. Annette was an artist; John Sr. owned a moving company and coached St. Cecilia's basketball team. It didn't take a detective to see that the couple's life revolved around their youngest son. The Atkinsons' home was filled with his basketball trophies.

John Jr. was the captain of his high school team, the leading scorer, and an honor student to boot, the Atkinsons told the detectives. He'd known Eddie Polec since second grade and they'd remained friends through the years. They were a funny pair. As John grew to 6 foot five, he dwarfed Eddie, who was more than a foot shorter. But they always seemed like equals. When John played in basketball games, Eddie kept score; when Eddie worked at Boston Chicken, John was one of his best customers. It was only yesterday morning that John had learned the gang that beat him had killed Eddie. "I found him slumped on the kitchen floor with the phone in his hand," said Annette. "He was sobbing, 'Little Eddie Polec is gone. They killed him; they killed little Eddie Polec.'"

As his parents spoke to the detectives in the kitchen, John Jr. huddled in the corner with an ice-filled towel wrapped like a turban around the baseball-sized lumps on his head. In addition to depression, he'd been suffering blackouts and had trouble focusing his thoughts. And he remembered very little of what had happened Friday night.

He recalled cutting across the Septa tracks heading to McDonald's from a party at the Rec when someone started yelling, "Run . . . run!" The next thing he knew, he was on the ground and there was a kid standing over him with a bat raised above his head. "I remember screaming," he said. "I remember curling up into a ball." But that was all; he didn't remember what the kid with the bat looked like. He started crying.

"This really sucks," Mee said as they walked back to the car. He could practically see his own house from here; Perks lived only a few miles away. The older detective shook his head sadly. A good boy like that with a bright future, now he was a mess. All that care, all those family dreams; it might take him years to recover. Maybe he'd never be right again.

Still, Perks thought, the Atkinsons were better off than the Polecs. He didn't even want to think about what they were going through.

4

John Polec was alone in the basement the next morning, wondering how he was going to get through another day. Upstairs, his usually vibrant wife was curled into fetal position on the couch, staring straight ahead, unable to talk above a whisper. At five feet tall and less than one hundred pounds, she was a wren of a woman normally, but now she looked as if she'd shrunk by half, as if her body had collapsed to fill the void inside. He was afraid she might actually die from grief.

For his part, John was still functioning, albeit in zombie-like fashion, working his way through a surreal things-to-do list:

Tell my elderly, ailing parents that their oldest grandson was murdered.

John's mother just sat there on her living-room couch staring straight ahead, frozen in disbelief. His father was asleep upstairs; she'd tell him when he awoke. After several minutes of silence, John stood up and left. He had to get back to Kathy and the kids.

Identify Eddie's body at the morgue.

It wasn't like on *Quincy*, with the body in a pull-out freezer drawer. There was a plain metal desk with a TV monitor. A doctor sat across from him and read aloud part of the autopsy report, but all John heard were the words "multiple blunt-force head trauma." The doctor called someone on the phone and told John to look at the TV. The picture came on and he saw a close-up of a boy's body lying on a table. The boy seemed to be sleeping. He didn't look at all like Eddie. "Is that your son?" the doctor asked. John stared hard at the image, trying to find the face of the teenager he'd rousted out of bed at 6:15 Friday morning. Eddie could sleep like there was no tomorrow, John thought. Eddie held to the notion that a civilized society should never start the day before 10:00 a.m. Unfortunately for him, the first period bell at Cardinal Dougherty rang at the decidedly uncivilized hour of 7:40. "Okay, okay," he'd say when John stuck his head in the room to announce the time. Then he'd flop back onto the pillow, hoping he'd be able to sleep a little longer.

"Is that your son?" the doctor repeated. John focused again on the TV screen. The boy on the table was dead, his face battered and colorless, but yes, John had to admit, he did look somewhat like Eddie. He nodded his head and the screen went black.

Make arrangements for my son's funeral.

John walked to Wackerman's Funeral Parlor two blocks from the house, carrying with him Eddie's favorite picture of himself—the one with the white knit shirt buttoned to the neck, the smoky, serious look, and the hair just so. Eddie had given it to Kathy as a Mother's Day present, and the family always joked that it was his "*GQ* picture." John wanted Mr. Wackerman to have it so he could make Eddie look more like that and less like the boy on the TV screen at the morgue. Mr. Wackerman showed him an array of caskets in white, blue, and brown. John chose the brown because he thought the white and the blue looked too feminine. He didn't want Eddie to be embarrassed by the coffin.

Now John stood in the basement with a steam iron in his hand, pressing the clothes that Eddie would wear in that coffin. Determined that his son would spend eternity in comfort, he rejected the conventional coat and tie and chose instead the white pullover shirt Eddie always donned when he went out someplace special, a pair of well-worn jeans, and sneakers.

John stared down at the outfit laid out on the pool table. His father had bought the table twenty-five years ago and his mother had given it to him and Kathy when they bought their first house on Spencer Street. Now the battered old table sat smack in the middle of the basement at Solly Place, dominating the room and forcing people to walk around it on their way upstairs. In recent months, he and Eddie had gotten into a habit of shooting pool before they went to bed.

The nightly matches started simply enough. Eddie fancied himself a pretty good pool player, better than his dad, who never really used the old table. To Eddie's way of thinking, his old man was stuck in a time warp. Styles and fashions had changed a lot since 1970, when John was sixteen, but not much of John's appearance had kept pace, particularly his hair. Except for a few gray streaks, it was pretty much the same style and length it had been twenty-four years earlier, a last vestige of nonconformity. Eddie had a good time razzing his dad about his old-fashioned appearance, and one day the razzing turned into a bet. They'd shoot for John's hair; if Eddie won, his dad would get his long locks shorn.

The game was simple: the winner was the first to sink twenty-five balls. No other rules; no shots called; just sink the balls using any combination of skill and luck. To Eddie's astonishment, he lost. With his hair on the line, John suddenly remembered how to shoot. Eddie demanded the best out of three, so they played again, and Eddie won, but John came back to win the third. They agreed to a rematch the next night.

The rematches ended up stretching out for almost three months, night after night. Saving his hair gave John a chance to see Eddie differently. His son had become a friend. The kid who got more phone calls in a day than most people got in a week would answer the phone in the basement and say, "I'll call you back when I'm finished shooting pool with my dad." At times John even suspected that Eddie threw a game when it looked as if he was finally going to win the bet.

Last Thursday night, they had finished two games by 11:05. Exhausted, John was heading up the stairs for bed when Eddie called out, "Yo, Pops, rack 'em up one last time?" So they did, and Eddie won. They marked it on the chalkboard on the wall: tied at five games to five. Then Eddie went upstairs to work on a project for religion class while John turned off the lights and closed up the basement. Walking through the dining room, he had to step over Eddie, who was lying on the floor, scissors and construction paper all over the place, drawing a cover for the assignment. John marveled at his son's ability to wait until the very last minute to finish a project. "G'night, Bear," he said, as he went up to sleep.

For the past two days, the basement had been John's refuge. He was a loner by nature, and the constant stream of neighbors and friends who comforted Kathy had the opposite effect on him. When everyone left at the end of the day, he'd go upstairs and sit with her and talk if she wanted, or just sit quietly. In the meantime, he preferred to stay out of the way.

The basement was also John's guardpost. Like many Philadelphia homes, the Polec house is perpendicular to the street, with its main entrance around the side and up a small flight of stairs. As a result, visitors unfamiliar with the house invariably approach the front-facing basement door for entrance. From his vantage point by the pool table John could intercept anyone not known by the family, thereby protecting Kathy from prying eyes. He was determined that no stranger would see her in her present state.

At 11:30 Monday morning, two men wearing dark suits rang the basement doorbell. They introduced themselves as police officers—Detective Tom Perks and Sergeant Tom Burke from the Homicide Division—and said they were heading up the investigation into Eddie's murder.

John was surprised the police would come calling, since there wasn't a thing any of the family could tell them to help find the killers. But he asked them in, prepared to answer their questions. "We don't have any questions," Perks said. "We're here to answer any questions you might have."

John knew a few cops—Kathy's brother Jerry and a couple of the guys who lived around Fox Chase. But he'd never had any official dealings with the police. He didn't expect the department to give the family a thought as it went about the investigation. "We keep the families of victims informed," Perks explained, "so they don't have to search the newspapers or watch TV to find out what's going on. It's department policy. We'll tell you in advance about any developments, arrests and such."

Until that moment, John had had little hope that anyone would be charged, much less convicted in Eddie's murder. He figured the police would find out who'd been there, but guessed that confusion and finger-pointing would preclude a successful prosecution. Something about the two officers made him a little less pessimistic, though. He invited them upstairs for a cup of coffee, even let them stick their heads into the living room and introduce themselves to Kathy. She didn't respond. The three men sat at the kitchen table and spoke as casually as they could. Sergeant Burke mentioned that his mother worked with Kathy as a crossing guard on Rhawn Street. After they left, John felt oddly buoyed. Nothing would bring Eddie back, but maybe his killers would be brought to justice, and maybe that would help ease the pain. Maybe.

His spirits were lifted again later in the afternoon, when Kathy suddenly rose from the couch and began readying herself for the prayer service for Eddie at St. Cecilia's Church that evening. She was weak and trembly and moved slowly, but she was determined to attend. Half an hour before they were to leave, the basement doorbell rang again. A stranger wearing a PECO Energy uniform stood on the doorstep. "Is this the Polec house?" he asked. John nodded, and the man handed him a condolence card. He worked clear across town and had driven out of his way at the end of his shift. He said he found the house by knocking on every door in the neighborhood until he got the right one.

All day long the media had been arriving at St. Cecilia's, drawn by the crowds of youngsters standing vigil at the makeshift shrine that had taken shape on the spot where Eddie fell. What began as a simple way to cover the bloodstains on the pavement had grown into an elaborate display of teenage solidarity and grief. Scattered among the flowers, photographs, teddy bears, and testimonials were scores of ball caps bearing the insignias of schools all over the city.

It all made for great pictures, and the TV camera crews gobbled it up greedily. This would be the lead story on the nightly news, and the pressure to bring back compelling pictures was palpable. But the video they were really after was of the surviving family members, who hadn't been seen publicly since the murder. "Are the Polecs coming to the prayer service?" reporters asked anyone who looked as if they might know. "What do they look like? Will you point them out to us if you see them? Which entrance do you think they'll use?"

The reporters would be disappointed. Tipped to the presence of the camera crews, John arranged for a neighbor to drive them to the rear entrance of the rectory, and the Polecs entered the church through a passageway connecting the priests' residence to the sacristy, just behind the altar. Kathy was still wobbly and had difficulty negotiating the stairs, but she managed to make it to the front pew without falling or fainting. John saw that the church, which seats 1,000, was full of young people, some of them standing in the rear. The service began with a procession of 200 to 300 teenagers walking single file up the center aisle, each carrying a rose or carnation, which they laid at the foot of the altar. John learned later that Eddie's friend Glen Katchel, who didn't seem like the flower type, had gone to local florists asking for donations, and they'd responded with thousands of blossoms.

Midway through the service, Monsignor Dregar announced that Kristie was going to speak for the family. John was surprised; she'd said nothing to him about it. She walked to the front of the church, supported by her boyfriend, Brian. She'd been up most of the night thinking about what she was going to say. Truth be known, for most of her teenage years she hadn't wanted anything to do with Eddie. He was the quintessential kid-brother pest, forever doing things like sneaking up on her while she was studying and peering into her ears, just to annoy her. "Ed, get out of here and leave me alone," she'd holler, jumping up to shove him out of her room. Then he'd put on his puppy face and proclaim goofily, "But I love you so much, Kristie." It was hard not to laugh, but his inability to be serious about anything drove her crazy. She got along much better with Billy, who, like herself, had inherited their father's more serious nature.

It was only in the last year and a half that she'd begun to appreciate Eddie. She'd been working at Boston Chicken on Huntington Pike, and Eddie had hounded her for months to recommend him for a job there. Finally, she relented, even though he was only fourteen and had to get special working papers. To Kristie's amazement, Eddie turned out to be the most conscientious employee in the place, putting in long hours and priding himself on mastering each task in the operation without ever losing his sense of fun. When he worked the dishwashing station—the messiest job of all, guaranteed to leave you soaked to the skin and splattered with mashed potatoes and gravy at the end of your shift—he encased himself from head to fingertips to toes in plastic trashbags, so that he looked like a cross between a bio-hazard worker and Gumby. The other kids would gather around and howl with laughter. But at closing time, while they were picking bits of chicken out of their hair, he'd peel off his protective coating and stroll into the night as clean and cool as Cary Grant on his way to a cocktail party.

Working side by side with Eddie, Kristie got to see his effect on other people. She met all his friends, who began patronizing the restaurant just because he was there. And she saw how his co-workers, especially Chris Regel, the manager, adored him. She'd heard that when Chris learned of Eddie's death, he went to the restaurant before dawn, sat alone in the darkened kitchen, and cried.

She wanted to explain all this to the people gathered in the church, and she wanted to deliver a broader message. For the past two days, newspaper, TV, and radio reports had been saying that the murder might have resulted from long-standing bad blood between kids in Fox Chase and Abington, and that there was talk in Fox Chase of retaliation. But Kristie knew the news reports weren't true. Boston Chicken was located in Abington. The kids who worked there and hung out there were equally divided among the two neighborhoods, and there was never any trouble. She and Eddie had lots of friends from Abington.

"All of you who knew my brother know what kind of person he was," she said. "He was a gentle person, a forgiving person, and the last thing he'd want is for any of his friends to get hurt. So please let the police handle the investigation and don't do anything yourselves. Eddie was the kind of person that if you got mad at him he'd always bounce right back. I remember my dad sitting at the dining-room table trying to help him with his algebra. But Ed was so goofy and he wouldn't catch on. No matter how many times Dad explained it in the simplest terms, he wouldn't get it. Then Ed would start fooling around, saying, 'Oh, Dad, what's this for anyway? I'm never going to need this.' And then Dad would get so frustrated that one time he even threw the book across the room and hollered at Ed. But the next night Ed was right back there again asking Dad for help. He never dwelt on things. He never held a grudge. So let us heal. I have to believe the system will handle this. No one else should suffer and go through what my brother went through. I know that the best way to handle this is through the law."

Back at the house after the service, Kathy returned to the couch. John was down in the basement when his twenty-two-year-old nephew, Steve Esack, stopped by to see if there was anything he could do to help out. Steve asked for a beer, but all John could offer was some cognac from a dusty half-full bottle he found stuck in the back of a cabinet. They sat in the back yard and polished off two stiff drinks apiece before Steve decided cognac was not a good substitute for a cold Bud. So they walked two blocks to Sweeney's Tavern at the corner of Rhawn and Veree to buy a six-pack.

John had never been inside Sweeney's before, but everyone there seemed to know who he was. Several men at the bar offered to buy John a drink. John wasn't a drinker. With only sporadic sleep and little to eat since Friday night, he was already feeling the effects of the cognac. Still, he pulled up a stool and accepted one drink, then another. Ten minutes later, Steve had to help him out of the bar. One of the patrons who observed the scene was Pat Randles, the brother of Kristie's best friend, Ann. Randles's father, Pat Sr., coached softball with Kathy.

Pat immediately called his dad on the phone. "John Polec just left here in pretty bad shape," he said. "I think somebody ought to give him a hand." Pat Sr. threw on a coat and bolted out the door.

Kathy was drifting in and out of sleep when Steve burst into the living room. "You gotta get yourself off that couch and save your family," he said, grabbing her hands and pulling her to a sitting position.

"John's drunk and I lost him. The last time I saw him he was with some bald-headed man."

Kathy couldn't imagine John drunk. In twenty-four years she had never once seen him drink too much. John prided himself on being in control; he didn't know how to be drunk. Panicked, she called Mary Ellen Douglass, who came over immediately with her husband, Mark. The four of them piled into Mark's car and began driving up and down the streets of Fox Chase. Steve, who was more than a little potted himself, tried to explain what had happened. They'd walked from Sweeney's to the church so he could take some photos of the shrine. That's when the bald man had come up and started talking to John, and while Steve was snapping pictures, they disappeared.

Kathy racked her brain for every bald man she could think of. Matt McDonald? No, Matt told them he hadn't seen John since the prayer service. Johnny Anastasia was bald, but there was no sign of them at Johnny A's house; all the lights were off. After fifteen minutes, Mark finally spotted John in the middle of Wiley's Field, two blocks from home. Kathy jumped out of the car and ran to him. As she approached, she was relieved to see that the mysterious bald man was Pat Randles, Sr. himself. Funny, she never thought of him as bald. "It's okay, Kathy," he said, putting his arm around her shaking shoulders. "He's going to be all right."

John was sitting on a log, head down, legs splayed out in front of him, a picture of despair. "We have to try to go on, John," she said. "Kristie and Billy are at the house and they're scared. We're all scared. Please come home."

He looked up at her and she could see that he was crying. "I couldn't help Eddie," he sobbed. "I couldn't save him."

5

"Eddie, Eddie, the magical teddy; Eddie the wonderful bear."

Kathy sang softly to the child nursing at her breast. She loved the stillness at 2:00 a.m., the way the moon slanted through the window, the sound of the rocker on the hardwood floor. This was the only time she had alone with her year-old baby.

Gently stroking his cheek with her thumb, she searched his face. Just today she'd asked the doctor if there was something wrong with him. He seemed almost too sweet, too placid, "like he doesn't have a shell," she said.

"There's nothing wrong with this boy, Kathy," the doctor had chuckled. He pointed to Kristie, who was careening around the office and prying into everything. "If you want to worry, worry about that one; she's possessed."

Kathy had been reassured, but now, in the dark, her doubts returned. As if on cue, Eddie looked up, giving her that soulful smile that only mothers and lovers know. Kathy was overwhelmed by the feelings she'd had since the day he was born. This child needs protection, she thought, hugging him closer.

6

By Tuesday morning, Tom Perks had a massive investigation under way. He'd used every cop from Two Squad and a couple from Three Squad and had asked for backup from the Special Investigations Unit.

More than thirty kids had been brought in for interviews, some of them twice. Still, he had no one in lockup, no one had confessed, and there was not enough evidence to make any arrests.

What he did have, though, was a developing picture of what had happened that night:

Several carloads of kids drove from Montgomery County to Fox Chase for a fight that had been brewing for a week. The rumble had been the talk of locker rooms and study halls at Abington High School, where a soda-throwing incident at the Fox Chase McDonald's the previous Friday night had grown into a rumor that an Abington girl had been raped in the parking lot. The mob went to Fox Chase to avenge her honor. Problem was, there'd been no rape.

The girl who allegedly started the rumor had been questioned by Homicide detectives Sunday night. Now, there's a piece of work, Perks had thought to himself when sixteen-year-old Diane Costanzo walked into the squad room. With teased brown hair, long legs, and a defiant, hard edge, she looked closer to twenty-one. She seemed to intimidate her father, a small balding man who sat passively through the whole interview, as if there could be no question about his little girl's story. Perks got the feeling that Diane could tell him a lot, but she never did. Given her middle-class background, he kept thinking she should know better and feel worse. But to hear her tell it, she was a victim, too.

Punctuating her version of events with a great deal of sobbing, Costanzo told how she'd gone to Fox Chase the Friday night before the murder with her friend Jessica. They drove her red Plymouth Duster, following three male friends from Abington who pulled into the McDonald's on Oxford Avenue. The girls were eating a "two cheese-burger meal" in the car when some kids from Fox Chase started yelling at their friends, "You wanna fight? You wanna bang? I'll f—k you up, then I'll spit on your girl." Diane and Jessica yelled back at the Fox Chase kids, and before long there was a group of four or five of them in the parking lot. The Abington boys took off, she said, leaving her and Jessica alone, surrounded by the Fox Chase "mob."

"One guy got in my car as I was trying to leave. It was really horrible. They were throwing our food at us, and as we left, someone threw a soda in my car and spit all over us." When they got back to Abington, they told all their friends what had happened. "Anyone would," she told Perks with a toss of her hair. But no, she insisted, she'd never told anyone she'd been raped, no matter how many people said she did. As for Eddie Polec, he wasn't there that night, nor did she see him the following Friday. "When I heard he died, I got really upset," she said earnestly, "because I knew people were going to blame us."

"Jeezus," Perks sighed as he read through the witness statements. It was all such petty grounds for such a brutal killing. And no one who really knew what happened had been brave enough to come forward.

All that changed at 8:30 a.m. Tuesday when Thomas Crook walked into the Roundhouse accompanied by his girlfriend, Jennifer Carr, and his mother, Lois Rocanella. Several witnesses had told investigators they'd seen Crook throw a bat out of one of the cars on the night of the murder. Detectives Jimmy Dougherty and Leon Lubiewjewski were just about to pick him up for questioning when the desk sergeant called the squad room: "Hey, your guy's here."

A gangly, grungy eighteen-year-old with bad skin, bad teeth, and three silver earrings, he was red-eyed and shaking as he stood in the lobby. Looks like a poster boy for the term "scared shitless," Dougherty thought as he identified himself. The girlfriend and the mother were doing their best to calm him down, but they were a mess, too.

"My son wants to tell you something," Lois Rocanella said, struggling to get the words out. "A terrible thing happened. If my boy had been killed, I would hope someone would step forward and tell me who did it."

Dougherty immediately softened. This was one brave lady, he thought, turning her child over to the police with no lawyer, no nothing, just because it was the right thing to do. "Let's go talk upstairs," he said gently.

Tom Crook gave his statement in Interview Room A, an airless space furnished with a metal desk and a backless metal chair that was bolted to the floor. Dougherty could see that he was terrified and hurting, partly about what happened to Eddie Polec, but more about the pain he'd caused his mother, who'd raised him and his little brother and sister by herself.

At first pass, Crook provided a detailed narrative of the night of the murder. He told how he'd been recruited from Willow Grove Mall by a kid named Bou Khathavong. He, Bou, Carlo Johnson, and Zach Dallas picked up Rob Colefield, and the five of them then headed to Fox Chase, looking for a fight. Along the way, they met up with more cars full of kids that arrived almost simultaneously at the Fox Chase Pizza Hut.

"We all got out of the cars and started running toward the back of McDonald's to the tracks," he said. "We saw about twenty or thirty guys from Fox Chase back there. Some ran away; others started fighting with us. It seemed like we were fighting for five or ten minutes. I was fighting with some kid there, and then I seen Rob bleeding from the head and I just stopped fighting, because I was afraid the cops would come."

Crook described how the Montgomery County crowd piled back into their cars and drove to Rhawn Street near St. Cecilia's. "I seen about ten kids running back toward the church. All the cars pulled in and we jumped out. I could see one kid laying on the ground up near the front of the parking lot. It was the kid, Polec. He was laying on the ground and I ran up and punched him three or four times. He was covering his face. There was a lot of people hitting and kicking him. After that, I ran back to Zach's car and all of us went to Abington Hospital and Rob got about nine stitches."

Crook's story tracked with bits and pieces detectives had gotten from other interviews. Clearly, Bou Khathavong was one of the prime movers of the mob. In the hours before the murder, other witnesses said, he'd boasted in front of the Fox Chase 7-Eleven that he and his friends were "packing," and had hollered at a group of kids standing on a street corner, "Tell the Rec we'll be back for them at 10:15 and tell them there's no place to hide, baby." Then, only minutes before the attack, Bou was back at the 7-Eleven jumping up and down and yelling, "I'm so psyched I could kill someone."

But Jimmy Dougherty knew instinctively that Crook was holding back. "The truth's always the best way," he said. "Eventually we're going to find out everything anyway." The detectives left Crook alone in the interview room to think things over. When they returned fifteen minutes later, Dougherty was carrying a bat found at the murder scene. "We lifted your prints off this bat," he said. "What can you tell us about that?" It turned out later that the bat did bear Crook's thumbprint, but for now it was just a bluff, and it worked. Crook cried harder, and buried his face in his hands. Finally, he gave it up.

"Everything I told you was the truth," he sobbed, "except what happened at the church. As I was running up the hill, I seen a bat laying on the ground, on some grass. I picked it up. When I got to Polec he was still on the ground covering his head with his arms. I hit him three times with the bat, on the back of his shoulders by his ribs. Nick was there, too; he had a bat."

Nick Pinero was Crook's best friend. They'd met at Lakeside, a school for kids who'd been expelled from public high school or who had been placed there by the juvenile justice system. Crook had been sent to Lakeside after cutting twenty-eight days of school in two months. Bou Khathavong had been there, too.

"Did you see Nick hit anyone with a bat?" Dougherty asked. "Not exactly," Crook replied, "but at Abington Hospital he told me he hit the kid four or five times with the bat. Nick didn't know for sure, but he thought the kid was dead, and he was scared." Crook looked at the two detectives. "We didn't go there to kill anybody."

Perks was ecstatic. Crook not only provided the detectives with a detailed choreography of events leading up to the murder, he also drew them a diagram of the five cars in St. Cecilia's parking lot and named the drivers and most of the occupants of each vehicle—twenty-four kids in all. Before he was finished, he'd given investigators enough to charge himself and his two Lakeside buddies—Bou Khathavong and Nick Pinero—with murder.

It was time for Perks to keep his promise to John Polec. He picked up the phone. "We just wanted you to know it looks like we're gonna make three arrests today," he said. "We wanted you to hear it from us before you saw it on the news." John thanked him but didn't push for details, not even the names of the suspects. In Perks's experience, most people who have a loved one murdered tend to take out their pain and frustration on the police. They make demands that can't be met and ask for promises that can't be kept. John Polec was a man of tremendous dignity, Perks thought, a man who trusted them utterly.

Just before noon, Art Mee and Manny Santiago drove to Roslyn to pick up Bou Khathavong. The high school senior had been readmitted to Abington High that fall after a two-year stint at Lakeside. But even though it was a school day, Bou was home, suspended for cutting classes. He was standing in the open garage with his father when the detectives pulled into the driveway, a seventeen-year-old street punk: five foot three, baseball cap turned backwards, scraggly goatee, one ring through each ear and one in his nose. Quite the fashion statement, thought Mee, taking note of Bou's oversized T-shirt and baggy jeans, made for someone six foot four, with one pant leg rolled up to the knee and the other bloused around his sneaker. Bou came with an attitude to match his outfit. Sullen and insolent, he seemed to be put-out that he had to talk to a couple of cops. His father seemed resigned to the fact that his youngest son was in trouble again. He looked tired as Bou got in the back of the police car.

Art Mee chose the "scenic route" back to the Roundhouse, through Fox Chase and right past McDonald's. He watched in the rearview mirror as Bou went pale at the sight. Mee relished the moment. "That ought to knock you down a few notches, you cocky little son-of-a-bitch," he said to himself with a chuckle.

Manny delivered Bou to Interview Room B and started filling in the "229," police form-speak for a background report. This wasn't Bou's first encounter with the cops. His rap sheet included arrests for criminal trespass, probation violation, and resisting arrest. He was slouched down in his chair, mumbling his name, age, and address when Detective Frank Jastrzembski walked in and grabbed him by the nose ring. "Sit up and take your hat off or I'll pull you up by this," he barked, nearly bringing Bou to his feet. "You're a suspect in Eddie Polec's murder, and you know what you did."

At first Bou denied everything. "You got the wrong guy," he told them. "I wasn't even there."

"You're a liar," Jastrzembski spit back. "Your friends gave you up, so you'd better start talking."

"Okay, okay," Bou said. "I was there, but I didn't hit him." It was all the other guys, he said, naming Crook, Pinero, Kevin Convey, Dewan Alexander, Jeff and Jason Lange, Jason Mascione, and Anthony Rienzi as people he'd seen punch, kick, or club Eddie Polec. He described a sickening tag-team between Pinero and Rienzi, whom he called "Ants." "Nick starts to hit the guy with the bat, then I seen Ants hold the dude up and Nick is hitting the guy with the bat, then Ants drops the guy and Nick is still hitting him with the bat. By this time, we're all back in the car and it's just Nick and Ants; then Ants drops him and it was just Nick."

When detectives left him alone in the interview room for a few minutes, Bou added a kind of coda to his formal statement. He took a ballpoint pen out of the desk drawer, tagged the wall with the date, and scrawled, "Bou was here, murder is da case." Was it defiance or simply stupidity? It didn't matter to the investigators. They'd take it to court.

Nick Pinero didn't wait for the cops to come get him. His lawyer, Bernie Siegel, called Perks around 5:00 p.m. "What's the status of your investigation?" he asked. "Your client's about to be charged with murder," Perks replied.

Shortly thereafter, the youngster the cops considered the main "doer" in the Eddie Polec murder arrived at the Roundhouse with his parents and Siegel. Perks was prepared for sobbing, prepared for excuses and finger-pointing, even hysteria. He wasn't prepared for cold indifference. The sixteen-year-old walked into Homicide looking bored, as if he was being dragged to a photo session for a family portrait. He stared past Perks while his lawyer did most of the talking. He was a good-looking kid, five foot eight, with dark, slicked-back hair, deep brown eyes, and a struggling mustache. Perks could see why someone might mistake him for Puerto Rican. At Siegel's instruction, Pinero refused to answer questions about the night of the murder, providing only the information needed to fill out the "229"—name, rank, and serial number. Perks thought he'd never seen such arrogance. As far as he knew, here was a kid with no police record, no previous experience with the justice system, now looking at spending the rest of his life in prison. Yet he showed no fear.

At 8:00 p.m., Art Mee was escorting Bou to the men's room. Just as they got to the door, it swung open and Pinero walked out. The two friends paused for a moment, then Pinero spoke more than he had all night. "Hey, Bou, what up?" he said with a slow smile. "This ain't no thing. I'll see you tomorrow night at the Mall."

7

It was a Winnie-the-Pooh kind of blustery day, with the rain blowing sideways, bending trees and stealing hats.

Kathy stood in the doorway at 193 West Spencer Street, wondering if everything she owned would get soaked in the move. She ran her hand over the solid oak front door. She and John had saved months to buy it, and she'd refinished it herself, carefully staining the wood, then adding a hard polyurethane finish. It was a real beauty, inset with panes of amber glass framed by hand-carved flowers. If only she could take it with her to the new house.

Spencer Street had been the center of their universe for eight years. They had moved here when Kristie was only three months old, the first young couple on a street of immaculate 1920s row houses with double front windows and open porches, trimmed hedges and closely cropped lawns. John worked long hours, while Kathy taught Kristie to climb trees and ride a tricycle. Six months after Eddie was born, Spencer Street began its own baby boom. Mary Ellen and Mark Douglass moved in with a three-month-old boy, Sean. Shortly after that, a pregnant Linda Baraniewicz and her husband, Ed, arrived.

In Linda and Mary Ellen, Kathy found lifelong friends. They felt lucky that they "got in under the wire," as Kathy put it, before so much social and economic pressure pushed young mothers into the workplace. John was all for her staying home. His kids were going to have the benefit of a stay-at-home mom even if he had to work two jobs. And he often did.

Soon Kathy could count more than thirty kids on the block. "It's like watching a garden grow," she told John. Every day an assortment of mothers and children paraded up Second Street to Sturgis Park, the strollers and tricycles tied together with string so that none of the kids could stray. Kathy was the heart of it all, a tireless organizer who cleaned her house before the kids woke up, got dinner half made by breakfast, and packed a picnic lunch by 9:00 a.m.

Now Kathy's eyes rested on the oak banister, rubbed shiny from the many bottoms that had taken the express route from the second floor to the living room. She remembered the kids leaping from the stairs onto a pile of cushions on the floor, whooping and tumbling, pillows flying everywhere. She loved their athletic high jinks, though she had to admit they took it a little too far last winter with that toboggan trick.

The first good snow of the season they were all in the front yard putting the finishing touches on a snowman, when Kristie and Eddie complained about the cold. So she led the troops back inside. Somewhere between getting two-year-old Billy out of his snowsuit and making the hot chocolate, she realized that Kristie and Ed were being awfully quiet. Suddenly she heard the thump-thump-thump of plastic hitting furniture. She flew into the living room just as Kristie and Eddie launched their new toboggan from the top of the stairs—whoosh, across the foyer, out the front door, off the porch, down the front steps, across the yard, and smack into a snowbank. "Holy Mother of God," she hollered as she ran to them. "You kids could have broken your necks . . ." She stopped when she heard her mother's voice in her head, saying, "This is why God gives you children when you are young."

Besides, wasn't she the one who dragged the kids around rodeo style on the vacuum cannister while she cleaned? Didn't she join them as they jumped from rug to rug, shouting, "Watch out for the alligator pit." And hadn't she been the one to teach the kids to ride the couch cushions down the staircase. "Be sure to pull the pillows up between your legs; it gives you a little extra curl and you won't pitch forward." As Billy would say to her years later, "Mom, you were always the biggest kid of all."

But Spencer Street had changed, had grown less family-oriented. The kids outgrew the yard, and people with a scary dog moved in next door. Suddenly it seemed as if there was too much concrete and not enough country.

The new house, set in a leafy neighborhood of brick twin homes, seemed ideal. The place was a comparative palace, with four bedrooms, three bathrooms, and a back yard big enough to hold the steel swing set with T-bar and slide. The rooms were so open and airy that Kristie could practice her gymnastics easily, cartwheeling from the living room to the dining room. But the real reason Kathy was drawn to Solly Place was its feeling of safety, and its proximity to Pennypack Park, which had a creek, hiking and horse trails, and acres of hilly woodlands. Kathy pictured herself and the kids wading in the creek, tracking frogs and snakes, stalking deer, and swinging from the trees on the "Tarzan" rope. It was just the kind of Tom Sawyer paradise she'd been praying for.

A pounding on the door brought her back to the task at hand. Two moving men, soaked from the rain, pushed past her. "Where do you want us to start?" they asked. She pointed to the kitchen and watched as they splashed dirty puddles across the floor. She closed the door to the wind and the rain and sighed, "Why do we always have such awful weather whenever big things happen in our life?"

8

Wednesday morning, November 16, dawned to a hard, driving rain, the tail end of a hurricane that had swept up the East Coast from the Caribbean but veered back out to sea just before it was supposed to hit land near Atlantic City. At 7:00 a.m., John slogged half a block through the downpour to get a newspaper, hoping to learn more about the kids who'd been arrested. He got more than he bargained for. The front page of the *Inquirer* carried a picture of Nick Pinero as a youngster and another photo of Bou Khathavong. The accompanying article reported that a witness heard Eddie, surrounded by the mob in the church parking lot, screaming what were probably his last words: "I didn't do anything; I'm innocent."

John felt as if he was choking. The newspaper account stole from him the image he'd conjured of Eddie's last moments—running, then tripping, then being rendered instantly and painlessly unconscious. But no, Eddie had known, had seen, had felt the blows. John staggered back to the house and stashed the paper in the basement so Kathy wouldn't read it. She was upstairs, getting dressed for the funeral. John expected it would be a gut-wrenching replay of the scene at Wackerman's Funeral Parlor the night before.

First there'd been a private ceremony for the family. John had not wanted an open casket. He didn't want the world to see what the mob had done to Eddie. But Kristie argued forcefully that that was exactly what they should see, and finally John gave in. Mr. Wackerman had done a good job. Eddie was laid out in the comfortable clothes John had selected, with a Cleveland Indian cap placed almost jauntily atop his head. Around his neck was the gold chain with the letter *K* that the kids had given Kathy for her birthday years before. In his hand were Uncle Jerry's rosaries. Beside him a teddy bear, a special pen (he had collected pens), his favorite pool cue, and the Pearl Jam CD he'd listened to night after night during the pool tournament.

Then the crowd came—a line of people that circled the entire block and never seemed to get shorter. Judging from the signatures in the guest books, more than four thousand people waited for at least an hour and a half to pay their respects. John stood in the reception line, shaking a seemingly endless number of outstretched hands. His head pounded in the stifling heat and his right hand throbbed. Eddie's best friend, Nick, who'd flown in from Florida, had devised a little game to keep him going. Once or twice an hour, he'd warned, he would come through the line to see if John's grip was flagging.

Kathy sat in a hard-backed chair, arms upstretched, hugging each person who passed. She knew every child's name, and she seemed to inhale them as they came by. "They smell like Ed," she said, "like that combination of Drakar deodorant and hair gel he always wore."

"Do you want to go home?" Father Olson asked after several hours. Kathy shook her head. "I have to stay," she said. "It's one of the last things I'll be able to do for Eddie."

The kids kept coming, hundreds of them, sobbing and looking scared. They placed flowers in the coffin, more teddy bears, even their varsity letters. John Atkinson made an appearance but fainted when he got to the casket. "It just doesn't look like Eddie" was all he could say when he came to.

The very last person to pass was Jean Kohl. She'd been Kathy's high school English teacher and later taught Kristie. This year Ed had been in her class. All last summer Kathy and Kristie had teased him about what a tough teacher Mrs. Kohl was, warning him that all his charm wasn't going to help him get good grades with her. To their surprise, Eddie thrived in the class. When Mrs. Kohl presided over a mock murder trial of Oedipus Rex, he played the defense lawyer with gusto and got an A for his effort. "Mrs. Kohl really scares me," he told Kathy, "but I respect her and want to do a good job for her." Still, Kathy was skeptical when he chose *Dr. Zhivago* for his senior thesis project. She was sure he'd picked the book as an easy way out, because she remembered that *Zhivago* had been Kristie's senior thesis, too. But Eddie worked hard on the project and Kristie swore he never asked her for help.

As Jean Kohl leaned over to embrace Kathy, she whispered, "I corrected the preliminary papers on the senior thesis, and Eddie's was the best in the class. It was honors work." Kathy gulped. "My God," she cried. "He did it. He got honors for the first time in his life, and now he'll never know."

As John stood in the basement doorway, watching for the limousine that would take the family to the funeral, he noticed a police car parked just across the street. He ran out into the rain. "Is there anything wrong?" he asked the patrolman. "No, sir," the cop replied. "We're just keeping an eye on the house while you're gone, making sure there's no trouble."

Just another department "courtesy," but it unnerved John. What kind of trouble were they expecting?

The limo arrived at 8:30 and took the family to Wackerman's for a short final viewing and the agonizing closing of the casket. Afterward, they waited in the limo while Eddie's casket was loaded into the hearse. The windshield wipers kept a monotonous beat as they headed up Ferndale to Rhawn Street, then down Bridal Street toward St. Cecilia's. It was a short drive, less than half a mile, but it took nearly half an hour because of the massive traffic jam around the church. The funeral Mass was set to begin at 10:00 a.m., but by the time they pulled into the parking lot it was already 10:04. No one in the limo missed the irony. How many times had they said, as Eddie rushed out the door, "Ed, I swear you're gonna be late for your own funeral."

Once again, the church was packed to nearly double its capacity, the pews and aisles jammed with parochial-school children in their colored blazers and school emblems. The entire senior class of Cardinal Dougherty was in attendance. A thousand more people spilled into the street and parking lot, where Matt McDonald had hooked up a loud-speaker so they could hear the sermon and Mass as they stood in the rain.

"Anybody who knew Eddie Polec knew he was one of a kind," said Father James Olson. He recalled how Eddie had made the grade for altar boy so young that when he sat in the ornate side chair during the sermon, his feet didn't touch the ground and he swung them back and forth in the most distracting fashion. He remembered the undersized wrestler a few years later who was so determined to compete in the lightest weight class that he ran laps swaddled in trash bags to sweat off critical pounds. And he conjured the klutzy kid whose exuberance often ran ahead of his feet, telling about the time that Eddie, hurrying down the stairs of the rectory, had spilled a basket of strawberries destined for parish shut-ins into a puddle of oil in the parking lot. Eddie bent down and blithely began putting the berries back in the basket. "Don't worry, Father," he said with a grin. "We'll just kiss 'em up to God. A little motor oil never hurt anybody."

After the church service, there was another long, slow ride as the mile-long funeral procession wound its way to Our Lady of Grace Cemetery. It was still pouring rain as Kathy and John made their way to the tented gravesite. She was so close to blacking out that John practically carried her. Even the rose in her hand seemed too heavy to lift. "This can't be," she said to herself as she looked down at the coffin perched on the precipice of the grave. She remembered how afraid Eddie had been when her father, his "Pop-Pop," was buried. "It scares me so much that you have to be put in the ground," he told her. She had tried to be reassuring, saying, "That's not where Pop-Pop is; he's in our hearts and with God." Now all she could think of was how frightened Eddie must be. This can't be where my child is going to sleep, she thought, and she vowed never to return to the spot.

Back at home that night, John and Kathy resumed their positions—she curled up, almost comatose, on the couch; he in the basement, alone with the pool table and a pile of sympathy cards, at least a thousand of them. Billy came down the stairs, and John could see he was in bad shape. His face was swollen with pain, and there were dark circles around his eyes and lines pulling at the corners of his mouth.

"What's up?" John asked, thinking it must be the dumbest question in the history of parenting. Kathy was the one who talked to the kids, knew their friends, gave them answers. But this time Kathy couldn't be there for them. Billy paced back and forth but said nothing. "Come on, Bill, what's on your mind?" Billy stood at the basement door, glowering. John persisted. "Bill, I think you have to talk about how you feel."

Finally, Billy exploded. "Are you kidding?" he shouted. "Eddie's dead and I was there and I couldn't do anything about it and nothing's ever going to be the same again. What the hell else is there to say?"

John was standing now, too, his voice rising to meet Billy's. "You can't keep this in. You gotta talk about it; you can't handle it yourself." They were two feet apart, squared off as if ready to punch it out, all the pain and frustration of the past five days boiling out of them.

"I can't believe that you are doing this to me," Billy hollered. "Who are you to tell me how to handle this? What makes you think you know how to deal with this any better than I do?"

John knew Billy was right. What did *he* know about talking? The man whose kids called him "the world's biggest introvert" was asking his son to do what he couldn't do himself. He lowered his voice. "This isn't easy for me either," he said. "I just know neither of us can handle it alone."

They collapsed together on the couch. "I love you," John whispered, realizing that it wasn't something he'd said much as a father. Now he had a need, an urgency to say what he felt. For more than an hour they talked as they never had before. And with the pool table reminding them of Eddie, they made a pact: no matter what happened, they wouldn't snap under the pressure for at least forty years. They'd wait until Billy was fifty-four and John was eighty before going nuts.

They leaned against one another, propped up like a house of cards. They knew that if either of them caved in, the whole house would come down. But that wasn't going to happen.

9

For nearly a week, the Polecs managed to avoid reporters. But on Thursday, November 17, the media entered their lives—for better, for worse, and possibly for good.

The *Inquirer*'s headline read: VICTIM WAS HELD FOR OTHERS TO BEAT. Citing police sources, the article reported that "at least one and possibly two teenagers grabbed Polec by his shirt and pants after the mob knocked him down. Polec was then yanked to his feet and held upright so that two bat-wielding assailants could have a clean swing at him." For John Polec, reading such specific details of his son's death was the psychological equivalent of a bat blow to his own head.

Around 9:00 a.m. he heard Kristie hollering upstairs. "You should check your stories. All you print is hearsay." He found her standing in her bedroom, phone in one hand, the front section of the *Inquirer* in the other. "You should be ashamed of yourself," she practically screamed into the receiver, "twisting the word of a priest just to sell papers."

He knew immediately what she was on about. In a relatively innocuous paragraph buried deep in the article, the reporter referred to the funeral eulogy, writing that "Rev. James Olson remembered Polec as a mischievous teen with a knack for getting into trouble—and an even greater knack for getting caught."

Kristie didn't see John until he grabbed the phone from her hand. "Who is this?" he asked calmly. At the other end of the line was a mystified editor at the *Inquirer*'s city desk. "Listen," John said. "I'm sorry about that. Things are very upsetting right now; we didn't mean to bother you."

He hung up and turned to Kristie, who was standing with arms folded, furious. "Kris, there is nothing horrible here; no one wrote anything bad about Ed." She was unmoved. "They're making him sound like a bad kid, a troublemaker. I don't want anyone thinking that." But John figured it was really the other information in the article she was reacting to. Once again, he took the newspaper and stashed it in the basement, so Kathy wouldn't see it. A few minutes later, the basement doorbell rang. He looked out the window and saw a red Jeep Cherokee parked at the curb, with the logo *Inquirer News Tonight* emblazoned on the side. That was fast, he thought, assuming Kristie's phone tirade had triggered the visit. They probably think Eddie comes from a hysterical family.

But the woman on the doorstep wasn't from the newspaper. Margie Smith worked for the television arm of the *Inquirer* and she knew nothing of the phone call. In fact, she loathed the idea of knocking on the door of a bereaved family and intruding on their private grief. But she was a reporter and she had a job to do. This was an extremely high-profile case and no one had heard from the family. The Polecs had an unlisted phone number, and people in Fox Chase were being very protective, refusing to tell reporters where they lived. Apparently she was the first reporter to dig up the address.

As the door opened, she took a deep breath. "Is Mr. Polec home?" she asked, peering through the screen at the slightly built, graying man on the other side.

"I'm John Polec," he answered quietly. "Can I help you?"

"I'm so sorry to bother you," she said. "We were just wondering if you would like to talk to us. Everyone's saying what a great kid Eddie was, and we thought maybe there's something you'd like to say about him."

John paused for a moment. He'd never talked to a reporter before. "Let me discuss it with my wife," he said, turning and disappearing up the stairs.

No sooner had he left than Kristie appeared in the doorway, picking up right where she'd left off with the *Inquirer* editor. "All you news people," she railed, "you don't know anything about Eddie; you have no idea who he was. Why don't you get your stories right?"

Smith was stunned by the diatribe. "If you'd like to straighten us out, we'll listen," she said. "We want to get it right, so why don't you tell us what the real story is." She stood silently while the teenager vented at her. By the time John reappeared, Kristie was calming down, even apologizing for being so overwrought. John looked at Smith. "You did something for me," he said. "You showed her that not all newspeople are monsters. Now what can I do for you?"

What Smith wanted, of course, was the exclusive, the first interview with the Polec family. "As I said, we'd just like to talk to you on camera for a few minutes. We'd like to hear about Eddie."

It was John's baptism by sound bite, and he was fortunate to have a gentle coach. "Just look at me and pretend he's not there," Smith said, referring to the cameraman. "If you don't like something you've said or you stumble on a word, don't worry, we can start over."

In fact, John found speaking on camera surprisingly easy. "I think we raised these kids right," he said. "You say good night to them as they walk out the door, and you expect them to come home. You think back, *you* always made it home. Most kids make it home." He said Eddie's death had been particularly tough on Billy, who'd lost his best friend. "Are you afraid for Billy?" Smith asked. "Petrified," he said. "I could have had two sons murdered the other night, just like that." He snapped his fingers. "But the only way I can protect him is to lock him in the house. I sure wouldn't want to live like that. I know my Ed didn't want to live like that."

It was better than Smith had hoped. There was something so straight-from-the-heart, so unselfconscious about the way John spoke.

She turned to the kids. "Do either of you want to say anything?" Still a little suspicious, Kristie declined. But Billy agreed to take a turn. He started out speaking straight into the camera. The cameraman stopped rolling. "The only people who look directly into the camera are sleazy politicians," Smith said. "Regular people just talk to the reporter." Everyone laughed. The ice was broken.

Billy didn't want to talk about Eddie's murder or his own feelings. He wanted to talk about the kids in Abington. That morning's edition of the tabloid *Daily News* carried an inflammatory banner headline, next to a graphic of Abington's school crest. MURDER HIGH, it read, with the subhead "They're suspects in Fox Chase beating—and they're walking the halls in Abington." Billy was offended by the smear. "There's this misconception that Abington kids are bad," he said, "that this is the normal thing in Abington. But that's not how it is. I know from talking to people that these were just the very few kids who came up here. That's not what they are all like."

For the second time in as many days John had cause to marvel at the maturity and wisdom of his children.

Back in Margie Smith's newsroom, an editorial meeting was under way. "The papers are reporting a nun from St. Cecilia's called 911," said the news director, a recent transplant from Los Angeles. "So let's get hold of the tape and find out what she saw or heard." Others in the room were skeptical. Unlike in Los Angeles, they explained, the police department here never released 911 tapes outside of a trial. The Philadelphia police considered those tapes confidential intelligence information, not public record, despite the fact that the citizens of Philadelphia paid for the 911 system through a monthly surcharge on their phone bills.

"Great," said the news director. "First we'll ask for the tapes, and when they refuse, we'll sue the city for them. And I bet we'll win."

Across town at police headquarters, *Inquirer* reporters Tommy Gibbons and Jeff Gammage sat by themselves in the Roundhouse pressroom, just down the hall from the radio room, where 911 dispatchers take their calls. The two police reporters were trying to figure out how to keep the Polec story alive when a high-ranking police official came out of the radio room and walked over to them. "I've heard the tapes," he whispered, "and they're gonna blow the roof off the department."

Gibbons eyed the door nervously, hoping no other reporters would walk in. "What do you mean? What tapes?" he asked. "The tapes from the night the Polec boy died," said the official. "They are unbelievable, very damning to the department." He told them that the tapes indicated the 911 operators took repeated calls from Fox Chase residents that night warning of teenagers on a rampage with baseball bats. But the operators dismissed the callers and waited more than half an hour before dispatching a patrol car to the scene, a delay that probably cost Eddie Polec his life. "Anyone who's heard the tapes is fucking outraged," he said. The two reporters nodded calmly as they took notes, but as soon as the officer left they looked at each other and said simultaneously, "Hol-eeeey shit!"

On Thursday afternoon, John drove to Our Lady of Grace Cemetery. He'd screwed up on Saturday when he made the burial arrangements, buying only a single plot. He later realized there should be room for at least Kathy and himself there, too, so he went to buy the plots on either side of Eddie. That wouldn't be possible, he was told, because those plots were already sold, but he could buy the plots opposite Eddie. "Okay," he said as he wrote out the check. "When that day comes, I doubt any of us will care."

Afterward he walked over to the grave. There were at least a dozen people standing there, looking at the pile of dirt and all the flowers. The shrine outside St. Cecilia's had been dismantled and restored at the burial site. The poems, caps, mementos, and stuffed animals were all there, wet from the rain. He sorted them out and put them in the trunk of his car, because he didn't want them to be destroyed. He left a single koala bear propped against the metal marker that bore Eddie's name. It seemed right—a little bear for the son they'd called "Bear."

Back home, he found that Solly Place was rapidly becoming rumor central for worried parents. The story was all over the place that Friday night, the week anniversary, would see another round of bloodshed. The Abington kids were going to finish what was started; the Fox Chase kids were going to get even. The newspaper and TV reports were full of foreboding. "A grieving community is demanding that something be done to stop the violence," intoned one over-the-top TV reporter. "The police are braced for trouble," said another.

"What are we going to do?" visitors kept asking John. "How can we let our kids go out tomorrow night knowing there might be more trouble?" John had no answers for them. He was a computer programmer, not a cop or a social worker. He worked with machines, not people.

This was totally out of his league. Nonetheless, when a group of agitated neighbors came to the door at 9:00 p.m. asking him to go with them to patrol the neighborhood, he reluctantly agreed.

They drove to the Rec, which was eerily devoid of kids but full of cops. As they tromped through the bushes and across the playing fields, the others fell in behind him, as if he were their leader. Four police cruisers were parked on the grounds. John approached one and asked, "What's going on?" "Nothing," the driver replied. "Everything's quiet. And we'll be out in force the next couple of days to make sure things stay that way." John reported back to the group, hoping the officer's response would ease their fear. But it didn't, and he went home feeling miserable. What did they expect of him? He hadn't been able to save his own son. How the hell could he protect *their* children?

Kathy was asleep on the couch. John flipped on the TV to catch the news, partly to see if there was anything new about the investigation and partly to see if he'd made a mistake by talking to Margie Smith. He was relieved to see that she treated them kindly, even tenderly, and that nothing they'd said had been lost or distorted in editing, as he'd heard often happened with TV reporters. He switched to Channel 3 and saw the mayor, Ed Rendell, talking about the murder. "It's touched everyone in this city," Rendell said. "To have kids do that to other kids is almost unfathomable. The tragedy is just enormous." He switched to Channel 10, just as anchorman Ken Matz turned to the camera and announced he had "something to say to Mr. and Mrs. Polec." The night before, in a report about the arrests, a Channel 10 reporter had made a mistake during a live standup, saying that Eddie had been in reform school when he meant to say Tom Crook. The mix-up hadn't upset John, because it was so obviously a slip of the tongue, but apparently the station had gotten a lot of irate calls from Fox Chase. So now Ken Matz was looking right at him from the TV and saying, "We just want you to know we are sorry if we've caused you any more pain."

Sitting in his dark, silent house, John was hit by the unreality of it all. A week ago they'd been a normal family going about their quiet, unremarkable lives; now they were grist for politicians and newscasters, their most intimate loss on everyone's lips. All he wanted was to rewind the videotape to a week ago, when Eddie was still with them and the world knew nothing of the Polecs.

The next morning, lawyers for Philadelphia Newspapers Inc., publisher of the *Inquirer* and the *Daily News,* along with *Inquirer News Tonight,* formally requested that Police Commissioner Richard Neal release the content of the 911 tapes, arguing that it was public record under the state's Right to Know Act. To no one's surprise, the department denied the request. By now Tommy Gibbons and Jeff Gammage had obtained a partial log showing that 911 operators took a flood of calls from Fox Chase in the half hour leading up to the attack, but delayed sending a patrol car to the scene. They'd confirmed through numerous high-level police sources that the operators were rude to callers, even hung up on one. They'd learned that Commissioner Neal himself had listened to the tapes and had ordered an internal investigation. Clearly there'd been a major breakdown in the system on the night in question. Smelling a cover-up, the newspapers' editors immediately instructed their attorneys to challenge Neal's refusal in court.

Meanwhile, word of Margie Smith's scoop had flashed around all the newsrooms in town. Apparently the Polecs were finally talking. Calls from reporters started while John was having his morning coffee. "I'm sorry," he told each one. "There was a reason we did that one interview and we really want our privacy." Just before noon he got a call from Monsignor Dregar, the pastor at St. Cecilia's. Kristie was at the church with a bunch of other kids from the neighborhood. They'd heard talk of retaliation, there'd been an argument, and Kristie was upset. "John, I'm afraid somebody's going to get hurt tonight," the priest said, and although he never asked directly, John heard the message: everyone wanted him to go to the media and call for calm. So that afternoon he stood in the driveway for an on-camera interview with David Henry from Channel 6. Henry showed him a letter that had been sent around to parents of Abington High School students, urging them to keep their kids at home over the weekend. What did he think about the letter?

"It's probably a good idea," John said, "but I really don't think there'll be any further problems. The kids in Fox Chase would never shame Eddie's name by resorting to violence." He believed that people lived either up or down to your expectations. So all day long he kept it low-key, refusing to get drawn into any us-versus-them controversy. "We just want this whole thing to die down," he told Channel 3's Walt Hunter, "and for all the kids to go back to playing soccer and basketball and doing whatever kids do."

Late in the afternoon, police officials in the Northeast section of the city followed his lead, holding a joint press conference aimed at heading off further violence. "We urge the parents of Fox Chase and Abington to talk to their children," said Second District Commander John Norris. "Know where they are going this weekend, have them home before curfew, and find alternatives to hanging out on street corners or recreation centers." Abington Police Chief William Kelly added, "We are going to be out in force this weekend and we are going to be enforcing the law to the fullest extent. We urge kids in the various neighborhoods to listen to the Polec family—they have called for calm over and over again."

With the evening came rain, torrents of it, enough to deter anyone from taking to the streets in search of trouble. John would never know if it was his words or the weather, but there was no retaliation that weekend or any weekend thereafter. But there was trouble of another sort. At 6:30 Friday evening John got a call from Detective Tom Perks. "I'm wondering if I could come talk to you for a few minutes," he said.

Half an hour later, Perks and Captain John Appledorn, the chief of Homicide, pulled into Solly Place. They found John standing under a tree at the end of the street, smoking like a chimney. He was worried about Kathy's condition, and he didn't want her to know the officers were coming. Nothing they could say would make it better, and there was always the chance they'd make it worse.

The three men huddled under the branches in the rain. "There's going to be some news reports tonight," Perks said softly. "They're going to say the police were slow getting to the scene." John nodded. What difference did that make, he wondered. He already knew that Sister Judy at St. Cecilia's had called 911 when she saw the kids beating Eddie from her window. By the time the cops got there, it was too late anyway. Perks didn't have much to add. "We just wanted you to hear it from us," he said. John was touched by the visit, but a little confused. Why take the trouble to drive all the way out to the house when a phone call would have sufficed?

The whole family was in the living room at ten o'clock, when John switched on the news. The lead item on *Inquirer News Tonight* was the story Tommy Gibbons and Jeff Gammage had been working all week. Margie Smith was the reporter. "The attack that ended in Eddie Polec's death may have begun here last Friday night, at the McDonald's on Oxford Avenue," she said. "It was here that police dispatchers got their first call of a disturbance in the area, while Eddie Polec was still alive. The first call came in at 10:11 p.m."

John stared wide-eyed as a red-and-black graphic appeared on the screen and ticked off the call times: 10:14 . . . 10:21 . . . 10:35 . . .

"At 10:41," Smith said, "dispatchers finally notified police officers to go to the scene."

John grabbed the remote and switched off the set. Fortunately, Kathy had missed most of the story, understanding only vaguely that there had been a delay in the 911 response. But Kristie hadn't missed a thing. "Thirty minutes!" she cried. "Eddie wouldn't be dead if they'd answered those calls." John wouldn't let himself believe it. Accepting that Eddie had died because of a spilled soda was hard enough; to hear that it could have been avoided if the cops had done their job was more than his mind could absorb. "The story is wrong," he insisted. "What makes you think that this time the media got it right?"

IO

Kathy moved around the kitchen slowly, like a sleepwalker. It had been more than a week since Eddie's death and still she could manage to stand for only a few minutes at a time. Her friends Mary Ellen Douglass, Linda Baraniewicz, and Terry Gara were bustling about—cleaning up the house, putting away the dishes, covering the food, writing down the names of people she'd need to thank later for their kindness.

The three women were part of a larger female support group that had formed spontaneously the minute the news about Eddie broke. Their goal was to make sure Kathy was never alone. Working in shifts, beginning at daylight and stretching into the evening, they took turns holding her hand, bringing her water, feeding her, reading to her, or just sitting beside her as she slept on the couch. The first couple of days, they even helped her up the stairs, stood by while she bathed, and then tucked her into bed. They figured it was the least they could do. She'd poured so much energy into their lives, and the lives of their children, over the years. So for however long it took, they'd neglect their own households, husbands, and children to be there for her.

Their initial concern was that she might actually die from a broken heart or, worse, kill herself. It was a fear John shared. "I'm terrified of losing her," he'd confided to Mary Ellen. "I'm afraid she's never going to come back and be what she was before." His solution was to try to keep her sedated. Whenever she attempted to get up from the couch, he'd be ready with another dose of Tylenol PM, softly stroking her brow and saying, "Sleep, Kath, sleep."

Suddenly the boiling teakettle began to shriek behind her, and she collapsed to the floor as if she'd been shot. *"Eddieeee!"* she wailed.

Linda quickly turned off the gas flame. Mary Ellen lay beside Kathy on the blue-and-white linoleum, cradling her in her arms. "Listen, I'm going to tell you something right now," she sobbed. "This is the most selfish thing I'm going to say to you in my whole life: I need you. I can't lose you. You have to come back for me. You can't go away, because I love you so much."

Kathy opened her eyes. "I'm all right, Mare," she said, smiling weakly. "I'm gonna be okay." Then she got to her feet.

The other three women exchanged glances. There was something of the old Kath in the way she'd pulled herself up, almost laughing at her frailty. It was the first sign they'd had that she wasn't going to drown in her grief.

The next time John tried to give Kathy a dose of Tylenol, Mary Ellen took the pills, nodded earnestly at his instructions, and then threw them away. Kathy began to ask for the newspapers, which she knew John was hiding downstairs. At first Mary Ellen just told her what was being reported, but soon Kathy was sneaking into the basement when John was gone to read for herself.

Gradually, the women came to understand that Kathy wasn't going to kill herself, but she *was* trying to will herself to the other side. "Kristie, Billy, and John are strong," she told them. "They'll be fine. But Eddie is so vulnerable; he needs his mommy." Something would trigger a memory in her and she would go with it instantly, as if watching a videotape with slo-mo and stop action that allowed her to linger over every image. Whenever she was on the couch staring into space, "in that other place," as John put it, she was really with Eddie, reliving in excruciating detail every minute of her life with him.

II

A warm breeze blew through the bedroom window, lifting the yellow curtain and messing up his hair. He quickly brushed it back with one hand

and smoothed the thick white-blond waves with the other. Then he checked himself in the mirror, making sure every strand was in place. Ready now for the final inspection, he climbed up on Kathy's bed for a full-length look, searching the reflection for any flaws in the white polo shirt and blue shorts.

Kathy laughed. At three and a half, Eddie was already as fashion-conscious as Kristie, who'd just taken a turn twirling in front of the mirror, pigtails flying over the strawberry shortcake dress and bolero jacket. Only Billy fussed as Kathy pulled on his denim overalls and orange shirt. "This will all be over soon," she assured him, keeping up a constant patter from the house to the car to Sears, where the photo session began at 10:00 a.m. sharp. "We'll have lunch at McDonald's," she said on the escalator, "then we'll go home, get changed, and go to the park."

In the studio, the photographer arranged them in a tableau: Kristie in front with Billy on her lap, Eddie seated in back and a bit off to the side. "Tilt your head a little," she instructed, as she draped him in the same black material that hung on the wall behind them, covering him from the neck down. For the first time Eddie looked uncomfortable. "You'll love this new technique," the photographer told Kathy. "This will be a picture you'll always remember."

Kathy wasn't convinced when she picked up the proof sheets a week later. The kids looked beautiful, their faces clear and sweet, but she wasn't crazy about the way Eddie seemed to just hang there, suspended in the background. "I wish I could see all of him," she told her mother. But "Mom-Mom" Esack loved the picture and hung it on the sun porch in her "rogues' gallery" of family portraits and snapshots.

Two years later, Kathy and Eddie were rolling around on the porch, laughing and tickling each other, when all of a sudden he stopped still and stared at the photograph. "What is it, hon?" she asked. "What's wrong?"

"I don't like that picture," he said. "It makes me look like I'm not real, like I'm just a thought in Kristie and Billy's heads." He stared into her eyes. "I don't ever want to be just a thought in your head."

12

John was right. The media did get the 911 story wrong, sort of.

When Tommy Gibbons and Jeff Gammage's full story hit the news-stand Saturday morning, the facts were far worse than initially reported. At least fourteen calls to 911 had gone unheeded. The early calls were wrongly assigned a "low priority," so that officers weren't sent to check on the fight at McDonald's for more than two hours. As more calls flooded in, dispatchers treated them as isolated incidents rather than as part of a worsening situation. Most disturbing of all, some operators verbally abused the increasingly frantic callers. Police sources were quoted as being "horrified" at what they heard. "When you listen to these tapes," said one, "you want to cry."

City officials no doubt felt the same way as they tried to deal with the fallout from the story. Reporters caught Police Commissioner Neal as he was leaving his home Saturday morning. "I have some concerns about why cars weren't dispatched earlier," he said. "Also, concerns about the interaction between dispatchers and the people who were calling." Asked about his decision to withhold the tapes, Neal said he "might consider" releasing them at some future date, but only after conferring with the district attorney's office to make sure it wouldn't jeopardize the case. D.A. Lynn Abraham promptly replied that releasing the tapes "at this time" would do just that.

Reporters weren't surprised by the official response. They knew that Neal and Abraham were taking their cue from the most powerful man in the city, the man to whom they owed their allegiance and their jobs—their boss, Mayor Ed Rendell. Nothing was said in the name of Philadelphia without the approval of the mayor.

The Rendell administration was an exceptionally media-savvy machine. At the boss's instruction, aides befriended reporters, returned their phone calls promptly, and generally fed the News Beast enough quotes and sound bites to keep it satisfied without revealing too much of the arm-twisting and ball-busting that went on in the back rooms of City Hall.

And it worked. Since Rendell's election in 1992, the former district attorney had enjoyed a run of almost unrelentingly positive news coverage. Seen as brilliant, tough, and temperamental, the mayor was genuinely liked and generally admired by the Philadelphia press corps, for both his energy and his accomplishments.

There was much to admire about Rendell. He had inherited a city drowning in debt and down on its luck—a third-rate town with a fourth-rate image. But under his leadership the city had gone from deep deficit to modest surplus, enough to reduce a long-standing and much-hated business tax. The cut was more symbolic than real, but it sent a message that this Democratic mayor was business-friendly.

Rendell built a new convention center that attracted hundreds of thousands of additional visitors to the area annually, and he proposed grand ideas for an "Avenue of the Arts" in the shadow of City Hall. A tireless cheerleader, he worked seven-day weeks and eighteen-hour days promoting everything that had anything to do with Philly, wolfing down cheese steaks and TastyKakes from one end of the city to the other. Restaurants flourished and businesses that had planned to leave stayed. Philadelphia was suddenly being touted as an urban phoenix risen from the ashes.

As the city's fortunes rose, Rendell's political stock soared—friend of the President, potent party fund-raiser, outspoken advocate for urban revitalization. Dubbed "America's Mayor" by no less than *The Wall Street Journal,* he was widely regarded as a politician with national potential and ambitions to match.

But now this 911 thing was threatening to tarnish his carefully polished image. *The New York Times, The Washington Post,* and *USA Today* all had reporters working the story, and they were calling Rendell's office for comment. Uncharacteristically, he began ducking the questions, having spokesmen respond with the refrain "The matter is under full investigation by the police commissioner."

Confronted by reporters at a charity photo-op, Rendell acknowledged there were problems with 911, but expressed confidence that those problems could be corrected quickly. "There's no question there will be some changes in the system and some changes in personnel," he said. "Rudeness to people is not something we'll accept under any circumstances." Then, in an attempt to downplay the seriousness of the situation, he added, "Some of the rudeness that's been reported in the papers is not really so bad when you hear the tapes."

So it went for the entire weekend. Wherever Rendell and Neal appeared, reporters showed up to shout questions about 911, until the pair grew visibly irritated at the hounding. During a joint appearance at the police department's annual Thanksgiving turkey giveaway, they were reduced to sputtering lamely that Philadelphia's 911 system was at least better than New York's.

While the Rendell administration circled the wagons and held tight to the tapes, irate citizens who'd dialed 911 that night were talking a blue streak. Vicki Petroski, a waitress at the Fox Chase Pizza Hut, told reporters that when she called at about ten o'clock to report the disturbance in the parking lot, "it took them three to four minutes just to pick up the phone." Residents along Ridgeway Street, where the Fox Chase kids regrouped after the fight at McGarrity's, told how they had provided 911 operators with a running account of the "riot" in progress. One man even demonstrated for TV camera crews how he had held his cell phone out the window for operators to hear the pursuing caravan of cars roaring up the street toward St. Cecilia's.

Monday's newspapers brought the news that the police department had known about the 911 problems for years and had done nothing. A study conducted in March 1993 by a citizens' committee cited widespread dissatisfaction with response times and found that "many of the call-takers are often rude and abrasive and often lack class in their questioning of callers." The panel had submitted twenty-five recommendations to the police brass for improving the system, predicting that if something wasn't done there'd be a tragedy someday.

The controversy had some of Rendell's longtime enemies licking their chops. The city's many labor unions loathed the mayor for his hard-ass tactics in contract negotiations and his privatization of many city services. He may have been America's Mayor to the media, but to the rank and file he was a union buster who'd balanced the city's budget on the backs of municipal employees and who cared more about big business and sports interests than workers. Predictably, union leaders laid the blame for 911 almost entirely on Rendell.

"This is a clear example of the lack of manpower," shouted Rich Costello, president of the Fraternal Order of Police. Pointing out that 98 percent of the radio-room staff had been replaced by civilian employees in recent years, Costello claimed, "There was no priority problem when we had enough cops. But until someone gets killed in the Super Box at Veteran's Stadium we're not going to get the mayor's attention."

Rendell responded with some audacious spin. First, he appeared to throw his police commissioner to the dogs, telling reporters he'd ordered Neal to look into the 911 problems "months ago." Then he one-upped Costello on the manpower issue, saying, "The main problem with 911 is what I've been saying since I was a candidate—we don't have enough police officers. If we could get a thousand more officers on the street, that would do more to cure the problems of 911 than anything else."

It was a nice try, but this was a story that couldn't be spun. On Tuesday afternoon, lawyers for the city and the media faced off in Judge Bernard Avellino's courtroom over the issue of the tapes. After listening to both sides, Avellino said he was persuaded that the tapes did indeed fall under the state's Right to Know Act, and he gave the city twenty-four hours to release them voluntarily before he made his official ruling.

For the cops in Two Squad, the 911 controversy was little more than a sorry sideshow, and one they'd seen before. They all had their favorite 911 fuck-up stories. "You can get a pizza faster than you can get a cop," joked Art Mee. "If you get in trouble, don't call 911, call Domino's."

Tom Perks and the rest of the squad were working the Polec case "24–7," coming in on their days off and staying until well after their shifts were over. It was painstakingly slow work, and it drove Perks crazy that some of the kids who killed Eddie were still walking the streets. It wasn't exactly a secret who they were. "Inside Abington High," the *Daily News* reported, "students say they still sit in class with murderers, pass them in the hallways, eat with them in the lunch room."

Perks knew that some of those kids would never be arrested. There were just too many of them; it would be nearly impossible to prosecute every kid who was at the church that night. The best he could hope for was to identify main doers and build strong cases against them.

One of "them" was seventeen-year-old Kevin Convey, a senior at Bishop McDevitt High and the grandson of a cop. Each time Convey was brought in for questioning, he showed up with his lawyer Joe Kelley and tried to present himself as an eyewitness to the murder rather than a participant. "We're not going to sit here and listen to your lies," one detective told him. "Come back when you're ready to tell the truth."

They knew from witnesses that Convey was at St. Cecilia's and was among the first, if not the very first, out of the cars. Investigators also knew that Eddie had tripped while running, but something was missing. "*How* he tripped is what you need to find out," taunted one witness who refused to elaborate further.

Finally, an Abington teen who'd been a bystander to the beating filled in the blank. Polec tripped because Kevin Convey threw a bat at his legs, he said. It was dynamite information, but Perks felt he needed corroboration of the bat-throwing before he could arrest Convey. He did have enough to charge two others—sixteen-year-old Anthony Rienzi and seventeen-year-old Dewan Alexander. Alexander was another one of Pinero's Lakeside buddies and a former student at Abington High. Witnesses not only put him in the caravan that ran Eddie down, they also claimed Alexander kicked him with steel-toed boots as he lay on the ground.

It was just before sunrise when Perks, Dominick Mangoni, Sergeant Tommy Burke, and several uniformed officers headed for Alexander's house in Montgomery County in two cars, hoping to surprise him while he was sleeping. For the past five days the newspapers had been reporting that three additional arrests were imminent. COPS READY TO POUNCE, shouted the *Daily News* headline, with detailed descriptions of each suspect, his age, and what role he had played. There were days when Perks picked up the morning paper and read as fact something he and the guys had kicked around as theory the night before. He was sure the information wasn't coming from anyone in Two Squad, that it was the "higher-ups" who were leaking like sieves. He understood that the department was under pressure from the public, but he had multiple cases to solve and a mountain of evidence to gather, and the leaks were making his job a lot harder.

"What a fucking joke," Perks snorted as they all climbed out of the cars. "If Dewan doesn't know we're coming, it's only because he doesn't read the papers." He banged on the front door and windows of the Alexander house. An elderly man let them in. He didn't seem surprised to see cops on his doorstep. Without a word, he motioned to a door on the first floor.

Perks entered first. "Police," he shouted, jolting Alexander awake. "We've got a warrant for your arrest. Get up, get dressed, and don't make any fast moves." As the teenager swung his feet to the floor, Perks noted the black steel-toed boots arranged neatly beside the bed. "And one more thing," he said, trying not to smile, "don't forget to wear your boots."

The police didn't need to pick up Anthony Rienzi. At 11:00 a.m. on Wednesday, the seventeen-year-old turned himself in. Head down and jacket collar up, he walked into the Roundhouse with his lawyer, John McMahon, a former D.A. in Montgomery County. TV cameras recorded the arrival, tipped off early that morning by police officials eager to promote the department's progress on the evening news.

Along with his pal Nick Pinero, Rienzi was considered a principal doer in the case. And like Pinero, he showed no remorse or fear as Perks processed him through booking and charged him with first-degree murder for first hitting Eddie Polec over the head with a bat and then holding him up for the others to hit.

Perks shook his head. Rienzi was from an upscale neighborhood in Warminster. His father was an architect. How did these kids get so cold? he wondered.

Not far away, another veteran cop was wondering how his police bosses and city officials could be so cold. Early that morning, he'd been handed a small cassette tape by an old friend at police headquarters. He knew what the tape was without even asking.

"This is the piece of gold the press is trying to get its hands on," his friend said. "If you want to listen to it, fine, just get it back to me quick, because I'm supposed to secure it in the safe. There are only two copies, and the commissioner has the other one."

Out in the parking lot, he slipped it into his dashboard tape deck. When he had heard it all, he drove to another friend's house two blocks away and dubbed a copy, then took the original back to headquarters without telling anyone what he'd done. For the next half hour he drove around Center City, playing the tape over and over. Then he headed toward Roosevelt Boulevard, where his buddy Mike operated a hoagie shop. He wanted a layman's opinion.

Mike's jaw dropped as he listened. He thought about his own kids and his nephews and nieces. "The system has to be straightened out," he said. "We gotta get this to the media."

First they called a lawyer they knew, who counseled them to forget the whole thing. "The court's probably going to order it released anyway," he said. But they didn't think it was going to be that easy. Given what was on the tape, they figured City Hall was going to stonewall to the end.

They started calling newsrooms. First they tried anchorman Steve

Levy at Channel 10 and got his voice mail. Same for Larry Kane at Channel 3. One assignment desk assistant after another put them on hold, hung up, or seemed clueless as to what they were talking about. It was as if they were speaking to 911 operators.

"I'm sorry, we're not interested in audio of the police calls," said a desk assistant at Channel 10. "Not *police* calls, the actual 911 calls," Mike explained. He was put on hold again. "Yes, we would be interested," the assistant said a minute later. "You can bring it here or we can meet you somewhere. We have a reporter doing a story at 30th Street Station right now."

"Tell him we'll be there in ten minutes. Meet us at the Bucks County Coffee service counter, by the condiments."

They pulled up in front of the train station feeling like a couple of characters in a Tom Clancy novel. "I'll make the drop," Mike said, knowing it would be a career-ender for his cop friend if anyone saw him with the reporter.

He was standing at the designated spot when a man approached. "Do you have something for me?" Mike nodded the way he imagined Jack Ryan would. "Over there by the napkin holder." Then he turned and walked away without looking back.

He was barely back at the hoagie shop before the shit hit the fan.

13

No one in the Polec house had watched the news since the 911 story broke Friday night. Reporters kept calling, asking John to comment about the alleged rudeness of the operators. But he was more troubled by the newspaper reports that calls had been miscoded and, as a result, cops on the street weren't sent to the scene in time. There were all kinds of rude people who did jobs, he reasoned. The 911 operators could have been as crabby as they wanted to be and still pushed the right buttons on their computers. No, something else was wrong with the system. But since he didn't know exactly what, he kept his mouth shut.

He spent a lot of time going through the mail. They were getting cards and letters from all over the country, from people who had heard the story on the news and were moved to write. Some of the letters arrived addressed simply "Eddie Polec's Family, Fox Chase, PA," with no street address or ZIP code. The post office always got such a bad rap in the press, John thought, but somebody there was getting these poorly addressed envelopes to the right house.

A lot of people were being very good to his family. Longtime friend and neighbor Kathy Goodwin had organized a feed-the-Polecs project, whereby anyone who wanted to do something for the family was asked to bring over a prepared meal. Folks out there must have thought they were the hungriest people imaginable, because there was more food coming into the house each day than they could eat in a week. Truth was, they weren't very hungry. They began sending meals home with Kathy's girl friends, who were spending so much time taking care of her that they weren't taking care of their own families. And they packed up hundreds of pieces of fruit before it spoiled and took it to the nursing home where Kathy's mom lived as an Alzheimer's patient.

On Tuesday, John got a call from the Melrose Country Club saying the staff there was preparing a full Thanksgiving dinner that would be delivered to their house in time for the holiday. Tom Perks phoned to alert him about the arrests of Rienzi and Alexander. John didn't ask what role the two had played in Eddie's death; he just figured the police were arresting everyone who'd been at the scene.

Around noon on Wednesday, Father Olson called and said he'd just heard a promo for the evening news on Channel 10. They'd obtained the 911 tapes and were playing snippets of the conversations. "Don't watch TV or turn on the radio," the priest advised, "because it's pretty disturbing stuff."

At five o'clock John turned on the TV in the basement and heard, along with the rest of the city, what police officials and the mayor had tried so hard to keep secret.

The first call came in at 10:01 p.m.—a "pack of kids" creating a disturbance at McDonald's. (Eddie was laughing and joking with his friends at the Rec.)

At 10:13: "Juveniles throwing rocks" on Rockwell Avenue.

At 10:20: "About fifty kids are busting up cars."

At 10:33: "We have a gang of at least fifty young kids with bats outside, beating each other, chasing each other." (Eddie was walking along the railroad tracks, headed to the Rec playground. He'd heard about the fight and was looking for Billy.)

The calls were coming in every few seconds now, the callers growing more frantic, agitated that no police had come. At 10:37 came this exchange:

> OPERATOR: Police 225.
>
> CALLER: I don't believe this; it rang about ten times. There's a big commotion going on outside our home, like a gang fight.
>
> OPERATOR: Where is that, ma'am?
>
> CALLER: Ridgeway Street, 7900 Ridgeway Street.
>
> OPERATOR: Okay.
>
> CALLER: They got clubs out there; a kid's hurt.
>
> OPERATOR: All right.
>
> CALLER (exasperated): Did you get that?
>
> OPERATOR (sounding bored): Yeah, a kid is hurt outside and there's a fight. All right? Is that it?
>
> CALLER (furious): Yeah, that's it. Send a police car to . . .
>
> OPERATOR (cutting her off, shouting): Wait a minute, wait a minute, wait a minute. You asked me a question and I'm asking you. I have the information. You can hang up now.

John sat frozen in his chair, sickened by what he was hearing. He figured that by this time Eddie and Billy had met up with the other Fox Chase kids on Ridgeway and were walking up the street toward St. Cecilia's. It was 10:42.

CALLER: We got a near-riot and there's no damn police around.

OPERATOR: Where?

CALLER: On Ridgeway Street, come on.

OPERATOR (irritated): Well, I don't know that.

CALLER: We been calling, the whole damn neighborhood's been calling there. I called the district and they told me to call 911. What are we supposed to do here? There's cars, a whole damn convoy of cars coming up here. You got a damn riot going on up here.

John's stomach constricted. It was 10:44. His sons were running for their lives.

CALLER (shouting): They're beating the hell out of people with baseball bats up here. When are you going to send somebody?

OPERATOR: Who's got a bat, sir?

CALLER (indignant): Who's got a bat? Some gorilla. What the hell do you mean?

OPERATOR (shouting): Wait a minute, wait a minute. Don't talk to me like that. I asked you a question. Who's got a bat? Is he black, white, or Hispanic?

The most gut-wrenching call came in at 10:45, as Eddie lay on the parking lot with his head crushed. John recognized the caller. It was Theresa Wech, a seventeen-year-old neighborhood girl who came along at the tail end of the beating and tried to comfort Eddie after the attackers fled. When no police arrived, she ran a block to the library to call 911 from a pay phone. She was covered with Eddie's blood and hysterical.

> THERESA: My friend, my friend is bleeding. He needs a hospital.
>
> OPERATOR: He's what?
>
> THERESA: He's at St. Cecilia's and he needs a hospital.
>
> OPERATOR: He needs what at the hospital?
>
> THERESA (crying, confused): He's at the hospital.
>
> OPERATOR: Slow down, slow down. He needs what at the hospital?
>
> THERESA: I mean, he needs a hospital. He's bleeding.
>
> OPERATOR: Where's he at?
>
> THERESA: He's at St. Cecilia's at the church.
>
> OPERATOR: He's where?
>
> THERESA: St. Cecilia's.
>
> OPERATOR: I can't understand you. Give me an address.
>
> THERESA: He's at St. Cecilia's.
>
> OPERATOR: Where's that at?
>
> THERESA: Oxford Avenue.
>
> OPERATOR: Oxford and what?
>
> THERESA: Oh God!
>
> OPERATOR (shouting): Listen, listen. If you don't calm down, he gets no help. Do you understand that much?
>
> THERESA: I'm trying.
>
> OPERATOR: All right. You gotta tell me. Oxford and where?
>
> THERESA (sobbing uncontrollably): It's like, oh God. Do you know where Fox Chase School is?
>
> OPERATOR: No, I don't.
>
> THERESA: Okay. It's . . . it's Oxford Avenue and Veree.
>
> OPERATOR: Veree. All right, what happened to him?
>
> THERESA: He got beat with a bat.
>
> OPERATOR: All right. Are the people that beat him still there?

THERESA: No.

OPERATOR: Hold on, I'm gonna connect you with Rescue. You tell them where he is.

THERESA: He got beat with a bat. He's at the church.

RESCUE: What?

THERESA: St. Cecilia's.

RESCUE: What's your address? Where's it at?

THERESA: It's right across from Fox Chase School, which is by Rhawn.

RESCUE (to operator): Please, could you tell me where she's calling from?

OPERATOR: She's calling from 501 Rhawn Street, by the free library.

THERESA (overhearing): Yeah, I'm at the free library, but my friend is at St. Cecilia's Church.

OPERATOR (sarcastic, to Rescue): She told me it was at Oxford and Veree first. She can't seem to get it together.

John switched off the TV, unable to take any more. He trudged up the stairs feeling as if he was going to vomit. Before he fell asleep in the green chair that night, the tapes were aired repeatedly on every TV station in Philadelphia, courtesy of Mayor Rendell, who finally ordered their release after they'd been leaked. By the next morning, they were being beamed from coast to coast, on their way to becoming the audio equivalent of the Rodney King beating tapes, broadcast over and over again on virtually every TV newscast in America.

14

This year, Thanksgiving seemed like a cruel joke. Kathy forced herself off the couch to sit at the table with the rest of the family. She stared at the meal that had been delivered in a box from the swanky country club they could never afford to go to. It looked delicious, but she couldn't eat. It was the first time that she hadn't prepared Thanksgiving dinner herself, spending all day basting and stuffing the bird, making apple and mincemeat pie from scratch while the kids poked their fingers in the pie crust and asked, "What's a mince?" They had a silly ritual of waltzing around the kitchen with the uncooked carcass—"Thomas the Turkey," they called it. She could see Eddie just last year, doing a loopy Fred Astaire and telling her, "Mom, no matter how old I get, no matter where I go or how far away it is, I'll always be home for your Thanksgiving turkey dinner and apple pie." But now his chair was empty, and all she wanted to do was go back to the couch and sleep.

Eddie's friend Nick called from Florida after dinner. He'd heard the 911 tapes on the news down there—ABC's *World News Tonight* led its newscast with the story, and so had the *CBS Evening News*. John felt strange knowing his family's business was the stuff of the national news, but at least no reporters called the house all day. He assumed they took the day off like everyone else.

That wasn't the case. The 911 tapes were practically the only news in Philadelphia that day. Every newscast played them repeatedly, and all day long, reporters did live standups from the street in front of St. Cecilia's and even from Solly Place, with the Polecs' house framed over their shoulders. But no one knocked on the door or called the house for comment. No one wanted to intrude.

The single exception came around 9:00 p.m. A telegram arrived from *The Phil Donahue Show* asking if the Polecs were interested in appearing on the program. They weren't.

They all fell asleep in the living room with the television on. John woke up several times and went back to sleep. At 4:30 a.m. he awoke again just as *ABC Overnight* was introducing a story—"Grief and rage in Philadelphia, as the 911 system fails and a young boy dies"— that turned out to be much more about the tapes and the controversy than about the young boy who died.

On Friday morning he called the mayor's office. "Tell him I'm not irate," he told the operator who took down his name. "I'm not going to scream and yell or anything. I just want to talk and find out what's going on."

Rendell called back a few minutes later. "I'm not calling to demand that anything be done," John told him. "I'm just curious if those people who were rude are still answering the phones."

Rendell said he didn't know, but would check it out and call John back. "We will take some disciplinary action," he promised, "but with the holidays coming up, it might not be right away." That was okay with him, John said. "I just think they should be off the phones, since they're not exactly doing a very good job."

Early Sunday morning a young woman appeared at the door with a box of doughnuts and a request that the Polecs appear on *American Journal*. John recalled vaguely that *AJ* was one of those quasi-news programs that came on early in the evening and tended toward the sensational. He politely declined. The *Today* show called a little while later. Mayor Rendell was scheduled to be interviewed live the next morning and they'd like John and Kathy to appear on the program with him. John said they weren't interested.

It seemed as if the whole world wanted his opinion on the fiasco, and he had nothing to offer. But the Sunday papers were filled with background stories and sidebars on the city's 911 system, so he sat down with a pen and notepad and began his education.

Operated at a cost of $16 million annually and paid for by a $1-a-month surcharge on every phone line, the system funneled three million calls a year through the radio room at police headquarters. The radio room was staffed by about 200 civilian employees and 50 police department supervisors. The staff was divided between operators, who took the calls from the public, and dispatchers, who directed patrol cars to trouble spots. On any given shift, each operator handled as many as 300 calls, or 1.6 calls per minute. The high volume translated into high stress and high employee turnover. With salaries starting at $21,000 a year and only a week's worth of training, fully 50 percent of radio-room employees quit during their first six months on the job. The union representing the civilian employees had repeatedly requested stress training for its members, only to be turned down by the city.

The more John read, the worse it seemed. Originally, the system had been run entirely by police personnel. But in a move to save money and put more cops on the street, the city had all but removed police from the radio room in 1977. The police union, the Fraternal Order of Police, subsequently sued the city and won back its supervisory positions. But rancor and bitterness remained, with the cops criticizing the civilians for not being streetwise and the civilians knocking the cops for not taking the job seriously. Indeed, the supervisory positions usually went to officers on temporary assignment who saw the job as drudge work.

A reorganization of the radio room in 1988 only added to the problems. Before, five or six operators and two dispatchers sat side by side at consoles covering twelve geographic sections of the city. Each operator-dispatcher group knew its area—the street names, landmarks, and cops on the beat. If a rash of calls came in from one neighborhood, they could see it immediately and react accordingly. But the 1988 reorganization separated the operators from the dispatchers and replaced the consoles with individual computer screens that were set up to take information on one incident at a time. With operators now isolated in cubicles, it was nearly impossible for any single operator to know what calls the others were receiving. And the only communication between operators and dispatchers was via computer.

John was profoundly disturbed by what he read. Like most citizens, he had always assumed that a call to 911 was a fairly direct link to the police on the beat. As a computer programmer, he knew that computers were only as good as the information they got. From what the newspaper reported, it seemed to him that Eddie hadn't stood a chance.

Mayor Rendell called again around 11:00 p.m. Sunday. He said he'd been in meetings about 911 all day. A committee was forming to study the system and recommend reforms. They were going to restructure management, replace the current watch commander, and bring in more supervisors. There would be better training for the operators, and the ones identified on the tapes would be disciplined. Not for their rudeness, Rendell explained, but because the tapes showed they hadn't asked the right questions and, as a result, had assigned the wrong priorities.

Rendell could have said a lot more, but he waited until he had a national audience. The next morning he told Bryant Gumbel on *Today* that the city was, in fact, firing three of the 911 operators and suspending three others for misconduct. Two hours later, Rendell held a press conference at City Hall to announce the disciplinary actions and to unveil a plan to overhaul 911's command structure and operations. "The system clearly didn't work," he said. "There was human error. There are flaws in the system and they must be corrected immediately. There's no excuse for some of the conduct and treatment of citizens who were just trying to stop a crime."

The commanders in charge of the radio room, Chief Inspector Charles Farrell and Captain Orville Ballard, were being transferred, replaced by a new management team led by Chief Inspector William Bergman and Inspector Carl Bittenbender. Three new police captains—one per shift—would be assigned to the radio room, along with eight additional corporals. There now would be stress and sensitivity training for 911 operators, random monitoring of calls by supervisors, and a requirement that operators notify their superiors anytime they got a repeat call on an incident.

With Police Commissioner Neal standing by his side, Rendell said he was going to appoint a task force to study the 911 system and recommend additional changes within sixty to ninety days. The task force would be made up of elected officials, community groups, union leaders, and radio-room operators and dispatchers. In addition, Rendell revealed that Patrick Murphy, a nationally respected law-enforcement expert and former police chief of New York and Washington, D.C., had agreed to consult with the city at no charge and make recommendations to the task force.

The throng of reporters present immediately piped up with their requisite impertinent questions, like "Why did a kid have to die for the city to start fixing a problem it's known about for a long time?"

Rendell countered that the city had been studying the system for months and had already made some changes. He said they had been "socking away millions of dollars" for the purchase of a $50 million 800-megahertz radio system that would dramatically increase the number of radio bands to police. "Were we working on every single one of these issues as quickly as you would have liked or I would have liked? Probably not," he said. "If the system had functioned right and there had been no human error, could this boy's death have been prevented? There's no way we'll ever know that. But could we have improved his chances? Sure, we could have.

"I spoke with John Polec last night," he told reporters. "I pledged to him that this won't be just an investigation to get you guys off my back, that we will make meaningful changes. And by the steps we've taken here today, we've begun down that road."

It looked at first as if Rendell had turned the corner on the crisis. By putting forward a sweeping, bold-sounding plan of action, he reestablished himself as a can-do mayor, diffusing the controversy and disarming the press with his candor and humanity. But there was a big bump in the road that Rendell didn't see coming. Unbeknown to him, all six 911 operators that he'd ordered disciplined were black.

Almost immediately the mayor was under attack. "Rendell is taking a futile but politically expedient course in blaming those at the bottom of the system for the problem," said Nan Lassen, the attorney for District 33 of the American Federation of State, County and Municipal Employees, which represented the 911 operators.

Within an hour of Rendell's City Hall appearance, three of the operators held their own press conference, appearing angry, unapologetic, and even defiant as they proclaimed themselves "political scapegoats."

"The city is looking to throw someone to the dogs and it's us," said Osborne Walker, who was fired for his handling of the call from seventeen-year-old Theresa Wech. "We're being portrayed as incompetent buffoons, as people who don't care, with no mention of the lives we do help save." Walker insisted that he wasn't being insensitive or sarcastic to the teenager when she called crying from the pay phone by the library. "She was hysterical and rightly so, but I was never disrespectful. When you hear the tape, I sound like some kind of monster, but it was impossible to understand her."

Linda Carroll was fired for her handling of the call in which she shouted at the caller, "Wait a minute. Don't talk to me like that . . . Who's got a bat? Is he black, white, or Hispanic?"

"To say there was a gorilla on the highway, I thought that was highly inexcusable," she said. "That's a zoo problem, not a police problem. If you want help, you need to cooperate. He got hysterical and I asked him to calm down. He used a lot of profanity."

Yes, she said, she considered the word "hell" profanity. Asked why she demanded to know the race of the person with the bat, she replied that the information was needed so officers could identify the suspect when they arrived on the scene. After all, she said, "Our number-one job is to protect the police."

"I have a clear conscience," said Nicole Burton, suspended for the call in which she shouted, "Wait a minute, wait a minute . . . You asked me a question and I'm asking you. I have the information. You can hang up now." But it turned out she didn't have the information. The caller reported that "they got clubs out there," but Burton miscoded the call as a report of a "disturbance" rather than a higher-priority "person with a weapon." She claimed that she didn't hear the part about the clubs in the din of the radio room. "I handled my calls to the best of my ability."

It was Burton who raised the race issue. "The dispatcher in charge that night happened to be a white male who you do not see among us because he was not subject to disciplinary action."

Ronald "Reds" Mauldin, the head of AFSCME Local 1637, took it even further. "Every life is important," he said, "but why—and I have to be choice in my words because I don't want to offend the family of this young gentleman—but what is so different about one Caucasian being killed that we get all this publicity, when 119 [blacks] have preceded him in death and nothing has been done?

"The city has known for some time that the 911 system was inadequate. They knew that. We had a meeting and I told them that, and they chose not to do anything about it. Unfortunately, a tragedy like this had to happen to make the city look at it. But if this incident had happened in North Philly or West Philly, I don't think the story would be this big."

Mauldin and the operators had a point. Residents of the poorer, largely black and Hispanic sections of the city had been complaining for years about the lack of police response, 911 and otherwise, in their areas. The situation had gotten so bad that folks from troubled neighborhoods in the west and north sections of the city routinely reported "man with a weapon" when they called 911, figuring that was the only way to assure that help would ever arrive. But crying "weapon" sometimes made the problem worse.

A few months before Eddie's murder, the family of thirty-three-year-old Moises DeJesus called 911 because the tow-truck operator was running around the neighborhood out of control on crack cocaine. What they really wanted was for the authorities to get Moises to a hospital, but they told the 911 operators that he was wielding a knife. Carloads of cops arrived within minutes, braced for an armed and dangerous suspect. In the ensuing scuffle, Moises was fatally injured by a blow to the head from a police flashlight. There was no knife.

The people of Fox Chase didn't know about "man with a weapon."

They assumed that reporting a band of fifty teenagers rampaging through a neighborhood busting up cars with bats was enough to get the attention of the police. They were naïve.

Of course, all this subtext was lost on John Polec as he followed the news coverage with growing dismay. From his perspective, Eddie's murder was being transcended by the politics of the tapes. A kid was dead, a group of kids had killed him, and suddenly people were blaming 911 for his death. Sure, the cops might have stopped the murder if they'd been there, but if the Abington kids had not decided to launch a mob attack over a spilled soda, there would have been no need for the cops in the first place. The beaters, not the 911 operators, were guilty of murder. He wanted the killers to be punished, and he didn't want the tapes to excuse or overshadow their crimes.

He spent much of Tuesday giving interviews to every reporter who called or came by the house. His message was always the same: "911 did not murder Eddie. Five people murdered him with bats. Those people being disciplined did not murder him. If they had done their jobs better, he might not have been murdered. But he's dead because of the five people in jail."

He kept to his mantra even after the news broke that between thirteen and twenty-two patrol cars were available in the Northeast section of the city during the forty-five minutes leading up to Eddie's murder and could have arrived on the scene within minutes, had they only been dispatched. That contradicted the official line that part of the 911 problem was a manpower shortage. If there were 22 patrol cars free to answer calls, then 100 more cops in Northeast Philly wouldn't have gotten there any faster. There was no shortage of cops the night Eddie was killed, there were no cops sent to a different location because the priorities that allocated personnel were wrong. There were cops who could have answered the calls but did not. That told John that whatever was wrong with the 911 system went way beyond a handful of rude operators; it was something that would take more than sensitivity training to fix.

He tried all day to reach Ronald Mauldin. He'd been seething ever since he read Mauldin's comments at the 911 operators' news conference. He was not a racist, and he and Kathy had raised their kids not to make assumptions about people from the color of their skin, their religion, or their ancestry. But he was outraged that a union leader—a leader of the same union that represented Kathy and the school-crossing guards—would bring race into this issue. When Mauldin finally called him back around dinnertime, John took the phone out into the back yard and let loose.

"Your comments yesterday were uncalled for," he said. "How in the world could you make such a statement? We've spent a good deal of time making sure no one made the murder a racial issue, so I find it disgusting that you would bring race into Eddie's death and the 911 fiasco. This is the last straw. If you keep up this rhetoric, I'll do whatever I can to turn this into a Rodney King issue in reverse."

He had no idea what he meant by that. But it sounded good and it apparently struck a chord. Mauldin apologized immediately. What's more, he said, he would be appearing on the TV talk show *AM Philadelphia* tomorrow and he would tell everyone that it was wrong to raise race in connection with Eddie's death.

Mauldin turned out to be as good as his word. On *AM Philadelphia* the next day, he took back his statement, saying, "I think the Polec family has suffered enough without going through the aggravation of the race issue. I'm not going to talk about race anymore. It's time to get off that."

This being Philadelphia, however, the race issue was not going to fade away. Emboldened by the sight of their once indomitable mayor on the ropes, members of the City Council came out swinging, criticizing the administration first for its slow response on 911's longstanding problems and then for its hair-trigger firing of the operators. "Political expediency," they cried. "Cynical scapegoating."

City Council president John Street, Philadelphia's most powerful black politician and normally a strong Rendell ally, said he would raise the issue at the next council meeting. "Any racial implications or overtones need to be put on the table. I think there is always a concern that people in the African American community end up getting the short end of the stick. That's something we all have to take a good look at. It cannot be ignored that African Americans believe that, at least in part, the quick response [against the operators] was because there wasn't an African American victim."

911: THE RACE DEBATE, blared the banner headline in the *Daily News,* over an article that speculated on whether the controversy spelled trouble for Rendell in the mayoral primary just six months away. "The 911 debacle really exposes the mayor for what he is—a person more concerned with a handful of money interests than with neighborhoods," said long-time foe Lance Haver, head of Philadelphia's Consumer Education and Protective Association. In Washington, leaders of AFSCME held a strategy session on how to unseat the mayor they'd long loathed as a union buster. "Maybe there are some chinks in his Teflon," said one AFSCME official. "I don't think he'll survive this," said another. "This goes to the heart of putting budgets before people."

Unaccustomed to such public criticism, Rendell began to lose his cool, telling reporters at an impromptu news conference outside his office, "These last two or three days have made me feel a lot less happy in my job. It's made me think about how rotten some people are in this city and how they start trouble for the sake of starting trouble." Asked who he thought was rotten, Rendell shot back, "Anyone who says this is racial. Right now I just feel sick and tired of being mayor of a city where people can make that allegation."

The race debate and the political sideshow all but obliterated the news on Wednesday that police had arrested seventeen-year-old Kevin Convey and charged him with first-degree murder. Several witnesses had confirmed that Convey was the first out of the car at St. Cecilia's and the one who knocked Eddie to the ground by flinging a bat at his legs while he ran.

On Thursday, John Polec got a call from Thornhill Cosby, who identified himself as the head of the Philadelphia office of the NAACP. Cosby said he wanted the Polecs to know the NAACP was issuing a press release and holding a press conference to announce it was offering the family whatever financial assistance it needed in filing a $50 million lawsuit against the city.

"But we're not suing the city," John said. Surprised, Cosby explained that the NAACP was troubled by all the racial implications in the news reports and wanted to make the point that this was not a racial issue, it was a human issue.

"We appreciate that," John replied. "But we couldn't take one penny in exchange for Eddie's life. We'd pay whatever was necessary to get him back."

The idea of suing the city had been swirling around the Polecs for days. Everyone, including city officials, assumed they were going to do it. They'd received letters from lawyers, phone calls from friends who knew lawyers, personal visits from people who knew people who could help them get a lawyer. But John had made up his mind. A few years back, Kristie, Eddie, and Billy had learned that some neighbors who had been involved in a minor car accident had gotten enough money from a lawsuit to buy a fancier new car, fix up their house, and take an expensive vacation. The kids thought that was pretty cool; John did not. "I don't agree with that sort of thinking," he lectured them. "To profit from an accident is not for me. You earn money the old-fashioned way—you work. Money doesn't come from mistakes." If it was wrong to profit from a car accident, he argued, then it was much less acceptable to profit from a murder.

The NAACP issued its press release anyway, a rambling three-page statement that decried the racialization of Eddie's murder and at the same time attacked Mayor Rendell for privatizing city services, mismanagement, and "the destruction of the unions." A reporter from the *Daily News*, Kevin Haney, showed up on the Polecs' doorstep around 10:30 Thursday night, asking for John's response.

"We're not suing anybody," John told him. "We will not profit from this tragedy. I don't want Eddie's name and 'lawsuit' mentioned in the same sentence."

Haney told him that the City Council was going to conduct an inquiry into the 911 debacle at its next session on Tuesday. Was John going to testify?

No, John said. "But I'll be there. I'm going to see if they're just rehashing the news media stuff, or if they're really doing something constructive."

Haney's article the next morning was the best news the mayor had heard all week. DAD WANTS REFORM OF 911, NOT $50 MILLION, read the headline. Rendell immediately called John. "Don't get your hopes up that the City Council will do anything constructive about 911," he said. "The task force will solve the problems; the council hearing will be for show."

Rendell spoke as if he assumed John had a working knowledge of city politics. Truth was, John had always been apolitical. The way he saw it, government had little effect on him. The city picked up the trash, piped in the water, and, until Eddie died, gave him police protection, none of which had anything to do with the people who got elected. He couldn't remember the last time he'd voted. He'd never seen a politician who looked worthwhile to him, so he didn't try to figure out what their views were, and he refused to vote just for the sake of voting.

On Friday, December 2, the police arrested a seventh suspect in Eddie's murder—Carlo Johnson, a nineteen-year-old Abington High graduate. Unlike the others, Johnson wasn't charged with murder but rather with assault, aggravated assault, conspiracy, and possession of an instrument of a crime. Although he'd been at St. Cecilia's, he hadn't joined in the attack, police said. But he had played a crucial role in the murder: he was accused of supplying the bats.

Johnson's arrest drew even less media attention than Convey's had—barely a three-inch brief in the *Daily News*. The big news of the day was the appearance of Mayor Rendell, along with Police Commissioner Neal, on *Larry King Live*. The two squared off against fired operator Osborne Walker and union leader Ronald Mauldin to defend both the 911 system and their disciplinary action. If the appearance was intended to counter the embarrassing publicity Philadelphia had been getting, it backfired badly. The tapes were aired yet again, and before the weekend was over, Philadelphia was literally a national laughing-stock. As *Saturday Night Live* host, comedienne Roseanne Arnold appeared in a sketch as a Philadelphia 911 operator more interested in doing her nails than in saving lives. "I gotta send an ambulance?" she said in response to a call. "Hey, I work for the city. I don't gotta do anything."

For the Polecs, it was almost too much to bear—Eddie's death had become fodder for comedy programming.

On Tuesday, December 6, John arrived at City Hall at 7:30 in the morning, two and a half hours early for the City Council hearings. He wanted to make sure he got a seat. The doors were locked, the halls empty, so he sat alone on a bench in an echoing corridor reading the newspaper. When a guard finally came and unlocked the double doors, he took a seat by the back wall, behind a post. He wanted to be as far away from the proceedings as possible but still to see what was going on. He hoped to blend into the woodwork. For a while he did.

He watched as a TV camera crew from public access Channel 64 set up for what would be the first-ever gavel-to-gavel coverage of a regular council session. Then the chamber began to fill with union members in yellow jackets with AFSCME emblazoned on the back, carrying placards that read, "Remember 911 in '95, Rendell. We will," and "Want Rendell's 911 Response? Dial S-c-a-p-e-g-o-a-t." A man sat down next to him and immediately started in about unions getting "the short end of the stick" all across America, and how it was "time to take a stand."

Councilwoman Joan Krajewski, head of the Public Safety Committee, presided over the hearing, which was supposed to focus on the systemic weaknesses of 911 rather than a blow-by-blow account of what had happened the night of November 11. Police Commissioner Neal was the first witness called to testify. The mayor was a no-show. Informed that the council would like him to appear, Rendell declined through his chief of staff, David Cohen. "The mayor doesn't have much to add in terms of how the system functions," Cohen told reporters.

As John listened to council members grilling Neal, he concluded that the term "City Council hearing" was a misnomer. They'd ask a question, then talk among themselves while Neal answered. They weren't *hearing* anything he said. Still, they kept him in the witness chair for the better part of two hours, at one point asking him to read portions of the 911 procedure manual aloud. The mayor was right, John thought. This was nothing but playacting, posturing for voters.

He was about to leave when City Council president John Street took over the questioning of Neal. "Commissioner," Street said, "to the world we have to deal with the question of why everyone who was disciplined was an African American. There is a perception in the African American community that we have created six new victims with these firings."

The room exploded with applause and foot-stomping cheers from placard-waving AFSCME members obviously gathered for exactly that purpose. In a move reminiscent of a scene from *The Bonfire of the Vanities,* Street turned from Neal to the crowd and bellowed in his best Al Sharpton style, "I will respond to them: race is not an issue in this discussion; it is a fact, it is a fact."

Even veteran City Hall reporters accustomed to histrionics and race-baiting from Street were shocked at the grandstanding. He was making a campaign speech, using the hearing to curry favor with black voters in his district who constantly criticized him for being too close to Rendell and (white) Center City business interests. John Polec stopped taking notes, took off his glasses, leaned his head against the wall, and closed his eyes. After a few more minutes of rhetoric, Street left the council chambers to the thunderous applause of AFSCME members. On his way out, he walked right past where John was sitting. "Mr. Street, I wonder if I could talk to you for a few minutes," John said. Barely breaking stride as he disappeared through the door, Street replied, "Call my secretary and she'll make an appointment."

John walked out of the hearing a few minutes later. Stepping into the hallway, he was hit by the lights of a dozen TV cameras and the sound of reporters shouting his name: "Mr. Polec! Mr. Polec!" He'd never experienced a media "gang bang" before; all his recent encounters with reporters had been one-on-one. Now he was pinned against a wall, blinded by the lights, and unable to hear any question above the din. So he just stood there and said nothing until the reporters calmed down.

"I think these hearings are a waste of time, based on the outburst I heard ten minutes ago," he told them. "What I heard just then definitely is not what we're looking for. I heard nothing in there looking for solutions for 911. I heard nothing in there that gives me any feeling that these people can make a change. I didn't like anything I heard today from the council side of this."

He started down the hallway and ducked into the men's room, figuring no one would follow him there. But someone did, a young man who introduced himself as an aide to John Street and asked sheepishly if John still wanted to talk to the council president. Apparently someone on the staff realized who it was that the boss had treated so rudely.

The aide escorted him past the reporters and into Street's office. They got right to the point. The way Street saw it, the issue was black and white: the victim was white and the operators were black; 911 had failed black people many times in the past and no one was ever fired from their job, so the discipline appeared to be racially motivated.

"Look," John said, "I wish there'd been a fuss when 911 let a black kid die, because maybe the system would have been fixed and my son would have gotten the help he needed. But it seems to me that the black community should be glad that attention is finally being focused on a problem they've known about for years. If a white kid getting killed is the spark that causes things to improve, then both blacks and whites will benefit." He was wound up now, pointing his finger at Street's chest. "But if everyone keeps focusing on the discipline and ignoring the problems, then 911 will continue to fail the black community and nothing will be improved in the wake of my son's murder. It's your call." He turned on his heel and walked out of the office without waiting for Street to respond.

In the hallway, the pack of reporters pressed him. "What did you say to John Street? What went on in there?" His blood up, John wanted to blurt out exactly what he was thinking: Only a racist would accuse others of racism instead of focusing on how to fix the problem. Only a racist would ignore the fact that people of all races depend on 911 just so he could defend a small group of incompetent operators who happened to be black. But he held his tongue, not wanting to make things worse, not wanting to do anything that might derail the mayor's task force in its efforts to fix the system. "Why don't you ask Mr. Street" was all he said.

He didn't know it as he left City Hall in a funk, but John had scored a major victory: he'd shut John Street up. The city council president never again raised the race issue in connection with 911 and Eddie's death.

15

John stood alone at the end of Solly Place, smoking and watching for Tom Perks's now familiar Crown Victoria to round the corner. Perks had called the day before and said he wanted to stop by to talk about the preliminary hearing, which was set for Friday. He was bringing with him the assistant district attorney who would prosecute Eddie's killers. Fearing that Kathy was still too depressed to handle the visit, John had decided that they could take care of their business outside and out of earshot. At least this time it wasn't raining.

Fifty-four-year-old Joseph Patrick Casey towered over John as they shook hands. He was six foot two, with thinning gray hair, clear blue eyes, and a slight stammer. "I'm so sorry for your loss," he said quietly. "I'll do the best I can for you and Eddie."

With more than two decades under his belt in the D.A.'s office, Casey was a career prosecutor, one of the few who refused to use his position as a stepping-stone to the more lucrative field of criminal defense. "I'd rather die than go over to the dark side," he always said. He was glad he'd been assigned the Polec case. Not because it was a high-profile murder; he considered the cameras and dueling sound bites after court a huge pain in the ass. What Casey loved about his job was the courtroom battle itself, the almost biblical face-off between good and evil. He saw himself as the last line of defense between the victims and the bad guys, the one person who might restore a sense of dignity and justice to those who had been wronged.

As a philosophy major at St. Joseph's University, he'd been attracted to Rousseau's idea that society owes its citizens protection from predators. As a young law student at Villanova, he'd argued constantly with his more liberal classmates and professors that defendants had too many rights and victims not enough. His years in the D.A.'s office had strengthened those beliefs, but they'd also heightened his sense of frustration. The truth was, he'd begun to feel burned out when the Polec case came along. It energized him, gave him confidence that he could bring this family, at least, some form of justice.

The minute he was assigned to the Polec case he began to familiarize himself with every detail of Eddie's death. He'd driven the route from McDonald's to the Rec, climbed through the hole in the fence, walked the train tracks. As the D.A.'s director of training, he always urged young prosecutors to visit their crime scenes: "You need to understand the spirit of the crime," he would explain. "If you get there soon enough, you can still *feel* the murder."

Casey likened the Abington kids to an invading barbarian horde that swept into Fox Chase primed for battle and chose the most defenseless victim they could find. "Every son-of-a-bitch who went down to Fox Chase knowing there was a bat in the car should be tried for murder," he told anyone who'd listen.

Dealing with victims' families was one of the hardest parts of

Casey's job. "It will be a long day," he told John. "There will be confessions read, police statements, eyewitness accounts." He paused. "You should know that you will hear awful details of Eddie's murder, how Anthony Rienzi picked him up by the coat and belt loop so that others could get a better swing at his head." He hoisted an imaginary Eddie to his feet, then swung at him with an invisible bat, hating what he was doing. He had four children of his own, including a son who was exactly Eddie's age. But he knew that if the Polecs chose to attend all the court hearings, as most victims' families do, they would have to listen to the details over and over again.

"In order for us to make our case, we need to show the judge and jury just how brutal the murder really was," Casey said, "and that also means showing graphic—um—very graphic autopsy photos."

John had seen Eddie in the morgue. How could he stand seeing full-color photos of his boy, beaten and bloody, on display? And what about Kathy? "Kathy won't be able to handle the photos," he said. "I'll have to figure out some way to get her out of the courtroom." Casey nodded, glad that John made the suggestion.

John listened as Casey and Perks gave him a quick lesson in the possible criminal charges in a case like this. You get mad at someone, grab a bat without thinking, hit them over the head, and they die—that's voluntary manslaughter. But if you were just swinging the bat around like fool and someone walked into it and was killed, that would be involuntary manslaughter. It's third-degree murder if you hit someone on the leg with a bat, intending to hurt rather than kill them, and they get a blood clot and die from complications. If you hit someone with a bat in the course of a robbery and they die as a result, that's second-degree murder, whether or not you intended to kill them. Second-degree murder carries an automatic life sentence in Pennsylvania. But since there had been no robbery here, second-degree murder did not apply.

The way Casey saw it, this was a textbook case of murder one, the most serious crime you can commit under the penal code. The Abington kids went to Fox Chase with bats in hand, hunted for a victim for more than forty minutes, ran him to ground, picked him up, took aim at his head, and crushed it. That wasn't involuntary manslaughter, committed in the heat of passion. They weren't mad at Eddie; they didn't even know him. Nor was it third-degree murder. If you take a Louisville slugger and swing for the fences on a human skull, the only possible intent is to cause death. "This was premeditated murder, pure and simple," said Casey.

Casey was determined to prosecute six of the seven defendants for first-degree murder, Carlo Johnson being the exception. But the D.A.'s office could not seek the death penalty, because there were no aggravating circumstances such as lying in wait, kidnapping, torture, or multiple murder. That meant the defendants were entitled to bail.

John's eyes widened. "You mean they could get out of jail after tomorrow? They could be walking the streets this weekend?"

"Technically, yes," Casey replied. "In non-capital cases, defendants have a constitutional right to bail unless the judge rules they are a danger to the community or a flight risk. I'm going to argue to keep them locked up on exactly those grounds. I'm hoping the judge will deny bail, or set it so high their parents can't pay it."

John didn't like what he heard, but he liked Joe Casey. "Why don't you come in and meet Kathy?" he said, surprising himself.

Casey was accustomed to calling on victims' families; it came with the job. He was used to the grief and anger that always met him at the door. But Kathy Polec took his breath away. She was the most frail-looking woman he had ever seen. She was sitting on the couch engulfed in a pink bathrobe. Her hand shook as she lifted her cup of tea. "Are you going to bring my Eddie back?" she whispered. "Can you bring my son back to me?"

Casey flashed back to a case he'd prosecuted in 1975. A young police officer named John McEntee had been shot in the head as he sat in his car filling out a report. The killer, a kid named Anthony Hogan, showed no remorse. Casey won a conviction, but McEntee's father, whom he'd befriended, died shortly after the trial. Casey was so upset he asked for a transfer out of Homicide and stayed away for years. Now, looking at Kathy Polec, he wondered if he'd made a mistake getting back in.

16

Kathy shivered as she looked out the car window. Despite her thick socks, leggings, heavy sweater, and wool coat, she could not get warm. She put her hands between her thighs and rubbed them together, but nothing helped.

"You sure you can do this, Kath?" John asked, wishing he could light a cigarette in the car.

"I have to," she whispered, not sure at all.

It had been twenty-eight days since Eddie died. Today she would see the people who had killed him. She'd sneaked a few looks at them in the newspaper, of course, but it was hard to imagine they were real. Then again, nothing seemed real anymore. Even her own body was alien. A month ago, she'd been a strong, fit woman, able to outrun her kids in any race. Now her clothes hung on her as if they were meant for someone twice her size.

She could hear the tires on the road as the car sped down Roosevelt Boulevard. Family drives had always been loud and boisterous, with the kids laughing in the back seat, teasing one another and talking at the top of their lungs. Now Kristie and Billy sat there in stone silence. She felt as if a violent storm had torn through their lives and was hurtling them forward, blowing them like paper cups down the street.

A shadow passed over the car as they neared City Hall, a behemoth of a monument to great expectations never realized. With foundation walls 25 feet thick, 634 rooms, and a 40-story tower topped by the world's largest sculpture, that of city founder William Penn, it ranked as the largest masonry building in the world, bigger even than the U.S. Capitol. Its architects and designers had envisioned it as the world's tallest building and hoped it would help establish Philadelphia as an American Paris. But by the time construction was completed in 1901, the Washington Monument topped it by more than two feet and its ornate style was considered passé. Many now considered it a monstrous relic, its silver-white Berkshire marble disfigured by decades of car exhaust, black gypsum crust, and algae.

Kathy had passed the building every day in the years before the kids were born, when she worked for a lawyer in Center City. Even then she found it oppressive, representing everything she loathed about the city itself—imposing, impersonal, dirty, badly damaged, and too big to fix. The thought of spending the day inside those cold walls made her shudder.

John parked the car in the garage under City Hall, and the four of them walked the two freezing blocks to the district attorney's office. There they were met by Kathy Boyle, a representative from Families of Murder Victims, a nonprofit organization that worked with the D.A.'s office. John had already talked to her twice on the phone. She'd explained to him that the preliminary hearing was just the first step in an arduous process, one that could take a year or more to resolve. She said she'd stay with them for the long haul, helping them navigate the legal system and cope with the frustration that all grieving families feel.

"Nice to meet you in person," she said, holding out her hand. She smiled at Billy and then turned to hug Kathy and Kristie. "I know what you're going through," she said. "My brother Danny was a Philadelphia police officer who was murdered three years ago, shot in the head during a routine traffic stop. I remember the anger, the inability to sleep. My family all slept in the same room for weeks and weeks after Danny was killed."

She was describing the Polecs' life perfectly. They were still sleeping in the living room, though no one except Kathy was sleeping much.

They felt an immediate connection to this attractive young woman with dark hair, clear eyes, and a direct manner. What struck John most was how normal she seemed. She was working, going to college, having a normal life. Normal seemed so out of reach to him. Normal was something he would give anything to be again.

Like a team coach, Kathy Boyle went over the game plan for the day. The purpose of the hearing was to determine if there was enough evidence to hold the defendants for trial. Joe Casey would put on witnesses to establish the basic facts of the case. The defense would not call any witnesses of its own, but would cross-examine the prosecution's witnesses, challenging their version of events in an attempt to get the charges either thrown out or reduced. In the end, the judge would decide.

It was not yet 8:30 a.m, but a mob of reporters and spectators, cameras and cops already lined the halls outside room 253, the largest courtroom in City Hall. It would be no easy feat to avoid that gauntlet, thanks to City Hall's byzantine layout. According to legend, the building's design was intentionally complicated, so that political patronage jobs could be handed out to party loyalists acting as guides. But Kathy Boyle needed no guide. She took them in an elevator to the sixth floor, then through a maze of dingy hallways to another elevator, and back down to the second floor. It took ten minutes to reach the rear entrance to the judges' chambers, which led into the courtroom.

None of the Polecs had ever seen the inside of a courtroom before, and after the grubby corridors and dank elevators they'd just been through, they were unprepared for the grandeur of room 253. It was enormous—thirty-five hundred square feet with 25-foot ceilings, arched windows, Doric columns, and stern portraits of judges long dead. Looking around, Kathy Polec caught her breath. Perhaps in this magnificent place they would find some justice for Eddie, she thought.

The room was packed. On one side, Kathy saw dozens of familiar faces, friends and neighbors from Fox Chase and many of Eddie's pals. On the other side were faces she didn't recognize, people from Abington, she guessed, friends and family of the defendants. They seemed to stare at her with hard looks devoid of sympathy. She began to tremble. Suddenly the room felt dark and filled with echoes. It was the last place on earth she wanted to be.

Billy wasn't allowed in the courtroom because he was on Joe Casey's list of potential witnesses. He would spend the day in a room with the prosecution's other sequestered witnesses, mostly cops and detectives who'd promised to take care of him. Kristie followed her parents into the courtroom, clutching a photo taken the Christmas before on the family's annual visit to Hershey Park, Pennsylvania. It was a silly picture of her and her boyfriend Brian with Ed and Bill. Ed was wearing his favorite cap turned backwards and was trying to get out of the frame while Brian held him in place. Kristie knew the medical examiner would testify about Eddie's injuries, detailing the number of blows to his head and what had happened to his brain when the bats made contact. She also knew that her mother would leave the courtroom and that her father would feel compelled to stay. She had decided to stay with her dad, and she wanted something to remind her of the way Eddie really was.

As they filed into the front-row seats reserved for the family of the victim, Kathy heard grumbling from the defendants' side of the room. One man complained aloud, "Why do they get the best seats? Why are we forced to sit in the back of the bus?" Stunned by the racial overtones of the remark, she tried to focus on the people she loved. Ed's three best friends sat directly behind her—Colleen McGovern, Lisa Mahoney, and Ellie Stefano.

Ellie was the serious one, more like Bill than Ed. She always struck Kathy as a forty-year-old woman trapped inside a young girl's body. She had a wisdom about her and tended to anchor Ed. They'd been inseparable since sixth grade, a classic case of opposites attracting. Lisa was the free spirit, Ed's female counterpart. Like Ed she was small for her age, with a thousand-watt smile, freckles, and a child's innocence. She and Ed had known each other since they were seven and had remained close all the way through his senior year. Colleen was the sultry one, with curling auburn hair and a pretty, kitten face. She was a sensitive girl with a big heart that was always being broken. These were the girls at the center of Ed's life, who'd shared their most intimate secrets with him, the ones who'd become Kathy's second daughters. Now the girls she'd cared for and worried about were watching her, their eyes filled with concern.

Municipal court judge J. Earl Simmons, Jr., took his seat on the bench, and the seven defendants were led into the room. What a difference their defense attorneys had made. With heads bowed, chins shaved, hair cut and neatly combed, ear and nose rings removed, and coats and ties put on they looked more like a procession of choir boys than a pack of predators.

Joe Casey stood and called deputy medical examiner Ian Hood to the stand. It was Kathy's cue to leave. Kathy Boyle, Ellie, Lisa, and Colleen escorted her to a witness waiting room, where she was met by a small, thin woman with dark curly hair. "I'm Debra Spungen," the woman said. "I'm the head of FMV, Families of Murder Victims."

Spungen told Kathy that her daughter Nancy had been murdered in 1978 at the Chelsea Hotel in New York, stabbed to death by her boyfriend. "Maybe you heard of him, Sid Vicious of the Sex Pistols?" Kathy's eyes widened. Sid Vicious! Could it get any more surreal?

Kristie was not yet two years old when Nancy Spungen was murdered. Even though the killing took place only 90 minutes from Fox Chase, it might as well have taken place in another universe. Kathy remembered the news reports, the morbid descriptions of Sid and Nancy as the apotheosis of punk-rock depravity: the minimally talented bass player who injured himself and bled on stage as part of the group's act; the runaway girlfriend who descended with him into demented drug addiction and ultimately goaded him into slashing her to death in a seedy hotel room. Vicious was charged with murder but was bailed out of jail by his manager and died of a heroin overdose before standing trial. Somebody even made a disturbing movie about it all called *Sid and Nancy*.

"When Nancy was murdered, we didn't know that victims' families had any rights," Spungen told her. "We were alone and scared. I didn't want anyone else to suffer like we did. That's why I started FMV."

Kathy looked into Debra Spungen's eyes and saw herself. She remembered how all the news reports at the time seemed to focus on the rock star, while dismissing his victim as a pathetic drug addict. She recalled rocking Kristie to sleep, thinking that whatever Nancy had become, she'd once been just like Kristie, somebody's little girl, with a mother somewhere who loved her.

Back in the courtroom, John braced himself as Dr. Ian Hood was sworn in. He was determined to sit through every moment of testimony. It was hard to explain exactly why. It was a kind of penance. He couldn't shake his feeling of incompetence because he had so utterly failed to protect his son. The least he could do was learn everything there was to know about Eddie's death. He couldn't stand the idea that other people would find out more about Ed's last minutes than he.

Still, he was grateful when Joe Casey turned the screen for the autopsy photos away from him and the other spectators, toward the judge and the seven defendants. He didn't need to see the pictures to know just how awful they were. Tom Crook's face told the whole story. All the other defendants sat passively, eyes down. But Crook, who was closest to the screen, stared in horror. Little by little, his mouth fell open, until finally he turned away, seeming to gasp for air, his hands white-knuckled as he gripped the edge of the table.

"This is a picture of the head of Edward Polec," Dr. Hood began, "showing, as you can see, numerous abrasions. The bruising of the upper eyelids are called raccoon eyelids. That's due to fractures of the thinning bones of the orbital roots within the skull." Hood pointed at the screen. "The left side of the front of his scalp had this, a faint double-tram track abrasion about four inches long, which is typical of a cylindrical object hitting the human body. He was hit predominantly over the left side of the face," Hood explained, pointing to a bruise that stretched from the left eyebrow, over the eyelid, across the cheek, to the bottom of Ed's nose. "There's another typical tram-type of abrasion going from the left of the left ear, obliquely down toward the corner of his mouth on the left. This is associated with extensive bruising underneath."

As John listened, the sheer brutality of the attack began to sink in. A bat striking a head would normally leave a single bruise where the bat connected with a solid object. But Eddie's face was covered with tram-track bruises, which meant that when the bats were striking his left side, his skull had already been crushed on the right side, reducing his head to a sponge.

There was more: excessively bloody brain tissue; multiple fractures at the base, top, and middle of the skull; upper cheekbones caved in; lacerations of the temporal lobe; and most of the cortex of the brain's cerebral hemisphere destroyed and replaced by blood.

"What is the significance of that, Doctor, medically?" Joe Casey asked.

"Medically it means that, had he survived, which would have been virtually impossible with this extensive injury, he probably would have been in a persistent vegetative state. He would have lost all his higher cortical functions. The most that could have been hoped for, for this young man, was for him to retain only the brain-stem functions that look after your ability to breathe and your heart to beat and to maintain temperature and circulation." Dr. Hood paused, then added, "I guess that wouldn't be much to hope for anyway."

At that moment, John would have taken it. Ever since he'd told the doctors to turn off Eddie's life support he'd been haunted by the fear that he'd made a terrible mistake. Since then he'd heard several news stories of miraculous recoveries, of people suddenly waking up after years in a coma. Dr. Hood could be wrong, he thought. They all could be wrong.

Joe Casey moved close to the witness stand. John could see the muscles in his neck constrict. "Doctor, do you have an opinion, within a reasonable degree of medical certainty, that the injuries you've shown and described are consistent with the deceased being held by his shoulder, such as I am gripping now, and his belt, and that his head was hit while he was being supported by his shoulder and belt?"

The defense lawyers came out of their seats. "Objection," shouted Dewan Alexander's lawyer. "Motion to strike," said counsel for Rienzi. "Pure conjecture!"

How could it be conjecture, John wondered. Eyewitnesses had told the cops they saw Rienzi hold Eddie up by the shoulder and belt while Nick Pinero took shots at his head with a bat. But these lawyers were acting as if Casey were making it up.

Judge Simmons rephrased the prosecutor's question. "What Mr. Casey's hypothetical indicates to you was if he was held in the way Mr. Casey demonstrated, is that consistent with the injuries?"

"It is consistent," answered Hood.

"Doctor," Casey continued, "do you have an opinion, to a reasonable degree of scientific certainty, as to the minimum number of blows that caused the injuries you've described to the head?"

"If I count them, I come up with a minimum of eight impact sites to the head and one to the left hand. And if you considered that abrasion to the below and left corner of the mouth as, in fact, being two blows, then it would be nine to the head and one to the hand."

"Doctor, was a toxicological examination done on Mr. Polec?" Casey asked.

"It was," answered Hood.

"And what were the results?"

John and Kristie held their breath. If there was even the slightest evidence that Ed had been drinking, the defense would try to make him out to be a bad kid, somehow responsible for what had happened.

"No drug abuse, no alcohol, and no common prescription drugs were found," came the reply.

John was sure he let out an audible sigh. Kristie grinned. Good for you, Ed, she thought to herself. They can't lie about you now.

As Dr. Hood left the witness stand, Kathy returned to her seat and John prayed the most painful testimony was over.

Next up, Detective Jimmy Dougherty read Tom Crook's statement to the police into the record. "I heard a couple of stories," Dougherty quoted Crook as saying when asked why he went to Fox Chase for a fight that night. "One was that someone threw a soda on a car, one was somebody spit on somebody, one was that somebody got raped, but I doubted that one." Crook said in his statement that he didn't know how Eddie was knocked down, but he described a group of about ten teenagers encircling, punching, kicking, and hitting him with bats while he curled on the ground and covered his head with his arms. "No words," Crook told the detectives. "I just heard him say 'ah' when he got hit, that's all."

Kathy thought she was going to black out. The room swirled and the voices seemed far away. She gripped John's arm and fought to remain conscious, focusing her attention on Joe Casey as he led several Abington teenagers through their eyewitness testimony. They were cooperating with the prosecution, but she thought they seemed like questionable characters, nothing like the kids she knew from Fox Chase. They seemed listless and hardened, as if they'd left their youth behind a long time ago.

As Casey called seventeen-year-old Jason Mascione to the witness stand, he turned and looked at the Polecs, a signal that things were about to get rough and Kathy should leave. Once again, Ellie, Lisa, and Colleen escorted her out of the courtroom.

Mascione testified that he'd seen his best friend, Anthony Rienzi, strike the first bat blow to a person lying "scrunched up" on the ground. Then, he said, Rienzi dropped the bat, picked the person up by his pants leg and shirt, and held him for Nick Pinero to hit.

"When the defendant Rienzi struck the first blow to this person on the ground with the bat, can you describe how he swung the bat, the manner in which he swung it?" Casey asked.

"Like swinging a golf club," Mascione answered in a monotone.

"And the defendant Pinero, when he hit this person, how many times did you say he hit him, Jason?"

"About four, three or four."

"And how did the defendant Pinero swing the bat?"

"Like chopping wood."

The words hit the courtroom with concussive force. Several people gasped aloud. Reporters scribbled furiously, knowing they'd just been handed their headline.

The hearing dragged on for nearly ten hours. Eyewitness after eyewitness, the prosecution laid out its case against the rest of the defendants: Carlo Johnson provided the bats; Kevin Convey jumped out of the car before it came to a stop and, bat in hand, chased Eddie and knocked him to the ground; Dewan Alexander kicked Eddie several times with his steel-toed boots; Bou Khathavong stood by, cheering, "Yeah, yeah"; Rienzi and Pinero delivered the *coup de grâce*.

During cross-examination, attorneys for the seven tried to make the case that, however tragic the outcome, there was no intent to commit murder when the cars pulled into St. Cecilia's that night. Therefore, there'd been no conspiracy. They argued that the charges should be reduced to manslaughter or, at the very worst, third-degree murder, with bail set appropriately. The attorney for Carlo Johnson proposed that his client shouldn't even be sitting with the others in the courtroom. After all, witnesses had testified that Johnson never got out of the car at St. Cecilia's.

Joe Casey countered that as the oldest of the group, the one the others looked up to, Johnson was a prime instigator of the fight. And it was he who had armed the mob with the murder weapons. "If you hunt with the pack, you share in the kill, and you are part of the conspiracy," he told the judge.

As Judge Simmons looked down from the bench, prepared to make his ruling, Kathy and John clasped hands tightly, girding themselves for bad news.

"What I've heard here today," Simmons intoned, "is such a marked departure from civilized conduct that I can't put anything beyond these defendants. They are sophisticated young people. They drive around in cars; they have beepers. They are just as capable of fleeing as adults." He ordered all the defendants, including Carlo Johnson, bound over for trial on charges of first-degree murder. Bail denied. Pinero, Alexander, and Johnson were also bound over on assault charges for the beating of John Atkinson and another Fox Chase teenager in McGarrity's parking lot.

For the first time, John felt his heart lighten. He watched as Kathy was transformed for a moment into her old self, her face beaming as she jumped to her feet and threw her arms around Joe Casey's neck. He thrilled when he heard Casey announce to reporters in the hallway, "The most heinous crime in my twenty-two years as prosecutor is on the road to being avenged legally."

But the moment of elation passed quickly as reporters crowded around him shouting, "Mr. Polec, Mr. Polec, how do you feel?"

How *could* he feel? he thought. When he got home Eddie would not be there. That was something no judge, no court could ever change.

"We're satisfied," he said, wondering if that was the best he would ever feel again.

17

St. Cecilia's

Edward Polec   *March 22, 1988*

I was born during a blizzard on January 21, 1978. I weighed in at eight pounds and was twenty-one and three-quarters inches long. Not only was the weather something to arrive in, I also turned out to be my Dad's 24th birthday present.

My Mom and Dad and two-year-old sister, Kristie, took me home to our house at 193 W. Spencer Street in Olney. Life was very happy and included many trips to the playground and other parks together. I enjoyed being out and learning to play ball, climb slides and monkey bars. Shortly after my second birthday, my brother Billy was born.

My family continued to spend a lot of time together outdoors. We learned to play baseball, soccer and enjoy nature. Sundays we always started with mass together and then visiting each set of grandparents.

My parents never believed in babysitters and took us everywhere they went. The most memorable moments of my life came at the age of three during a trip to Sears to buy some clothes. My mom promised to buy me, Kristie and Billy and my friend Sean a pretzel when I discovered a bubble gum machine next to the pretzel stand. I didn't realize you had to pay so I put my hand up the machine where it became lodged before my Mom could stop me. A large crowd gathered, people called the fire department and then decided to try turning the machine upside down. My Mom calmly asked if anyone had some hand cream, which she squirted up the slot and gently slid my hand out just as the firemen came through the door with their axes. So at the age of three I learned you never get something for free.

The next few years passed quickly and happily. Family trips to the seashore and Hershey Park and Dutch Wonderland are some of my best summer memories.

I started kindergarten at Finletter School and went to first grade at St. Helena's in Olney. During March of my first grade school year we moved to our house on Solly Place. I finished first grade at St. Helena's and spent the summer making new friends and swimming at Fox Chase Pool. In September I started second grade at St. Cecilia's School. I made a lot of new friends and felt I lived there all the time.

Living at our new house gave me and my brother and sister more things to do. We play ball at a field down the street, play hockey at the top of the street, swim and dive in the summer at the pool down the block, nature hikes in Pennypack Park with our friends all year round.

I play soccer on a travel team for Fox Chase and baseball for N.E.O. I like the excitement of the games and being part of the teams.

My life has been very good to me and I like how it's going. I am always playing sports and going out to play. I hope my life continues to be like this.

18

Kathy opened one eye. She was not yet fully conscious, but two things were immediately clear. Someone was rubbing her head, and her insides ached. From her heart to the pit of her stomach she felt empty, as if she had been hollowed out and left with nothing but an unbearable physical pain. She started to cry.

"I know, sweetheart, I know," soothed Terry Gara. She was sitting cross-legged on the floor, stroking Kathy's head. "Maybe you'd feel better if you washed up," Terry whispered. Kathy slowly pushed herself into a sitting position.

It was Eddie's seventeenth birthday, a day that had no right to be. But somehow January 21 had come anyway, and there were people in the house.

Terry had already been there for hours, cleaning and doing her best to brighten things up. Tina Mason was in the kitchen, cooking. Mary Ellen, Linda, and Pat Esack would come by later to help out.

John walked through the living room and quickly disappeared into the basement. Poor John, Kathy thought. Today was his birthday, too. She'd always done her best to fête both of them, especially after the Humpty Dumpty incident.

It had been Eddie's third birthday, John's twenty-seventh. Kathy had ordered a cake from the neighborhood bakery decorated with Eddie's favorite character, Humpty Dumpty. It wasn't until she put the lighted cake in front of them that she noticed the mistake. In bright red, yellow, and green icing, the inscription read, "Happy Birthday Eddie and Dottie." She and John laughed, but she suspected that in his quiet way he was hurt. After that, she always made sure there was a cake for each of them.

Sitting on the floor with Terry, Kathy was hit by an awful realization. "Oh, John," she wept, "now you have your birthday back, and it's the last thing you ever wanted."

Down in the basement, John was lost in his thoughts. It was a state he'd tried hard to avoid in the weeks since Eddie's death. He'd returned to his part-time job at the Data Processing Trainers business school the week after Thanksgiving, when both Kristie and Billy went back to school. He taught computer programming from 7 p.m. to 10 p.m. The school had offered him a full-time administrative position just before Eddie was killed, and he'd accepted, but now he didn't know if he wanted to do it. He was still being paid by his old company, the Vanguard Group, where he'd accumulated several hundred hours of compensatory time during the past year. The company told him they'd keep paying him until the comp time was used up. Plus, he and Kathy had several thousand dollars they'd put away for Eddie's college. So they had enough money to get by for now, and he felt he needed to be home during the day. There was plenty to keep him busy. Just going through the mail took several hours. Every day there were sympathy cards from strangers, heartrending letters from other parents who'd lost children to violence, offers of free services from local merchants. And every now and then there was a letter that brought tears to his eyes, like the one from Albert Einstein Medical Center.

Dear Mr. and Mrs. Polec:

Your son's medical record came across the desk of our billing department today, and they called asking what we wished to do. It should not have taken that event to have us remember Eddie and to write to you with our condolences. The fast and frenzied pace of the Emergency Room continues and we try to proceed and concentrate on the next patient. However, we, the physicians, nurses, technicians, administrative and allied support staffs, want you to know that we haven't forgotten Eddie and the circumstances of his death. He was not just another victim to us, but rather a reminder of how fragile life is.

We do not wish to burden you or your family further. On behalf of the Emergency Department physicians, we have asked our billing company to cease any billing or collection activity. If you should receive a bill from them, please discard it. Again, we are sorry that we did not write to you sooner. Please know that our thoughts are with you and your family.

Sincerely,
William C. Dalsey, MD
Chairman, Emergency Medicine

Requests from national talk shows and news magazines continued to pour in. John returned every call, responded to every letter, and answered every question, but in each case he declined to be interviewed on camera. In his mind there was a crucial difference between the local and the national news media. Local reporters were covering the story almost daily and might end up changing the 911 system. But the national folks would do it once and then move on to some other ratings-grabbing tragedy.

Still, he tried to be helpful whenever he could. For *Dateline NBC* he drove producer Steve Eckert and anchorman Stone Phillips along the route the caravan of Abington kids took that night, from McDonald's to the Rec to St. Cecilia's parking lot. It was the same sad tour he'd given to at least a dozen local reporters, and it included the same bitter observation at one intersection along the way. "If they had turned left here instead of right," he said, "then Eddie would be alive, and you wouldn't know who I am."

A camera crew from *American Journal* came to the door one day, accompanied by the show's host, Nancy Glass. When John explained that he didn't want to talk on camera they said they understood, but they really needed some pictures of Eddie for their story. So he let them in and set up Eddie's "GQ" photo on the pool table for them to shoot. While the cameraman appeared to be busy doing that, Glass asked him questions about the 911 debacle, which he answered. It wasn't until a week later, when a friend sent him a tape of the *AJ* segment, that he realized they had tricked him and taped his comments surreptitiously, an act that was not only unethical but also illegal in the state of Pennsylvania. He was learning about reporters.

The producer for *The Oprah Winfrey Show* was the most persistent of all. A Philadelphia native, Elizabeth Coady tried through numerous phone calls and letters to convince John that Oprah, with her powerful reach and ability to focus national attention on issues, might do something to change the 911 system. John had never watched Oprah, but he knew the show had a studio audience, and to him that smacked of show business. He wasn't willing to take the slightest chance that Eddie's death would become entertainment. Even so, he found Coady's perseverance admirable, until the day she asked him over the phone, "Are you and Kathy divorced? We haven't seen her on TV, and I know a lot of people divorce after the death of a child." John hung up on her in mid-sentence.

He was surprised when Coady showed up at the house several days later and apologized profusely for her gaffe. She seemed so genuinely contrite that he ended up helping her with the 911 show, providing pictures of Eddie and background information for the broadcast. The show aired on January 18, John and Kathy's twentieth anniversary. John thought Cody had done a good job and he immediately wrote to tell her so. "Your show on 911 was nicely done and examined the Philadelphia issue in a professional, non-sensational manner. That was your promise. Thank you for keeping your word."

Letter writing had become John's therapy. Every day he tapped out dozens of pages—to the mayor, city council members, police inspectors, and "Whoever Might Care." Before Eddie died, John had loathed writing so much his friends joked that he was the only computer programmer in America who didn't know how to operate a word processor. But since the murder he'd set up the family's old computer in the basement and taught himself to use it. Writing became his way of grieving, of trying to take control, of trying to make people listen. It was the only therapy that worked for him.

John had no desire to talk to anyone about his feelings. He'd attended one grief-therapy session sponsored by the FMV. Given the number of homicides in Philadelphia, he figured the meeting room at Jefferson Hospital would be packed with bereaved parents. But only ten people showed up, and as the session got under way it became clear that most of them had been coming to the same meeting for years. The idea that the emptiness he felt would always be there left him more depressed than when he'd arrived. Still, he sat dutifully, waiting for the time to be up. He knew that the therapist and everyone else in the room recognized him from the news reports, and he could feel them wanting him to talk. But he couldn't think of anything to say. He could not imagine crying, nor could he figure out any way to help the others with their pain. When the meeting ended, he practically ran from the room.

Billy and Kristie had seen a therapist briefly, at the Counseling and Referral Agency, CORA, a few miles from home. But she'd only had them draw pictures of their anger, which Billy thought was crazy. By the end of January they'd decided not to go back.

Kathy had therapy occasionally at CORA, too. John met sometimes with Mary Doherty, a spirited woman with a big laugh, strong opinions, and a no-nonsense attitude. John knew Mary had appointed herself his unofficial guardian angel, to watch over him in case he started to snap. But even with her he refused to discuss his feelings, preferring instead to focus on abstractions like problems in the neighborhood or the ills of the world. Still, he trusted Mary and she quickly became a loyal and much loved family friend.

Kathy was still going to therapy twice a week, talking about her grief and getting medication to cope. John couldn't tell if it was making things better for her. Once, during the Christmas holidays, they'd opened the door to the CORA offices and the chime on the door began to tinkle "Oh, Little Town of Bethlehem." It was the only song Eddie had learned to play on the piano. They both froze for an instant, then John caught Kathy just before she hit the floor.

It took her days to get over the incident. He couldn't forget it either. The image kept playing in his mind of Eddie earnestly picking out the song on the piano. He could almost smell the Christmas tree in the background.

John saved his deepest anguish for paper. He'd always been an intensely logical and religious person, but Eddie's death seemed to defy the laws of logic and the tenets of John's faith. In an effort to reconcile what had happened to Eddie with what he believed, he turned to the one person he thought was powerful enough to make sense of this senseless loss. He wrote to the Pope.

> *Your Holiness,*
>
> *In all your years ministering to God's children you have seen the despair that life's experiences can provoke. As the leader of our Church, we are turning to you for your understanding of the tragedies that occur.*
>
> *You see, our son Eddie was murdered last November 11 when he was 16 years old. As he was walking home, he and his brother Billy were surrounded by some 20 people. My two boys ran from the mob, but they caught Eddie and beat him to death with baseball bats on the steps of a Catholic church.*
>
> *We are not asking for insight into why Eddie was beaten and murdered. Rather we are at a loss, based on our Catholic education, to understand how an all-merciful, loving and powerful God could watch as our son was beaten. Why did God not use His power to stop the attack and let Eddie live?*
>
> *While we at first felt that God singled us out for this tragedy, we have come to the realization that senseless tragedy occurs throughout the world on a daily basis. We were always aware of the wars, the famines and tyranny under which people live, but we never KNEW what those who suffered actually felt.*

We have found peace in knowing that our son suffers no more and is with God in heaven. We would love to see him once more just to say good-bye but we know that is not possible. We will rejoin Eddie when we die and go to heaven. In other words, our belief in God is probably stronger now than ever, for doubting God's existence would destroy our chance to ever hold our son again.

Our understanding of God, though, has drastically changed. As children we were taught to pray to God, for all things were possible. We prayed for the end of the Vietnam War and it ended; we prayed for the fall of communism and it fell; we prayed for our children to be good people when they grew up, but Eddie never had a chance to grow up. So maybe praying to God does not do what we were taught.

Is it possible that God really does not get involved in the affairs here on earth? We do not mean to say He chooses to ignore some and help others. Instead, does God have a hands-off policy and never alters the course of human events?

Then what is prayer for? Why do we go to church and pray for this to occur and that to occur? Is the purpose of our prayer misdirected? Is it possible that prayers just allow God to strengthen our soul to withstand the temptations of Satan? Is it possible that praying for anything to happen—like a plane landing safely, or a hurricane turning away from land—is really a waste of both God's time and our own? Because, from the number of times prayers are not answered, it seems that either God sometimes does not listen to our prayers or we asked for something that was not allowed.

So, there are a lot of questions in this letter. But, to sum up our current beliefs:

1. *God made earth and gives each of us a soul.*
2. *God created the laws of nature and never interferes.*
3. *God gives man free will to choose between good and evil and never alters one's right to choose.*

IN EDDIE'S NAME

4. *Satan, on the other hand, chooses to exercise his power on earth. Satan can cause a person to choose evil over good; he can likewise alter the natural laws to suit his purposes.*

5. *Prayers to God will not cause Him to change the natural laws. Nor will prayer cause God to interfere with another's free will. Prayer is a vehicle to talk to God and obtain the strength to deal with the temptations of Satan—through prayer, God enables our soul to choose good over evil.*

Your Holiness, are we close? Or do you have a better, more justified belief that allows you to believe in an all powerful, merciful and loving God when you see the Bosnian tragedies, the Chechnya war, the earthquakes in Japan and Los Angeles, and the atrocities of the Holocaust? If God does use His power on earth, then how does He decide when to use it and when to ignore our pleas for help?

Thanks for reading this. We know you are busy so, if you have someone else who is able to help us out, please let them see our letter.

John, Kathy, Kristie and Billy Polec

Several weeks later, they received a short reply from a Vatican functionary.

Dear Mr. and Mrs. Polec,

His Holiness is saddened to learn of the tragic death of your son Eddie. He asks God our merciful Father to fill you and your family with abiding peace and to sustain you with the consolation and hope offered by our faith in Christ's saving Passion, Death and Resurrection.

With regard to the questions you raised, I would suggest that you discuss these matters more fully with your parish priest.

Sincerely yours,
Monsignor L. Sandri
Assessor

It was hardly the answer John was looking for. The priests and nuns at St. Cecilia's were already doing everything they could for the Polec family. A day did not go by without one of them dropping in. Usually they were a comfort, but one day their attempts at kindness backfired when a young priest noted that the Virgin Mary and Kathy had something in common, the loss of a son. "The Blessed Mother walked where Kathy walks now and knows how she feels," he said. "That's true," John shot back. "But Eddie didn't show up again three days later." The priest cut his visit short.

The man who helped the Polecs the most was Father James Olson, the young priest who had given the homily at Eddie's funeral. Since the day Eddie died, Olson had either called or visited every day. It was his idea to celebrate a special Mass at the Polec house on Eddie's seventeenth birthday. He knew John and Kathy would need some extra comforting and figured that going to church and walking past the steps where Eddie died would be too painful. So he brought the church to Solly Place.

Father Olson was in the living room when John emerged from the basement. It was already dark outside and nearly thirty people were gathered for the Mass. Everyone seemed a little uncomfortable, not sure if this was really the right thing to do. Maybe the Polecs just wanted to be left alone.

Father Olson started in with the Apostles' Creed, words Eddie had repeated a thousand times as an altar boy. "I believe in God, the Father Almighty, the creator of heaven and earth . . ." The group joined in, reciting the words in unison. But somehow, somewhere in the middle of the prayer, they jumped tracks, Father Olson included, and ended up reciting the Gloria. Soon they were all lost.

"That's Ed," a voice piped up from the crowd, and the entire room broke up. Even Kathy was laughing. It was just the kind of flub Ed would have made. He must be in the room, she thought. He probably took one look at this somber assembly and decided to lighten things up a little. After all, today was his birthday, not his funeral.

She looked over at John and beamed. "Happy birthday," she whispered to them both.

19

Detective Bill Danks stomped his feet as he entered the squad room. "Jee-sus Christ, it's cold," he announced, hoping he sounded somewhat normal.

"Don't even bother to take off your boots and coat," said Frank Jastrzembski, on the phone. "There's two dead on Pallas Street and you're up."

Danks shook his head. "Do I at least have time for coffee?" he asked, already headed for the industrial-sized Bunn-O-Matic. Frank chuckled as he hung up the phone. "I'd be getting that coffee to go if I was you. Now you got a 'four bagger' on Pallas and no one else can get there because of the storm."

"All right, all right, I'm outta here," Danks grumbled. It was a hell of a welcome back to Homicide. He'd imagined a very different return to the Roundhouse, sitting around shooting the shit at the Mall Tavern after work and having Betty, the eighty-year-old waitress, get his order wrong, everyone laughing and giving him shit. That's the way it had been for the sixteen years he'd been a detective.

At forty-seven Danks had perfected a hangdog, butt-of-the-office persona. Everyone knew it was an act and that he could always be counted on to serve up the straight lines just to take the fall. But Danks liked the role and needed the laughter. Especially now, when he pretty much felt like crying all the time.

It was February 4. Less than three weeks earlier, he'd buried his youngest, Mary Kate Danks, the week after she turned thirteen. She had been sick since she was seven years old, fighting a losing battle with Fanconi anemia, a rare genetic disorder that keeps the bone marrow from producing white blood cells, red blood cells, and platelets. Only three hundred kids in America get it every year, and most don't survive. But Danks and his wife, Pat, had been hopeful in early November. After weeks of radiation, Katie had received her first bone marrow transplant. It was a good match, and the doctors at Cincinnati's Children's Hospital were telling them, "Katie's the one we save."

Danks got out of the car and stepped around the yellow crime-scene tape. Sure enough, he was the first investigator to arrive; even the crime lab technicians hadn't made it through the snow yet. He could see his breath as he headed into a small, run-down, two-story house. There in the morning light, crammed in a 12-by-12 back bedroom, lay four dead men, all in their early twenties. Two things struck him immediately. First, the victims had been caught unawares, playing Nintendo when they were shot. Second, there were probably two gunmen; two different kinds of 9-millimeter casings littered the floor. It had all the marks of a gang hit.

Better this than the Polec case, Danks thought to himself. That one would have been too tough to handle right now, and with his luck, he would have been the up man. But he'd been in Cincinnati with Katie when his Aunt Dot, a nun at Cardinal Dougherty High, called to tell him that one of the students had been murdered. Before long, Danks was hearing all about Eddie Polec on the evening news in Ohio, where the murder and Philadelphia's dirty 911 laundry were all over the local stations and CNN.

The Polec story became more personal to Danks as Katie grew worse. Her first transplant failed and she prepared for a second, but by Christmas no one was talking about Katie being "the one." Her liver failed, her kidneys failed, her brain hemorrhaged. In the end, he and Pat could only hold her as she died in their arms.

"At least we were there," he told himself. At least she hadn't been lying on the pavement in a parking lot, bleeding out her life, like poor Eddie Polec. One minute the boy is alive, the next his parents get a phone call. Even in his own pain, that was more than Danks could imagine. And yet there was this boy's father on TV calling for calm, telling people to let the justice system take its course.

Not me, Danks thought. I wouldn't have needed a courtroom or a judge; I would have been out for blood, I would have gone up to Abington myself. He turned to the four dead bodies in front of him and began taking careful notes, knowing that one day he would have to testify about what he found.

At least I won't be sitting on the witness stand with the Polecs looking at me, he told himself, not imagining that in less than a year he would be in court with them every single day, helping Joe Casey prosecute their son's killers.

20

The light from the television flickered in the darkened room. The Channel 6 anchor team blathered their closing inanities as Kathy waited for Ed to come home. She knew he would make his 11:30 p.m. curfew, just as Billy made his at exactly 10:30.

She was lucky, she thought. She had good kids who didn't argue much about her rules. Even Ed, who was a senior now, hadn't made a fuss when she told him he wasn't allowed to spend the night with friends. Kathy wanted the comfort of seeing her kids at the end of the evening. And she needed that good-night kiss, which was two parts affection and one part Breathalyzer. She would have made a good cop.

Lately, she'd been trying to give Ed a little more freedom, encouraging him to cut back on his heavy workload at Boston Chicken, and even agreeing that this year he finally could get his driver's license. Last winter, when he turned sixteen, she had said no, using the icy weather as an excuse to cover her real concern. "If anything could happen, it would happen to Ed," she always said. She was not anxious to have him on the road even in the best of weather. In recent weeks, he'd pestered her about buying a motorcycle. "No one in this house will ever have a motorcycle," she'd said with finality, and Eddie didn't argue.

Eddie Polec, age sixteen
(POLEC FAMILY)

(Left to right) Billy, Eddie, and Kristie on a family trip to Hershey Park, Pennsylvania, in 1984

John and Kathy Polec after the verdict
(AP/NANINE HATZENBUSCH)

Kevin Convey (top left) and the six defendants: (top row) Nick Pinero, Anthony Rienzi, Thomas Crook; (bottom row) Dewan Alexander, Bou Khathavong, and Carlo Johnson

Assistant District Attorney
Joe Casey
(AP/CHRIS GARDNER)

Lead defense attorney A. Charles Peruto
(AP/CHRIS GARDNER)

Kristie and Billy Polec, leaving the courthouse during the trial
(YONG KIM/*PHILADELPHIA DAILY NEWS*)

(top) Kathy Polec on her corner, guarding the students of St. Cecilia's
(MICHAEL S. WIRTZ/*THE PHILADELPHIA INQUIRER*)
(bottom) John Polec speaking to middle-school students about the causes and effects of violence
(ART GENTILE/*BUCKS COUNTY COURIER TIMES*)

When she heard the basement door slam at 11:29, Kathy breathed a sigh of relief: all her children were home safe. Kristie and Bill headed downstairs to greet Eddie, but stopped in mid-flight. Their talkative brother was even more animated than usual, and it was clear to them that he wasn't going to pass Kathy's breath test.

"You know, Mom," he slurred as he sidled toward the staircase, "I'm a senior in high school now and I think that if I can pay the insurance on a motorcycle, I should be able to get one."

He grabbed the banister for balance and rested his chin on the wrought-iron curve. Kathy couldn't help thinking how ridiculous and angelic he looked as he tried to make his case. "I'm a senior now, Mom, so it should be my decision," he said, slurring.

Kathy looked at him hard. "I'll let you know my 'dee-shish-un' in the morning."

"You're a great kid," she told him the next day. "You've never given us any trouble. You're doing well in school and this was the first time you ever came home like that. But you broke the rules and you know it. So now you've lost the chance to get your driver's license for another three months. That's my decision and there is no discussion."

Two months later she wondered, Was I too easy on him? If I had grounded him for three months he'd still be alive.

21

On February 15, Municipal court judge Carolyn E. Temin did what Joe Casey knew all along she would do. She granted bail to six of the defendants. The seventh, Tom Crook, hadn't asked for bail. His lawyer, Janis Smarro, had been blunt with him: Given the statement he made to the police, at trial he certainly would be convicted of at least manslaughter and be sentenced to a lengthy jail term. Since any time served now would count against his sentence, he might as well start getting it out of the way.

Attorneys for the six had made their case at a two-day hearing that at times approached theater of the absurd. In the confusion of reporters and spectators cramming into the small courtroom, the bailiffs had seated the Polecs in the front row on the defendants' side of the room, so close they could almost reach out and touch them. From that uncomfortable distance John, Kathy, Kristie, and Billy listened as a parade of character witnesses put forward a parallax view of the teenagers accused of murdering Eddie.

Carl E. Johnson testified that his son Carlo was a "good boy" who'd never been in any "real trouble" before. Never mind that Carlo's girlfriend and her mother had once filed a police complaint accusing him of violent and abusive behavior, Mr. Johnson said that what had happened at St. Cecilia's that night was a "mistake" and, of course, "everybody makes mistakes."

Billy couldn't hold his tongue. "Yeah, we all make mistakes," he said under his breath, "but we don't commit murder. Murder is not a mistake."

The Reverend Joseph L. Patterson, a leader among Philadelphia's black clergy, told the court that he'd known the Johnson family for years, since "Carlos" was born. He said "Carlos" was a fine young man, who regularly attended church and Friday-night choir practice.

"If you know him so well," Joe Casey said sarcastically, "why aren't you aware that his name is Carlo, not Carlos? And can you explain how he could be at choir practice every Friday night when he was very clearly in Fox Chase on the Friday night Eddie Polec was killed?" The reverend had no answer.

Boukay Khathavong looked tired and defeated as he pleaded, through an interpreter, for his son's release. But he gave the court no assurances that he could keep Bou out of trouble. Yes, he admitted, Bou had been arrested for criminal trespass, had run away from home, and had repeatedly cut class. Yes, he said, he had once asked the courts to place Bou in a residential treatment facility because no matter what he did, he just couldn't make Bou "show respect or obey."

Theresa Convey told the judge, "I absolutely want Kevin back home." But she acknowledged that she'd been called to school on numerous occasions because of her son's academic problems and disruptive behavior. "Sure, I told him every time to behave," she said, assuring the court that this time she would control him.

Casey countered the character witnesses with the official record of the defendants' antisocial and criminal behavior. Dene Harris, a Montgomery County juvenile probation officer, testified that Dewan Alexander had failed to appear at three successive hearings on assault charges. When Alexander finally did appear for the fourth hearing, he was released into the custody of his parents, then failed to show up for his next court date and ran away from home. After his probation was revoked and he served time in a residential treatment center, Alexander returned to Abington High and promptly got into trouble again. He skipped school fifty-four days in one year, was late another twenty-six days, and was finally suspended for holding down a student while others beat him.

Nick Pinero's record included arrests for "loitering and prowling at night, theft by unlawful taking, receiving stolen property, and conspiracy." Nick was placed on six months' probation for his scrapes with the law, but his probation was extended three more months after he was suspended from school for an eighth time. The probation was extended yet again when Pinero was cited for disorderly conduct and possession of alcohol.

Only Anthony Rienzi had no prior involvement with the juvenile justice system. His one previous infraction was a disorderly-conduct citation growing out of a dispute with a next-door neighbor over the volume of his stereo. Rienzi's lawyer, John McMahon, went so far as to claim that his client had no involvement in Eddie's death, that he was a mere "bystander." Casey reminded the court that witnesses had said Rienzi was not only the first to hit Eddie with a bat but was also the one who took a "golf shot" at his head. "A young man who would do that is capable of anything," he said.

Casey summed up by arguing that the six teenagers should remain in jail until trial because "their parents did not or could not control them, and they went about doing what they chose to do without any parental supervision." But in the end, he knew it would all come down to the Constitution, and that without "special circumstances," Judge Temin would have no choice. John seemed to comprehend the legal realities, but Casey could not make Kathy understand. Finally, he put it to her in the starkest of terms: "Their children may be able to go home, even though Eddie can't."

She was still trying to grasp the concept when the bailiffs began the ritual of handcuffing the defendants to take them out of the courtroom. It was always the same drill: first one person was handcuffed, then another, then two were hooked together into a pair. As he waited his turn, Nick Pinero stood looking into the crowd, probably searching for the faces of his family. But John could see that Kathy thought Pinero was staring at her. And the more Pinero looked, the madder John got. He was only inches away from the person who had beaten his son to death, near enough to reach out and choke him. Instead, he looked directly into Pinero's eyes as he was being led away and said calmly, "See ya later, Nick."

You'd have thought he'd fired off an Uzi. Kathy Boyle grabbed him by the arm and hissed, "Shut the hell up." Pinero's attorney, Bernie Siegel, complained to the judge that courtroom security was dangerously lax. He accused John of "threatening" his client.

Surely the world's gone crazy, John thought as he left the courtroom.

After the bail hearing, Judge Temin received a petition with a thousand signatures from Fox Chase residents urging her to keep Ed's killers behind bars. A group of neighborhood mothers even organized a demonstration: three hundred people marched through the streets of Fox Chase carrying placards that read, "Say no to bail" and "Eddie Polec can't go home, why should they?" To no avail.

"I find that under the law each defendant is entitled to bail," Temin announced from the bench on February 15. But she didn't make it easy on them: $1 million for Nick Pinero, Anthony Rienzi, and Dewan Alexander, $750,000 for Bou Khathavong; $450,000 for Kevin Convey; and $350,000 for Carlo Johnson.

The defense attorneys protested the amounts as punitive. "When you set $1 million bail and $700,000 bail and you know people are impoverished, that's like saying you are not getting any bail," complained Carlo Johnson's lawyer. Still, Joe Casey figured that at least three of the defendants—Rienzi, Pinero, and Johnson—ultimately would make bail, because the law provided that, in lieu of collateral in the full amount, defendants could be released upon posting only 10 percent in cash. "He'll be out within a week, absolutely," predicted Anthony Rienzi's father. There would be severe restrictions, however. Judge Temin went along with all of Casey's recommendations on that score. The accused would have to remain in their homes unless they were meeting with their attorneys. They would be fitted with electronic bracelets to monitor their movements, and they would be subject to random visits by court employees. They were not allowed to go to Fox Chase and were barred from passing within a block of Abington High School and two blocks of Cardinal Dougherty. There was an extensive list of people they could not contact under any circumstances, including the Polecs and any possible witness to the murder.

John knew it was the best that could be hoped for, but he was nagged by fears that Eddie's killers might still escape justice. Those fears were fueled by a story that had been all over the news the week before the bail hearing. Alex Kelly, a former high school wrestling and football star from Darien, Connecticut, had been accused of raping two teenage girls and arrested in 1986, when he was eighteen. Kelly fled the country after his wealthy parents posted $200,000 bail and spent the next nine years skiing, scuba diving, and mountain climbing across Europe, aided and abetted by his family's money. He had finally been apprehended last month, but his lawyers were fighting his extradition back to the United States. In a weird way, John understood Alex Kelly's parents. If Kristie, Billy, or Eddie were facing life in prison, wouldn't he, too, spend any amount of money, do anything short of murder to keep that from happening? All of which was in his mind on February 15 when he walked out of the courtroom and faced a pack of reporters shouting, "Mr. Polec, how do you feel about the judge's ruling today?"

For the first time since the ordeal began, John allowed his private bitterness to break through. "The best thing that could happen," he said flatly, "would be for them all to rot in prison."

22

Chuck Peruto leaned back in his leather office chair and said to himself, "This ought to be interesting."

After months of following it in the newspaper, the sixty-eight-year-old criminal defense attorney was about to become involved in the biggest murder case to hit Philadelphia in years. It was exactly the kind of case he relished: high-profile, complicated, and controversial, with a defendant already tried and convicted in the press.

"Mr. Peruto," his secretary's voice echoed on the speaker phone, "the Pineros are here to see you."

He'd already met Nick's parents, who'd come to him after deciding that Bernie Siegel should be replaced. Peruto figured the case against the kid must be so strong that Bernie, an excellent trial lawyer, had given them little hope for acquittal. Today he would meet Nick for the first time. The seventeen-year-old was let out on bail after his parents had posted $100,000 in cash for his release.

Peruto didn't need the police reports to tell him that his newest client was in deep shit. Nick was being portrayed in the press as evil personified, the most brutal killer in a brutal murder. In that sense, he was the perfect client, the kind Peruto had spent his life preparing for.

Angelo Charles Peruto, Sr., had made his reputation winning seemingly unwinnable cases. Over the years he'd successfully defended some of Philadelphia's most notorious criminals, including "Hunchback" Harry Riccobene, a major Mafia figure and the rival of mob boss Nicodemo "Little Nicky" Scarfo. He won an acquittal for a local judge who was caught on videotape accepting a cash payoff from the Roofers Union. More important, he'd never lost a murder case, prompting his colleagues to refer to him as "the white Johnny Cochran."

"The guiltier you are, the more you need Chuck," said one competitor. "He's an excellent trial lawyer—funny, entertaining, and able to throw up nine million red herrings to bamboozle a jury."

He was a small man, with a larger-than-life personality and a penchant for sarcastic one-liners that had earned him the sobriquet "clown prince of the courtroom." His mother had named him Angelo because "he has the face of an angel." But her son had grown up more full of fire than light. At seventeen he'd enlisted in the Navy as a radio gunner, then went on to flight training school, hoping to see some action as a pilot. But World War II ended before he got there, and while everyone else was celebrating peace, Peruto was complaining he'd been "screwed out of the fighting." In the years since, he'd managed to stay in the thick of battle.

Ellen Pinero entered the office first. She was a blond, slightly overweight woman with fair skin and sad eyes. Peruto had her pegged as a mother who might have loved well but not too wisely. She'd inherited a school for learning disabled children, but couldn't seem to accept the fact that her own son was a slow learner. From what Peruto could tell, she'd done everything she could to mask Nick's disabilities. Nick's father, Carlos, was a swarthy man with a barrel chest, bushy eyebrows, and a heavy beard. He was a social worker, and it was evident that Nick's behavior disgusted him. From what Peruto could tell, Carlos Pinero had never had much use for his oldest child. Nick was last. Clean-shaven, with a dark suit that matched his eyes, he seemed quiet and withdrawn. Peruto was sure he saw some remorse. He was also sure he saw a loser, an insecure kid who worked overtime to impress his peers. Nick reminded Peruto of his own son Joseph, who'd gotten into trouble as a teenager and never got out, traveling with the wrong crowd and taking drugs. He'd died of a heart attack at the age of twenty-six.

Peruto had not been able to save his son, but he thought maybe he could do something for this kid. His first order of business was to lower everyone's expectations.

"Look, I have vast experience in homicide," he said, looking straight at Nick. "There is no way you can get out of this. The best you can hope for is a lesser charge. My advice is to plead guilty to everything and make a deal for third-degree murder."

Nick listened in silence as his mother cried and his father sat stone-faced. Peruto continued: "The only way I can rescue you is to prevent you from spending the rest of your life in prison. If I'm successful, you will be out by the time you are thirty-two."

The family asked few questions, and Nick had nothing to say. Peruto got the sense that they would go along with whatever he recommended. "Let's see if Joe Casey will go for a plea," he said, escorting them to the door. "I'll let you know what he says."

Back in the office he speed-dialed the district attorney's office. "Joe, Chuck Peruto here. I want to talk about a deal."

"No deal, Chuck," said Casey. "No way are we *ever* going to cut your guy a break. We're going for murder one right down the line."

"Okay, have it your way," Peruto said with a smile. "I'll see you in court."

23

April 7 was a strange day. It was Billy's fifteenth birthday and the house was filled with friends trying to make up for the fact that his big brother wasn't there to celebrate with him.

But the festivities kept getting interrupted by reporters calling and knocking on the door to ask for the family's reaction to the big news of the day: all the disciplined 911 operators were getting their jobs back.

Responding to a grievance filed by AFSCME, a labor arbitrator ruled that the city had overstepped its authority and dealt too harshly with the union workers. According to the ruling, the three operators fired for mishandling calls and being abusive to callers were "discharged without just cause." As a result, Linda Carroll's punishment was reduced to a ten-day suspension, Victoria Randall was given a fifteen-day suspension, and Osborne Walker got twenty days. All three were ordered returned to their jobs with back pay and benefits. The transfers of the other three operators were nullified and their suspensions were drastically reduced. They were told they could go back to their old jobs after a period of "retraining."

"I feel as if I've been vindicated," crowed Nicole Burton. "It's not the 100 percent restoration that I expected, but I think [the arbitrator] was fair and it was the best he could do."

"I'm just happy that's it's over," said Osborne Walker. "I thank the Lord, because it had gone far enough."

Ignoring the overwhelming public sentiment against his members, AFSCME leader "Reds" Mauldin complained that the six never should have been punished in the first place. "Although I'm still not totally satisfied with the arbitrator's decision," he told reporters, "at least our people are back to work."

The Rendell administration acknowledged the defeat grudgingly. "We are disappointed but not surprised," said the mayor's chief of staff,

David L. Cohen. "It is almost impossible to discipline people in the current grievance-arbitration environment." The mayor was more blunt. "The system just stinks," he said. "The arbitrator is dead wrong." Rendell said the city had no choice but to bring the operators back, but he vowed he would stop them from ever answering 911 calls again. "The highest court we can go to is going to have to tell me to put them in the radio room before I will put them back there," he said.

The ruling drew the wrath of local editorial writers. The *Daily News* lampooned the decision, saying it was harder to fire a city employee than it was to "get ice water in hell." The editorial suggested it would be better to replace all the 911 operators with voice mail, "so you could call 911 and hear a pleasant pre-recorded voice saying, 'If you are reporting a murder, press one; if you are reporting a rape, press two.'" Such a system would "eliminate most human contact, and that would be a mercy to any Philadelphians unfortunate enough to need 911," the piece went on. "And it's a lot easier to fire a computer."

But the reporters who called or came by the Polec house expecting to land a fiery quote were disappointed. John low-keyed it as usual, telling them he had never wanted to see the operators fired in the first place, only removed from the radio room. He said he trusted Deputy Commissioner Bill Bergman, who told him that the operators would never again answer the phones, and that was good enough for him. In truth, though, it was getting harder for him to keep to his message that the Polec family would "respect the system." The more he learned about the justice system, the political system, and the 911 system, the less faith he had in any of them.

By now, John was something of an authority on 911. Some of what he'd learned came from the media. For example, *Dateline NBC* producer Steve Eckert informed him that, along with all the other mistakes made the night Eddie died, the first Rescue Squad sent to the scene never arrived because it was given the wrong location.

But much of what John knew about 911 he'd taught himself. He'd spent the night of Friday, March 31, sitting at the Roundhouse watching the system in action. The call takers themselves had pretty straightforward jobs, answering phones and typing the information into the system. The operators may have behaved badly and mishandled calls the night Eddie died, but from what he could see, the real problem wasn't with them, it was with the dispatch system.

While the operators sat at their computer terminals taking calls from citizens, the dispatchers worked like one-armed paperhangers—simultaneously taking in information from the operators and radio calls from patrol cars on the street. John likened the system to a huge funnel. At the wide end were all the people in Philadelphia who might call 911. In the middle were the call takers, passing their vital information on. And at the narrow end were the dispatchers, who broadcast the emergency calls to cops on the beat and who had an almost impossible job to pull off. What John saw in his mind as he watched were police cars lining the streets, waiting for calls that slowly dripped out the funnel, a form of water torture for those in need of help.

The reason the cops had to wait so long for the dispatchers, and the people had to wait so long for the cops, was that there was only one dispatcher in each section of the city who could broadcast calls. The system had been set up with a separate radio band for each section, and each radio band could handle only one call at a time. That might have been okay in the 1970s, when the system was first installed. But by the late 1980s, it was woefully inadequate. John learned that in the Northeast section on the night Eddie was killed, one dispatcher was handling calls to and from eighty patrol cars. You couldn't add dispatchers to relieve the backlog of calls because it was technically impossible to increase the number of radio channels. As a result, the amount of radio "air time" available for broadcasting emergency calls was permanently fixed at not enough. And the more calls that poured into the funnel, the longer it took for that information to get to the street.

City officials were aware of the "air time" problem, but they had no idea what the lag time was between a call coming in to 911 and a dispatcher sending it out to a cop on patrol. John figured it out. Using raw data supplied by the police department, he took records of calls and dispatches, picking days at random over a six-month period, and fed them into a computer. In less than six hours of programming, his analysis was complete: On any given Friday or Saturday night in Philadelphia, a typical 911 call languished in limbo for up to an hour before it was broadcast to a patrol car.

And that wasn't the only problem. Each dispatcher was spending an inordinate amount of time doing clerical work. It was the dispatcher's job to conduct driver's license and vehicle registration checks for cops making routine traffic stops, all on the same single radio channel. In 1994, a third of the three million calls dispatchers handled were for traffic stops.

Chicago, Los Angeles, and Las Vegas had adopted a new 800-megahertz radio system. The system was powerful enough to provide multiple channels, which meant more dispatchers could be put in charge of fewer patrol cars. And the new system allowed for the installation of small computers, called mobile digital terminals, or MDTs, inside each patrol car. That meant that officers on traffic stops could get license and registration information themselves, bypassing the dispatcher and increasing the available airtime. In addition, the MDTs helped police supervisors keep abreast of what was happening in their districts by telling them which officers were busy with jobs and which ones were patrolling. The supervisors would also have a window on the dispatch backlog that showed them if any 911 calls were waiting to be broadcast. If all the dispatchers were busy, a supervisor could send a cop on a call, in effect becoming a backup dispatcher.

John learned that the night Eddie was killed, 911 calls were delayed because the dispatcher was busy on a series of traffic violations, and because supervisors patrolling the streets had no idea that calls from Fox Chase were backing up. Had the MDTs been in place, they probably would have saved Eddie's life. But the 800-MHz system cost an estimated $50–60 million, and even the mighty Ed Rendell hadn't saved the city that much money.

John was on the phone almost constantly with Bill Bergman as the two tried to work out a solution to 911. They discussed the possibility of giving officers cell phones and assigning a group of people other than the dispatchers to perform the license and registration checks. Frustrated merchants in the city's touristy South Street area had already taken it upon themselves to bypass 911. They'd bought cell phones for the police assigned to patrol their street so that they could simply call the cops directly.

Bergman took the idea to Joe Martz in the managing director's office. Joe countered with an even better idea. Why couldn't the little MDTs be installed using a cell phone network instead of the 800-MHz system? Rather than laying out $50 million, the city would pay $3,000 per computer, plus the monthly cell phone fees. With five hundred patrol cars and other ancillary costs, Martz figured the city could have the 911 system it needed for a mere $3.25 million, plus $150,000 a year in cell phone costs.

Bill Bergman and Joe Martz told John they needed a month to clear some bureaucratic hurdles and they'd be back to him. John was ecstatic. But April came and went and he heard nothing. Frustrated, he requested a meeting with the mayor, and on May 2 he found himself in a small conference room on the second floor of City Hall waiting for his first face-to-face meeting with Ed Rendell.

Although he'd been living in the public eye for months, John was still nervous whenever he met "official" people. Even the homicide detectives intimidated him a little. He couldn't help addressing the amiable Tom Perks and Art Mee as "sir." But for some reason, he had no anxiety about talking to the mayor. Perhaps it was because he couldn't work up any awe for a politician.

Rendell rushed into the room, late as usual. He apologized for making John wait, then launched into what sounded like a campaign speech. "I know the system isn't perfect yet, but look at all the ways we've improved 911 already." He spoke quickly and with great enthusiasm. "The call takers have been given sensitivity training, the city is putting more police officers on the street, and we are searching for a way to have the call takers answer the phones faster."

John couldn't believe what he was hearing. This was nothing more than what John had read in the newspapers back in early December.

The mayor's own 911 committee had made virtually the same suggestions in March and further recommended better public education about 911 use, the creation of a non-emergency number and career counseling for 911 operators who felt their jobs were dead-end. They were well-intentioned proposals, John thought, but almost laughable in light of what he'd learned about the dispatcher problem.

"Do you really think the system will be fixed by having the call takers say 'Philadelphia 911' more quickly?" he asked. "That will save only a few seconds. What about the dispatching issue? What about the fact that it takes an hour to get the calls to the street?"

John could see the mayor reddening. "The biggest problem is that we don't have enough cops on the street," Rendell insisted. "There is federal money coming and we are going to use it to do just that."

John tried again. "There were plenty of cops available the night Eddie died," he said. "The problem wasn't the cops, it was that they weren't sent to Fox Chase until it was too late." But it was no use. John could see that Rendell thought he didn't get it, couldn't see the "big picture." The feeling was entirely mutual.

Two weeks later they met again. This time Joe Martz was there, too. And this time John thought they were getting somewhere. The city agreed to investigate whether the fire department's 800-MHz system was capable of handling radio traffic for five hundred MDTs in patrol cars. The study would be completed in a matter of weeks. At that point, the city would decide whether it was better to modify the fire department's system or to use the cell phone network. Either alternative would be an interim solution, until the police department got its own 800-MHz system. The city seemed to be moving in the right direction.

As usual, John took detailed notes during the meeting and wrote a two-page letter to Joe Martz the next day outlining his understanding of the city's plan. He ended by saying, "If I have misunderstood anything here, could you let me know?"

If John misunderstood anything, it was the way the city worked. By the end of June there would be no progress.

24

Kathy stood on the Fox Chase playground looking up at the darkening sky. It will rain for sure, she thought. Eddie always brought the weather.

This was to be her solo debut, the first time since the murder that she had appeared in public without John. He was at City Hall for another pretrial status hearing. She was at the Rec, where the staff of the Fox Chase post office was planting a tree in Eddie's name. Kristie, Mary Ellen, Linda, Terry, and Pat were all there to give her moral support, but it was up to her to say something. "I hope I don't blow it and start crying," she whispered to Kristie.

She had expected it to be a low-key affair. But the TV stations and newspapers sent reporters and photographers. Kathy's presence made it a bigger story. For months she had been an enigma, a wraithlike figure hurrying away from them with her head buried in her husband's coat. "You won't believe it," reporter Margie Smith said when she called her assignment desk on the mobile phone. "Kathy Polec is here and she's going to *talk.*"

Kathy looked around. It was a warm, overcast May day. Mothers with toddlers on tricycles and in strollers were coming and going from the playground. A month before, she'd ventured into the back yard one afternoon, drawn by the smell of the sweet spring grasses. But all she could feel was rage. She resented the bright new green of the trees, the soft clouds, the days getting longer. If Eddie couldn't enjoy it, then neither could she.

But she couldn't go back inside, either. Maybe it was the months of counseling, maybe it was the Zoloft finally kicking in, but she was becoming more and more aware of the world around her, especially of Billy and Kristie. If she stopped living because Eddie was dead, then it would be like telling them that she loved Eddie more than she loved them. So she began to say yes when Linda or Mary Ellen suggested a walk around the block. The exercise and fresh air seemed to help a little, lifting the depression and giving her energy. She even agreed to go Easter shopping for the kids.

For as long as she could remember, she had shopped in threes: three Easter baskets, three Christmas stockings, three goody bags for Valentine's and St. Patrick's Day. She knew that Ed was gone now, but "threes" were so ingrained in her mind that she couldn't stop from reaching for the Cleveland Indians baseball cap or the Marvin the Martian Looney Tunes pen. Everywhere she looked she saw something that would have made Ed's eyes light up. Each time she signed an Easter card she would start to write Ed's name, too. It always came right after Kristie and before Billy. How could she leave it off? How could she include it? People would think she was crazy if she signed his name the way she always had before. But she'd be leaving him behind if she didn't. In the end, she bowed to convention, knowing that for the rest of her life all her cards would look empty and unfinished, just like she felt.

But she'd begun to realize that the best way to keep Ed with her was to get involved in the world on his behalf. "I'm still his mom," she told herself. "The only way for people to know what a wonderful person he was is for me and the rest of the family to show them."

"We bless this tree in the memory of Eddie Polec," the priest intoned. Kathy lifted the shovel and turned over the first chunk of soil. Then Kristie took her turn.

"On behalf of the Fox Chase post office, we give you this certificate in memory of Eddie," said the postmaster, patting Kathy's hand as he struggled to find the right words. "Too much of today is about rights and privileges instead of responsibility," he said. "Hopefully, this will be a start in making changes."

Kathy looked at the framed certificate with Eddie's name embossed on it. There were tears in her eyes as she thanked the postmaster. But by the time the television crews reached her she had composed herself. "This tree is the perfect symbol for Eddie," she told Margie Smith. "He loved nature and he loved animals, so I can't think of a better tribute to him than to have a place where kids can climb and animals can live."

Every year since they'd moved to Solly Place, Kathy had tried to plant a garden and grow a healthy lawn. And every year, every living thing she touched died. "This is the Dr. Kevorkian Home for Plants," Ed had teased her. Last summer was the worst. The entire yard turned brown despite her efforts. "It's a dust bowl back there," the kids joked. "Give it up, Mom."

But in recent weeks the yard had suddenly begun to flourish. Kathy dug a trench separating her garden plot from the lawn. She read books on plants, studied up on fertilizers, and began putting in miniature daffodils, columbine, and hyacinth. The more time she spent in the garden, the closer she felt to Eddie. "He's there, John," she'd say, "I know he is." John would roll his eyes, but Terry Gara was sure it was true. As the weather got hotter and hotter, even the neighborhood's most experienced gardeners were losing their plants. But Kathy's back yard looked like Eden. "It's gotta be Ed," Terry told her, "because, God knows, you have a black thumb."

On June 9, 1995, Eddie graduated from high school.

The sky was bright blue over Philadelphia that morning, there was a light breeze, and the air smelled like summer vacation. It was a day made for Ed, who would have been at the center of it all, laughing and joking, waiting impatiently for the ceremony to begin and even more impatiently for it to end.

John and Kathy couldn't imagine being in the crowd of boisterous kids and proud parents at Cardinal Dougherty, but neither could they imagine missing Eddie's graduation. So Billy and the school principal, Father Paul Kennedy, devised a way for them to attend the ceremony and remain out of sight. They set up a wooden bench for Kathy, John, and Father Olson in the projection room above the auditorium. From the small square window, Kathy looked down on the stage where

Kristie had been handed her diploma two years ago and where she and John had received theirs two decades before.

This was a moment Kathy and Eddie had dreamed about for years as he struggled through one class after another. "I'm going to get you into that cap and gown if it's the last thing I do," she had vowed repeatedly, sometimes wondering if it really would happen.

Just getting him to sit down long enough to study was a challenge. But when he was in eighth grade she had found a solution. As soon as he hit the bathroom, she'd plant herself at the top of the stairs outside the door. "Give me the word 'invincible,' " she'd yell to her captive audience. "Spell it phonetically, then spell it the right way and then tell me where the accent falls." Eddie would groan, "Aw, Mom, not *now*." Then he'd dutifully launch into his vocabulary assignment.

Kathy promised him that high school would be easier, less structured. "You're the kind of kid who brings life and experience to a classroom," she said. "Teachers in high school like that." And they did. Ed did better at Cardinal Dougherty, but it was never easy. "I'm just not academic, Mom," he told her a few weeks before he died. "I don't think I'm ready for college."

Instead of being disappointed, Kathy was impressed by his clear-eyed assessment and his new goals. Eddie had always wanted to be a chef, but after working at Boston Chicken and watching his boss, Chris Regel, work nights, holidays, and weekends, he decided cooking wasn't for him. "I want a job where I can be home more with my family," he told her in their last lengthy heart-to-heart. "I think I'll go into the Coast Guard. I'll only be twenty-one when I get out and by then I'll be ready for college, and the government can pay my way."

Kathy wondered now if she'd given him fatal advice during that conversation. "You've worked so hard these past few years," she said. "Maybe it's time to work less and relax and enjoy life a little more."

He was pleased but suspicious. "I thought you wanted me to work and not hang out," he said.

"I did," she responded carefully, "but it's your senior year and you've earned a break. Why don't you cut back your work hours a little?"

If only he'd been at Boston Chicken that Friday night instead of at the Rec, she thought for the hundredth time as she looked down at the parade of cranberry-colored caps and gowns entering the auditorium. The sound of 10,000 Maniacs came through the loudspeakers—"These are the days, the sweetest we will know"—as smiling photographs of the senior class flashed on a large screen at the back of the stage, showing her just how much of his senior year Ed had missed. She watched as the 332 seniors filed onto the stage and filled every seat but one. They left one empty for Ed.

She looked over at John. He was biting his lip, his Adam's apple bobbing up and down. There was nothing to say. She was glad Father Olson was holding her arm.

One by one, the names of the graduates were called and they walked to the center of the stage to accept their diplomas. "Diane Marie Pescatore . . . Adam Edward Peterson"—Father Olson tightened his grip—"Jeannine Josephine Pierson . . . David Stanley Plewa . . . Edward William Polec."

The crowd began to clap. The applause built to a crescendo of whoops, whistles, and cheers as everyone rose from their seats to give Eddie a two-minute standing ovation.

Kathy could see him clearly now. His eyes were filled with light as he tossed his cap high into the air and shouted up to her at the top of his lungs, "I did it, Mom, I did it."

25

Kristie watched her boyfriend's nieces and nephews wrestling on the floor. She loved being at Kevin's house. He lived in Lawn Crest, only five minutes away from her house. But it was another world, a normal one.

She could smell the barbecue going in the back yard and was looking forward to a day of parades and fireworks. The Fourth of July was her only day off the entire summer. She worked at Boston Chicken weeknights, at Fox Chase Camp weekdays, and at Pizza Hut on weekends. She had figured that if she kept busy enough she would think less about Ed. But everywhere she went she was reminded of him. His friends were older now and hanging out more and more with her crowd. It was impossible to be with them without seeing the huge hole Ed had left behind. Boston Chicken was no better. The restaurant had moved to a new building, but Chris Regel was still there. He carried in his wallet the photo of her and Bill and Ed that she'd given him two years ago, and he took it out all the time to look at it.

She couldn't even get away from Eddie at camp, because camp was at the Rec, which had been renamed the Eddie Polec Memorial Recreation Center. The mayor himself had been there for the dedication ceremony. And even the youngest kids at camp knew who she was. Just yesterday, a five-year-old had turned to her as he was leaving and said, "I know you are Eddie Polec's sister, and I'm so sorry." Then his mother added, "I've taken my kids to every service for your brother. I want them to learn how much pain people can cause each other, so that they will never do that to someone else."

Kevin's six-year-old nephew tackled her broadside. "I'll get you," she laughed, rolling him over to tickle him on the tummy. The horseplay reminded her of how her family used to be.

"I'd better go check on my folks before the parade," she said to Kevin as she got up to leave. She dreaded going home. Every time she drove up the street she played a game with herself, pretending that nothing had changed. But the game lasted only until she opened the door.

The house smelled different now. It used to have the aroma of Kathy's cooking and Ed's latest aftershave. Now it smelled of other people's food and other women's perfume. Her mother, once the dominant force in the house, had retreated, giving up territory to John and her friends.

Kathy had always been the one who paid the bills, handled the money, and insisted that Kristie get a job. "You have to be responsible," she would say as she demanded payment for the car insurance. "Driving is a privilege, not a right, and if you want to drive you need to pay for it." Now John handled the bills, paying for everything without asking to be reimbursed.

The biggest change, Kristie realized, and the scariest one, was that she was no longer afraid of her mother. Kathy had been her best friend and confidante, but she had also watched her children like a hawk. "She sees everything I do," Kristie would complain to friends, half-relieved that she couldn't get away with the things they got away with. These days she could probably get away with anything, her mom knew so little of her life or Bill's.

What would Mom think, Kristie wondered, if she found out that she and Bill sometimes sat at Ed's grave, talking to him and each other and plotting revenge on the kids who killed him. "One, two, three, four, five, six, seven," they'd say, pointing out seven gravesites. "We know just who can go there." The visits always ended with the two of them wrestling on the ground, trying to do something—anything—to vent their rage. Bill always won. Then they'd drive home with Pearl Jam's "Alive" cranked up to full volume, singing, "Oh, oh, oh, I'm still alive" at the top of their lungs.

Poor Bill, Kristie thought. One day he was the fourteen-year-old baby of the family; the next he'd lost his brother, his best friend, and his mother, too. She was proud of the way he'd handled himself. Somehow he'd managed to finish his freshman year, walking out of the house by himself each morning and spending all day in a school that had become a concrete memorial to Eddie, where the lockers were festooned with farewell poems and pictures of Eddie and everyone stared at him with sad eyes. He was proud of being Eddie's brother, but he hated being the brother of the murdered boy, hated everyone knowing who he was and feeling sorry for him.

Kristie was the only person in the world who knew exactly how he felt. She, too, had come a long way in the last eight months. She had finished her sophomore year at Allentown College of St. Francis with good grades. She had promised herself and Ed that she wouldn't waste her life. As she put it, "When I see him again in heaven I'll have a lot to show for it."

The first day back at college had been almost unbearable. It was gray and rainy as she arrived for her 8:00 a.m. algebra class, hoping to slip into her seat before anyone noticed. She tried to tiptoe to her seat, but her wet sneakers betrayed her, squeaking with every step on the slick hardwood floors. In English lit, where the class was studying love and death in French fiction, the professor told her, "You don't have to read with the rest of the class, just pick anything that you want." The last thing Kristie wanted was a special favor.

She'd been particularly afraid to return to her dorm room, where she'd first gotten the news that changed her life. But her roommates urged her to enter the two-bedroom suite. There, tacked to the wall, was a huge computer printout that read, "Welcome Home, Kristie." They'd piled her bed with her favorite snacks. She sat on the floor and cried. Suddenly school had started to seem more like home, just when home was feeling more and more foreign.

Still, she made the hour-long drive home whenever she could. Usually the house was overrun with Kathy's friends. That might be good for Mom, she thought resentfully, but it's bad for me.

One day, unable to control her anger, she banged around the house like the high-strung thoroughbred her mom always said she was. Mary Ellen tried to intervene. "I know how you're feeling, Kristie; we're all hurting."

The very idea made Kristie furious. "That's easy for you to say," she shouted. "You get to go home, you have your whole family, and you are secretly glad this didn't happen to you. But what about me? My family will never be the same and I'm stuck here."

Mary Ellen looked surprised, then hurt, but Kristie was too angry to apologize. "I hate it here, I'm going back to school," she announced dramatically.

"Not in that condition," John bellowed. "You are in no shape to go anywhere."

"I'm going back and you can't stop me," she screamed at her father, but he had left the room. When he came back she was packed and ready to go. She looked at him defiantly, then marched to the door. John made no move to stop her. She couldn't believe it. Didn't he love her? How could he let her leave like this?

She flounced past him, threw her clothes in the back seat of the Saturn, and jammed the key in the ignition. The car wouldn't start. She tried again. Still, the engine wouldn't turn over. After the third try she looked and saw her father standing on the front stoop, holding something in his right hand.

"Looking for this?" he asked, holding up the ignition fuse. "If you can figure out where it goes, you can go back to school."

She took the fuse and started walking down the street. She'd show him. She rang a neighbor's bell. "Mr. Goodwin, can you help me figure out where this goes?" she asked sweetly. "It's come out and my car won't start."

The neighbor was waving goodbye to her when John came running out of the house. "I didn't think you'd figure out how to fix that," he yelled. "The only way I'm letting you go back to school is I drive you. We can't afford another tragedy around here."

"Fine," Kristie said. "You drive." They drove up Church Road toward Route 611. She knew John was furious, but she was furious, too.

"I hate this f—king stuff," she screamed. She rarely swore around her friends and never in front of her father, but it felt great to get it out. "I hate the f—king people who did this, I hate everything. My house is never going to be the same, my mom is never going to be the same, nothing is ever f—king going to be the same. I'm not coming home again until Christmas, and I've already told Mom that."

It was as if she'd slapped him in the face. It wasn't the swearing or the anger—he could take that—but the idea that she could be so cruel and insensitive to Kathy. "You selfish little bitch," he shot back. "How dare you!"

The words took her breath away. Her father didn't yell very often, and he never swore at her. They were in traffic now, moving slowly. "I don't have to take this," she said. Then she opened the door, jumped out, and began to run north on 611. He followed her. She darted into a parking lot, ran to the far end, and slid down a steep incline, grabbing branches to slow her descent. At the bottom she lay in the grass panting, trying to catch her breath. But up above she saw the car headlights and heard him calling. "Kristie Elizabeth, get in the car now."

It was no use. No matter where she went, no matter what she did, he would track her down, as if she were the Runaway Bunny. She was sure of it now, and she was glad. She stood, climbed up the hill, and got in the car. She was still crying, but her anger was gone. So was his.

"Kristie, I know you're feeling crowded," he said. "And I know you're sick of people telling you how to feel and what to do. But you don't have to do anything. We don't have to do anything. If you want to go back to school, you can. If you want to stay home, you can. The only thing we can't do is hurt the family. Other than that, we decide what we do, we decide what schedule we're on. We're in charge."

She had never had that kind of conversation with her father before. He had never really treated her like an adult before. For once, something had changed, and it was for the better.

It was a beautiful day, but John was in the basement, banging away on the computer. Kristie read over his shoulder. He was writing another letter to Mayor Rendell.

July 4, 1995

Dear Mayor Rendell,
You are probably aware that it's been almost 8 months since our son, Eddie Polec, was murdered. Since my first phone call to

your office, I have been patient, allowing both City Council and your own 911 committees to study the system that failed to send a cop to Fox Chase on November 11 . . .

While I was told in March that the MDT study would be finalized in April, it's now July and the study is not completed. In May we met and I walked away from our meeting sure the study would be completed by June and the pilot would be ready to start in November 1995. After leaving many phone messages, I found out the Managing Director's Office was still waiting to see what a couple of vendors had recently proposed for a trial down south. In effect, the City is still not sure what the MDTs are supposed to do and must continue to study the issue. I'm flabbergasted: it's been 8 months, I've been promised time and again meaningful reforms would be quickly implemented and it seems like a plan has not been formulated yet!

You are a father just like I am. What would you do in my shoes, when it is clear that my son's murder could have been avoided had the city taken an active hand in addressing the dismal emergency response system years ago when these problems first started to be noticed? I can understand how an organization could have ignored hypothetical potential problems as being statistical improbabilities. But there's a grave up on Route 1 that proves that the worse case scenario is no longer improbable; it is, as of November 11, most assuredly a statistical certainty. Are the committees and various departments hoping it never happens again? Or are they waiting for another citizen to die . . . to confirm that November 11 was not just a blip on the statistical charts of probability?

Is anyone really planning to fix the system?

John Polec

Good luck to those city officials, Kristie thought. They have no idea who they're up against.

26

Mayor Rendell never responded to John's letter. Joe Martz ignored repeated letters and phone calls over a four-month period. In fact, no one in the administration communicated with John through the entire summer and early fall of 1995.

It wasn't that the city did nothing. Reports were published. Sixty-two new operators were hired. Sensitivity training commenced. Word-processing capability in the radio room was upgraded and the dreary walls got a new coat of paint. Now, when multiple calls came from the same section of the city, an alarm went off at the supervisor's desk and the incident was automatically given a higher priority. Proud of their efforts, city officials encouraged reporters to write stories showing how much energy and expense was being directed toward improving 911.

But from John's point of view, not one of the "improvements" would have prevented Eddie's death or another one just like it, and that was unacceptable. In early October, he called Bill Bergman and asked what had happened to Joe Martz's idea of using cell phones to connect MDTs in patrol cars with the radio room. "They're still studying it to see if it's feasible," Bergman replied.

"What's to study?" John asked. "It either works or it doesn't. How long could it take to find that out?"

John decided to force a confrontation. He asked Bill Bergman to set up a meeting with Martz. Bergman scheduled it for November 3, a week before the anniversary of Eddie's murder.

John went to CompUSA and bought a laptop computer for $2,000. Then he purchased an inexpensive cell phone and modem and signed up for service. Back home, he laid all the equipment out on the kitchen table and pored over the operating manuals. In less than three hours he had linked the laptop to his mainframe computer at work via the cell phone network.

If he could do it in a single morning using equipment purchased off the shelf, then why couldn't the city do it in six months? He didn't believe they were even trying.

On November 3 he packed up the equipment, organized his notes in a folder, and asked Kathy if she was ready for her first face-to-face with city officials. She had made big strides since going back to work in September—not that the city had made her return easy.

As a crossing guard, Kathy was technically an employee of the police department, and the department at first refused to let her go back to work until she handed over all her psychiatric records from CORA.

"You know, dear," said a department functionary, "we are dealing with children after all, and we just can't be too careful."

Kathy insisted that her psychiatric records were confidential, but offered to undergo an evaluation by any psychiatrist they chose. When that failed, she turned to her union, AFSCME, which had gone to bat for the disciplined call takers. A union rep told her there was nothing they could do. John finally appealed directly to the police commissioner, arguing in a letter that since Kathy had not gone on disability and had not taken any money from the city during her absence, the city had no right to view her private medical records.

Two weeks later, Kathy got a call saying all she needed was an evaluation by a city psychologist and a letter from CORA saying she was fit to return to work. So she went back to her corner and resumed her role in society—protecting other people's kids as they went to and from the site where Eddie had been killed. It was hard at first, but the kids and the parents seemed glad to see her, and it felt good, almost normal, to be back.

Now Kathy felt strong enough to help John take on the city and the 911 problem. They met with Bill Bergman, Joe Martz, and three radio room supervisors in Martz's office in the Municipal Building just across from City Hall. A collection of baseball caps adorned the walls of the office. Eddie would have loved those, Kathy couldn't help thinking. She wondered if Martz had kids.

Much of the talk was too technical or too bureaucratic for Kathy to follow, but she understood that none of the deadlines had been met and that the pilot project for the MDTs wasn't even under way. She also perceived that no one except Bill Bergman was taking John seriously. They were just humoring him. "We're working as fast as we can, but there are certain realities the city has to deal with," Martz said. "The procurement department is concerned about competitive bids and there's also a question of getting a performance bond from the company that will install the system. Nothing can happen without that."

"Nothing *has* happened," John exploded. "It's been fifty-one weeks to the day since my son was murdered and this city, which could have prevented his death, hasn't even started to address the real problem. I have the solution downstairs in my car. *I* know it can work and *you* know it can work and no one is doing a damn thing except making excuses." He grabbed his folder. "C'mon, Kath, we're outta here. This is a waste of time."

She followed him to the elevator. He was pressing the down button furiously, trying to make the elevator come more quickly, when Bill Bergman came running out of the office. "I'm glad I caught you," he said. "Please come back. Joe feels bad. He wants you to know he really is taking this seriously." Kathy got the impression that Bergman was secretly glad John had blown his stack, as if he knew that was the only kind of language the city understood.

Back in the office, the mood had changed. This time, Kathy felt that they were really listening to John and realized, albeit grudgingly, that he knew what he was talking about. "We're committed to making this a reality," Martz said at the end of the discussion. "*I'm* committed to making this a reality."

John shook his outstretched hand. "I hope so," he said. "I really hope so." But he didn't really feel very hopeful. Maybe it was the one-year anniversary next week. Maybe it was the trial, set to begin January 2, only two months away. Or maybe it was O. J. Simpson.

John had never wavered in his public statements that he believed Eddie's killers would ultimately be found guilty of first-degree murder. But privately he was beset by doubt, made worse by the Simpson trial.

All summer long he'd followed the proceedings closely, making mental notes on how the prosecution presented its case and how the defense team tried to counter the evidence. After closing arguments, he was sure the jury would vote to convict on first-degree-murder charges. Then he heard the judge instruct the jury that they could find Simpson guilty of a lesser degree in the death of Ron Goldman if they believed that he hadn't meant to kill the young man.

The whole idea that you had to prove "intent to kill" in order to get a first-degree-murder conviction made John sick to his stomach. How could you stab someone repeatedly, or bludgeon him over the head with a bat, and not intend to kill him? Barring an accident, how could not *meaning* to kill someone mitigate the fact that you had? So when the jury found O.J. not guilty on October 3, John was beside himself. Now, when he told reporters he was still confident the system would bring justice for Eddie, he was haunted by the image of Fred Goldman—a father sentenced to a life of grief and rage. Would it be the same for him?

Word was coming from the district attorney's office and from reporters that the defense was planning to tear a page from the book so recently written by O.J.'s "Dream Team." They were going to try to put the kids from Fox Chase, Eddie included, on trial. The seven defendants had been denied separate trials, so they banded together, sharing resources and investigators who met every Saturday to discuss the seemingly impossible task before them—defending clients who had either confessed to the killing or had been fingered by several of their friends.

Charles Peruto became the lead attorney for the group. Janis Smarro, a former schoolteacher who'd become one of Philadelphia's top criminal attorneys, represented Thomas Crook. Michael Wallace, a former judge who'd been removed from the bench a few years back amid allegations that he'd taken payoffs from the Roofers Union, represented Dewan Alexander. Michael Applebaum represented Bou Khathavong. Oscar Gaskins, the only African American in the group, had recently been hired by Carlo Johnson. Joseph E. Kelley was already talking to the D.A. about a plea bargain for his client, Kevin Convey. And John McMahon, a former assistant D.A., had recently declared to reporters that his client, Anthony Rienzi, was "innocent of all charges; he's not going to plead guilty to spitting on the sidewalk in connection with this case."

"Let's get something straight," Peruto told the group early on. "Anyone who gets a deal should take it. No hard feelings. We all have tough cases here, and anything short of first-degree is a big win."

In the beginning, they were split six to one on the issue of venue. The majority wanted to move the trial out of Philadelphia because of all the publicity. As one of them put it, "We've got a victim who's a choir boy and a press that's already pro-prosecution."

But Peruto wouldn't hear of it. "What, are you crazy?" he said. "Anywhere else we go we're in the buckle of the Bible Belt. The folks outside the city are serious law-and-order types. For godsakes, the cops out there look like Marines, with shaved heads and patches on their sleeves. You want that kind of jury? No! We need a more callous jury, a jury more familiar with crime, more ho-hum about it. We need a jury from Philadelphia."

First of all, they would argue that it was too dark and too chaotic in St. Cecilia's parking lot for anyone to be sure about what they had seen. Already there were plenty of conflicting statements from the kids present. "Half the prosecution's witnesses are covering their ass, and it's obvious," Peruto said. "The jury's got to wonder about that, and they've got to wonder why only some of the kids from Abington were arrested and others were not."

And why weren't any of the kids from Fox Chase arrested? "It's politics," said Peruto. "Lynn Abraham [the district attorney] doesn't have to worry about voters in Montgomery County, she only has to worry about voters in Philadelphia. Maybe we can use it to our advantage, argue selective prosecution. Anything is worth a try."

The defense team also planned to cast the attack on November 11 in a different light. Instead of Joe Casey's invading horde of killers, they would paint a picture of a long-planned fight in which Fox Chase had the home-field advantage. "It will be warrior versus warrior, not devil versus angel," said Peruto. "And we can say that the kids from Montgomery County were not only outnumbered, they were also outsmarted, lured into a trap by the kids from Fox Chase."

They all knew it was weak, but it was the best they could come up with. "I'd give us a good 2 or 3 percent chance of winning," Peruto joked. But with less than two months to go until the start of the trial, no one else in the room was laughing.

27

It poured rain on November 11, one year to the day after Eddie was beaten in St. Cecilia's parking lot. As John watched the gray skies let loose, he felt betrayed by the weather. If only it had rained that day, the kids from Montgomery County wouldn't have driven to Fox Chase. If only it had been miserable like this, Ed would've stayed home that night. He was driving himself crazy with "if only's."

Reminders of Ed were everywhere. Reporters and TV camera crews had been crawling all over the neighborhood for a week, videotaping Kathy as she shepherded kids across the intersection behind the church, doing stand-ups at St. Cecilia's, and generally interviewing anyone who had a thought about the tragedy and its aftermath. The newspapers ran editorials about lessons learned and articles about community soul-searching in both Fox Chase and Montgomery County.

In Abington, the entire week was designated "Nonviolent Conflict Resolution Week," with teachers and clergy conducting classes and seminars focusing on alternatives to violence. In Fox Chase, members of the all-volunteer Town Watch patrolled the streets with extra vigilance. When Dennis Fenerty, head of the Fox Chase Homeowners Association, had first tried to launch Town Watch, only four people had shown up. After Eddie's murder, Fenerty had tried again and four hundred people turned up.

Christine and Christopher Rauscher were typical of the new enlistees. They didn't know the Polecs very well, but they were galvanized by Eddie's murder and dogged by guilt that they weren't on watch that terrible night. Now, Christine told a reporter, she relived the attack in her mind whenever she went out on patrol, each time trying to change the ending. In her reconstructed version, she and Christopher and other Town Watchers spot the mob that has Eddie trapped in the parking lot. Five carloads strong, they move in, creating a ring around the mob. "We would have been honking our horns, we would have turned on our high beams, we would have dispersed them," she said. "If we had been there, we know he wouldn't be dead."

The centerpiece of all the media attention was, of course, the Polec family, particularly John and Kathy. In the year since Eddie's death, John's appearances in court and at City Hall, his interviews with reporters, and his anti-violence speeches to youth groups had made him into something of a celebrity. His face was almost as familiar to the citizenry as that of Ed Rendell. Everywhere he went, he was recognized. Some people just stared and whispered among themselves. He could almost read their lips: "That's the father of the boy who was killed with baseball bats." Others approached him to say how sorry they were about what had happened or, less tactfully, to ask how he managed to carry on.

Having just re-entered the outside world, Kathy was beginning to come to grips with the fact that when they'd lost Eddie, they'd lost their cherished anonymity as well. Standing at the grocery counter, she'd notice that the clerk had stopped checking the food out and was staring at her. "Don't I know you from somewhere?" Realizing what was coming, she'd respond that she had "one of those faces that just seems familiar."

"No," the clerk would insist, "I know I've seen you on TV." Then recognition would dawn. "Aren't you Eddie Polec's mother?" Suddenly the idea that the world knew her because her child was dead would crash over her and all she wanted to do was turn and run away. But she couldn't turn away from the question. She could never deny that she was Eddie's mom.

"Yes, I'm Kathy Polec," she'd say. Then they'd catch themselves and apologize for intruding. They all meant well, she told herself, even when they inadvertently said something that wounded. Like the lady who blurted out, "I guess the Lord just wanted your boy more than you did." Still, she told John, "it helps that people do care. It helps us heal."

Kathy had healed to the point where she finally felt ready to face the media. When the requests began pouring in, she surprised both John and the reporters by agreeing to sit with John for the anniversary interviews. She wasn't at all intimidated. She thought it important to speak out, because she felt it would help people to understand Eddie. "Only if they see all of us," she told John, "will they know who Eddie really was."

By now John was an old pro with the press. He knew just how much they needed from him to write their stories, and he was always careful to give them just that much and no more. He didn't want anyone peering too deeply into his heart or those of his family. Which is why he sometimes cringed when Kathy was unguarded with reporters.

No, Kathy told Margie Smith, Eddie's death had not caused her to lose her religious faith. "But it changed the way I think about God. Before Eddie died, I believed that God had a plan for each person. But there's no way God could've meant for this to happen," she said. "So when I get to heaven, He better be ready for me, because we got a lot of questions for Him."

A memorial service for Eddie was scheduled for 10:00 p.m. at St. Cecilia's Church, and John dreaded going. He could handle the court hearings, the media interviews, and the meetings with city officials, but he hated attending church services in Eddie's name, particularly the part of the Mass where the congregation is asked to pray for the dead. Hearing Ed's name mentioned among the departed souls was still unfathomable to him, and it was at those times that he came closest to losing it.

He took some comfort from the fact that it would be a low-key affair, with just close family and friends in attendance. He was sure that Kathy and the neighbors were going way overboard in baking dozens of cookies and cakes for the reception after the service. After all, a year had passed, and while feelings for the family were still strong in the neighborhood, he figured the rest of the world had moved on. When the rain started, he wondered if more than a handful of people would show up.

But when they arrived at the church, the parking lot was jammed, and he could see dozens of kids gathered on the spot where Eddie had fallen. Inside, the church was filled to capacity. Kids who'd gone away to college had come home. Parents, neighbors, friends, and people they'd never met packed every pew and aisle. More than twelve hundred people turned out, a majority of them teenagers.

"It has been one long, hard year," Father Olson told the crowd. "We haven't come here today because of the 911 controversy or what's the matter with the world today. This service is instead a remembrance of a really good kid who died needlessly on the steps of our church. And you, his friends, are to be praised. Even in your pain and anger you did great service to Eddie's name. If anyone wants to know what Eddie was like, they need only to look at his friends."

Eddie's closest male friends—Glen Katchel, Michael Brontis, and Nick DiCarli—placed a white muslin cloth on the steps of the altar, covered with colorful Magic-Marker messages: "We will always miss you . . . Ed, always in our hearts." The boys were followed by more than two hundred other teens, each holding a red or white carnation. They wore baggy jeans and floppy sweatshirts; they had pierced ears and half-shaved heads. Still, Kathy thought they looked like a procession of angels as they walked in pairs up the long center aisle toward the sanctuary and, with heads bowed, placed the flowers at the foot of the altar. Colleen and Ellie were last, carrying an enormous heart-shaped wreath ringed by white flowers and a red ribbon with EDDIE spelled out in gold block letters.

At the end of the service, John and Kathy stood up to thank the congregation. John noticed that Sister Judith, who'd seen the beating from her convent window, was sitting in the back of the church crying softly. His heart went out to her—she always seemed to feel responsible for not stopping the fight. He wanted to tell her, "It's not your fault." There was so much to say to so many people.

"This is truly amazing," he began. "After we've seen human nature at its worst, we now see human nature at its finest. We believe that this terrible evil is just a small part of life and that all of you, with your kindness, are the biggest part of life. That is the part we are focusing on, because that is the part of life that Ed was about."

Kathy had planned to speak, too. Looking out into the crowd—Ed's crowd—she thought of all the acts of kindness, all the extraordinary gestures, all the people who'd helped pull her through. She wanted to tell them what a difference they'd made, but all she could manage was a choked whisper: "Thank you all."

As they made their way to the reception, John noticed Bill Bergman and Carl Bittenbender, the commanding officer of the police communication bureau, sitting in the back of the church. "We wanted to be here," Bergman said as they shook hands.

The reception went on until 2:00 a.m., with everyone sitting around sharing their favorite "Ed-isms."

"I remember having an argument with him one day," John said. "I can't recall what it was about now, but I told him that in my book you didn't do things like that. And he looked at me and said, 'You know what the problem is around here? *You* wrote the book.'"

Kathy remembered a scene on Kristie's twelfth birthday:

"All of Kristie's friends were lying on the floor eating pizza and watching television. Ed was ten and Bill was eight, and of course they had to be in on Kristie's pajama party whether she liked it or not. So this commercial comes on and the girls start to giggle. It's a Midol commercial and they think it's the funniest thing. Bill, of course, has no idea what's going on, but Ed, he's paying close attention. Suddenly his face lights up and he yells, 'That's it! That's why my stomach hurts. I have menstrual cramps.'

"Oh my God, the girls just roared. Ed was very upset. I had to take him aside and explain that menstrual cramps were something that only girls got. He looked at me like I was crazy and said, 'Then why do they call it *men*-stral cramps.'

"He never lived that down." She laughed. "For years afterward, every time he saw Kristie's friend Melissa, she'd ask, 'Hey, Ed, how are those cramps?' "

In the midst of all the laughter, someone asked, "I wonder what Eddie would make of this, being the center of all the media attention?"

"Oh, he'd like seeing his face all over the news." John chuckled. "He wouldn't like being dead, but he'd love the publicity."

By Monday morning the sun had come out, but Kathy's mood had darkened. The laughter and shared memories had almost made it seem as if Eddie was there with them. But now the well-wishers were all gone, and once again, so was Eddie. Shivering as she stood on her corner waiting for the kids to begin arriving for school, she wished she could crawl up on her favorite Aunt Cath's lap as she had when she was a little girl.

Suddenly she heard her father's voice, clear and distinct, as if he were standing right beside her. "Yo, Kath," he said. "I've got Ed."

Kathy froze. Then she started to laugh. "Yeah, Dad," she said out loud, "you would be the one to have him."

She had so many good memories of her father. She could still picture herself walking hand-in-hand with him to Heil's religious store in Olney when she was seven years old. She was going to help him choose a statue of St. Joseph, her father's favorite saint. "He's the quiet saint," he always said, "the one who works behind the scenes, like a true dad." She looked carefully at each figurine. "This one, Dad," she said, picking up a creamy white porcelain replica of Saint Joseph holding the baby Jesus. "This one is the prettiest." Now that Kathy's dad was dead, it occupied a place of honor in her living room.

A car stopped at the corner. Officer Jerry Gallagher, the head of Police Community Relations, got out and began to walk toward her. She recognized him because his son and Ed had played baseball together. "I've been wanting to give you something for a while," he said, handing her a small box. "Today seemed like the right day."

She unwrapped the box and nearly gasped out loud. Inside was a set of miniature stained-glass tablets that opened like hinged picture frames. Inscribed on the left was the "Prayer to St. Joseph." On the right was a picture of Saint Joseph holding the Infant Jesus.

"I can't tell you how much this means," she stammered. "It's just perfect."

She tried to steady herself as he walked away. She knew the kids would be coming across the corner soon and she didn't want them to see her in tears. She was sure this was a message. And it wasn't the first one. That had come one day last summer when Eddie's trial date was set. During a meeting in the judge's chambers, the defense lawyers had demanded a December start, arguing that their clients had waited long enough for their day in court. "But that's Christmas," Casey protested. "We can't put the Polecs through a trial during Christmas."

"Why not?" one of the attorneys shot back. "Their kid isn't coming home for the holidays."

"How could they, how could they?" Kathy had asked Father Olson, who sat with them in court. "They have no heart. They have no conscience." By the time they got home, Kathy couldn't catch her breath, she was sobbing so hard. "Where does that leave Ed? Where does that leave my Eddie?"

Father Olson took her hands in his and raised them, facing her palms to the heavens. "Kathy," he said gently, "that leaves Eddie in God's hands."

Looking into Father Olson's eyes and listening to his words, she had suddenly been filled with a sense of peace.

She had not mentioned the incident to anyone, figuring that John, and even Father Olson, would think she was a little nuts. But the very next day her niece Jeanie came to the house and handed her a small, beautifully wrapped box. "I found this and I just had to give it to you," she said. In the box was a pair of white porcelain hands cradling the figure of a little boy. An accompanying holy card quoted from Isaiah, chapter 49, verse 15–16: "I will not forget you; I have held you in the palm of my hand."

That was four months ago, and now she had this St. Joseph's statue, too. As she walked home from her corner she began reciting his prayer to herself: "Oh, St. Joseph, whose protection is so great, so strong, so prompt before the throne of God, I place in you all my interests and desire . . ."

All she had ever wanted was for her kids to be all right. Now it seemed God was telling her that Ed was okay, safely tucked away in heaven with the people she loved. Some people wait a lifetime for a sign, she thought, and I've already had two. I am truly blessed.

28

The week before Christmas, Center City was all dressed up. Giant snowflakes adorned the lampposts on Market Street, the windows of Strawbridge and Clothier featured a scene from Dickens's *A Christmas Carol,* and a thirty-foot Christmas tree warmed the cold courtyard at City Hall.

But Bill Danks was not in a holiday mood as he hurried past shoppers on his way to the district attorney's office on Arch Street. This would be his first Christmas without Katie, and he'd never be able to get the last one—in the hospital—out of his mind.

He imagined the Polecs must be feeling the same way, maybe worse, with the trial only two weeks away. The detective had been working on the case day and night for a month, ever since Tom Perks had asked if he could help out. "Joe Casey needs someone to carry all his boxes," Perks had said with a grin. "I said you'd be perfect."

In a way, it *was* the perfect job for Danks. Even though he'd have to sit through some painful testimony, it would get him off the streets and into a steadier routine. Somehow his old partner Tommy Perks had understood that the uncertain routine of homicide work—sitting around for hours doing nothing, then suddenly rushing out and spending all night on the street—wasn't helping him get back on an even keel.

Besides, "Chief of Staff," as they jokingly called it, was a pretty good job with plenty of overtime. In addition to carrying boxes of evidence, Danks was responsible for coordinating witnesses before and during the trial, consulting with the prosecutor, taking notes, and sitting next to Casey during court sessions. "Second Chair" at the defense table was usually reserved for the junior lawyer on a case, but with so many homicides in Philadelphia, a second prosecutor was a luxury. So Danks would sit there, to keep Casey from looking so alone, with all those defense attorneys on the opposite side of the room.

Danks flashed his badge as he passed through security. The highly polished solid oak walls, fourteen-foot ceilings, and marble fireplaces were a testament to the importance this law-and-order city placed on the D.A.'s office. Unlike the public defenders' office, which was cramped and decrepit, the building that housed D.A. Lynn Abraham and her 250 prosecuting attorneys had a sense of grandeur and style.

Like Ed Rendell, Abraham was a highly visible, extremely powerful city official with a national reputation. *The New York Times Magazine* had dubbed her "America's Deadliest D.A.," noting that the prim-looking fifty-four-year-old woman who loved cats and Impressionist paintings was, in fact, the prosecutor most likely to ask for, and get, the death penalty.

But Abraham wasn't seeking the death penalty in the Polec case. Even though the crime was extremely brutal, there weren't enough aggravating circumstances to make it a capital case. Danks knew that John Polec was relieved by that. He'd heard John say he thought the death penalty was state-sanctioned murder, and he couldn't in good conscience tell the kids not to avenge Eddie's death if he asked the death penalty for his killers. He's a better man than I am, Danks thought.

The elevator stopped on the seventh floor, where Joe Casey had turned his office into a command center for the Polec case. Dozens of boxes lined the floor. Inside the boxes, police reports, witness statements, autopsy photos, and aerial pictures of Fox Chase were carefully catalogued. Leaning against the wall was a large sheet of white cardboard with a schematic drawing of the intersection of Rhawn and Ridgeway Streets. The schematic showed the exact spot where the Abington kids had pulled into St. Cecilia's parking lot, where they chased Eddie, and where he fell.

But the dominant item in the room was a five-foot-long chart made from sheets of green graph paper taped together and tacked to the wall. Across the top of the chart were the names of the twenty-four people who were present when Eddie was beaten, grouped according to the cars they rode in. Down the left side of the graph Casey had written the names again, with a brief description of what each person had told the police. The result was an elaborate grid system by which he could cross-reference one witness statement with another. He was trying to match statements and piece together a narrative of the night of the murder.

The chart was making it painfully clear that there was a problem. "They're washing out," Casey said as Danks came in the door. "For every one thing a witness gives us, they take away two."

Danks knew exactly what Casey was talking about. In the past four weeks he'd arranged to bring dozens of witnesses into Casey's office. It was a frustrating process. Most of the kids from Abington arrived for their interviews looking as if they were heading for the mosh pit. Sullen and uncooperative, they invariably wore oversized pants and sloppy shirts, sported tattoos and lots of facial metal. Not exactly the kind of kids who would convince a jury. "But the worst part is, they just outright lie," Danks told Art Mee over beers at the Liberty Tavern. "Yeah?" Mee replied. "So tell me something I don't know."

The ones who didn't lie just couldn't seem to remember what they'd seen, even when confronted with the statements they'd given to the police in the days after the murder. Most of them denied ever discussing the murder with anyone. Danks would never forget an exchange between Joe Casey and the father of Zach Dallas, who had driven one of the cars that night. Mr. Dallas insisted that his son had no clear recollection of the murder. "Your son's a goddamn liar," Casey growled. "You know how I know? Because I can see the vein in his temple pulsing, and I can see the way his neck muscles clench."

But it was no use, as far as Danks could tell. Zach Dallas's father, like most of the parents, didn't seem to want his child to take any responsibility for what had happened. Instead, the parents lashed out at the police and the prosecutor for picking on their children. "If he says he doesn't remember, then he doesn't remember" was the common refrain.

Danks was disgusted. "The biggest event in their lives—a kid gets killed right in front of them—and they can't remember anything about it, never even talked to their friends about it? Gimme a break!"

Danks knew that if he was frustrated, Joe must be going insane. But Casey just kept moving forward, taking notes and trying to find the best witnesses. Unfortunately, one of those witnesses was charged with murder.

"We'll have to go with Kevin Convey," Casey announced. "Have him brought over."

The meeting took place in Casey's office. Tom Perks, Convey's attorney, Joe Kelley, and a retired homicide detective named John Cimino were already there when Danks brought the teenager into the room. Danks could barely muster a smile at Cimino. The guy was a friend of Convey's grandfather and had insinuated himself into the middle of negotiations for Convey. Casey couldn't stand him. "Cimino's pain in the ass," he told Danks. "He's trying to gorilla people into giving this kid a break."

Joe Kelley had been asking for a deal for months, but Casey always said no. Now, however, with so many witnesses falling out, Casey needed someone who could tell the whole story—explain to the jury what had led up to the fight, what had happened at St. Cecilia's, and where the carloads of kids went afterward.

"You testify," said Casey, "and I'll make sure the judge knows about your cooperation at sentencing."

"We've been over this a thousand times," said Kelley. "The only way it works is we agree on the numbers right here. Otherwise, no deal."

Kelley had insisted all along that they had to agree on the exact amount of jail time before a plea could be worked out. With no possibility of the death penalty, Casey didn't have a lot to bargain with. He wanted to offer Convey life in prison, but that was the worst the kid would get from a jury.

"We are prepared to go ahead with first-degree murder against your client. So I don't want to hear any more bullshit," said Casey. "Either he gives us the absolute truth here and now or it's over."

Kelley nodded. "He's prepared to tell the whole truth."

"All right," Casey said, "he pleads to third degree. We'll recommend five-to-twenty to the judge."

"Five years! You gotta be kidding," Cimino hollered. "I don't get it. He's giving you your whole case. We were told it would be one to two years at the most."

Perks and Danks exchanged glances. They couldn't believe what they were hearing, especially from a homicide guy. "Whaddaya talking about?" said Danks. "No one here ever talked about numbers." By now Cimino and Danks were facing off. "I came here in good faith," yelled Cimino, "and now you're backing out of the deal."

"We're not backing out of anything," shouted Danks. "There was no deal to back out of."

Perks stepped in. "How 'bout we all take a walk?" he said to Cimino. Out in the hallway, he tried to calm Cimino down. "Let's leave the lawyers to themselves," he said. "I'm sure Joe Kelley knows what's best for his client."

At the end of the day it was done. Kelley took Casey's offer. By Danks's calculation, it meant that Convey would be out by 1999. "That sucks," he said to Perks, "but what are you gonna do?"

On Saturday, December 23, John Polec arrived at the D.A.'s office. Even though it was a weekend, he was surprised to see Casey in casual clothes. He'd had the impression that Joe slept in a suit.

Casey cut straight to the chase. "We want the beaters convicted of first degree, and I think we can get it," he said. "But we've got a problem. Most of the Abington witnesses are pathological liars. I don't believe them and the jury won't believe them, so we can't use them."

John knew what was coming. He and Kathy had discussed the possibility for weeks.

"Our best shot is giving Kevin Convey a deal," Casey went on. "He's willing to testify and he can tell the jury the whole story. He was there, he gives us Pinero, Rienzi, and Crook on a platter."

John was sick to think that one of Eddie's killers might ever walk free. Still, he trusted Casey. If Joe said there was no other way, then there was no other way. "You're the expert," he said. "Do whatever you think is best."

John wasn't the only one having trouble digesting the news. Across town in Charles Peruto's office, the defense team was holding its weekly strategy session. Peruto was the last to arrive. It was not a happy scene.

John McMahon had his head in his hands. Janis Smarro was downcast. "What the hell is wrong with all of you?" Peruto barked. Five pairs of eyes stared back at him. "This is good news," he said. "No, it's great news."

"C'mon, Chuck, get real," they argued. "We're talking a fatal blow to our case. Kevin Convey's going to get on that witness stand and point a finger at every one of our guys. We got two weeks left and we have to come up with a whole new strategy. We're screwed."

"No," Peruto said. "We're saved. The D.A. just cut a sweetheart deal with one of the ringleaders of the fight. He's the first guy out of the car, for godsake. If it weren't for Convey, the Polec kid wouldn't be dead. Don't you see it? He's at least as guilty as everyone else and he lied every time he talked to the cops. Until now, we had nothing and the D.A. had everything. But Joe Casey just blew it, because now we've got the bad guy. And we can pin everything on him."

29

For days, TV and radio weather forecasters had been hyping a monstrous blizzard that was barreling down the East Coast. On the morning of Sunday, January 7, the so-called Storm of the Century hit Philadelphia with a vengeance. The snow was already falling hard when Kathy opened her eyes.

"We'd better get packed, Kath," said John. "They're talking twenty inches by tomorrow."

Kathy stared out the window. It was the same kind of snow she'd seen the day Eddie was born.

John prodded her again. "Joe's already on his way. He borrowed his daughter's sleeping bag and is taking it to the office. He thinks the whole city will be shut down by tomorrow."

Looking out at the swirling snow, Kathy couldn't believe that the judge would actually hear opening arguments the next day. But she could see Judge Jane Cutler Greenspan on Friday, glowering at the defense attorneys as they whined about the impending storm. "I don't care if you have to sleep in your offices," she'd said sternly. "Court will start on Monday at 9:00 a.m. sharp."

Greenspan was so adamant about starting on time that she sent out a citywide teletype announcing that even if the courthouse was closed, room 304 would be open. No one—not Tom Perks or Bill Danks or Joe Casey—had ever seen that happen before.

The Polecs had already spent nearly a week in court, sitting through pretrial motions and jury selection. But the trial would begin in earnest tomorrow with opening arguments. It would be the first time the prosecution and defense faced off in front of a jury and delivered their conflicting narratives of what had happened in Fox Chase on the night of November 11, 1994.

The pretrial motions had been an indication of what was to come. Joe Casey and Charles Peruto seemed to argue over everything, starting with the autopsy photos. Casey wanted to show the jury color slides of Eddie's damaged brain. "I think it's important for the jury to see the severity of the beating," he told Greenspan. "That shows malice."

"They're repulsive and frightening," Peruto said. "There's no need for the jury to see that."

Greenspan rolled her eyes. "I found them anatomical and not the least bit gruesome," she said, ruling that three of the slides could be shown to the jury.

With her dark hair and expressive rubber face and nasal voice, the forty-eight-year-old Greenspan reminded Kathy of Lily Tomlin. She'd been on the Common Pleas bench for nine years and had a reputation as a serious jurist who knew the law, but she also had her critics when it came to murder cases. Many in the police department and the D.A.'s office felt that her five years on the Superior Court of Appeals had made her nearly phobic about being reversed, and as a result, she let defense attorneys get away with, well, murder. "In an abundance of caution, I'll allow it" seemed to be her favorite courtroom response to objections from the prosecution. She had said it so often during pretrial proceedings that reporters and court personnel alike took to doing their own Greenspan impressions, rolling their eyes, stroking their chin, and intoning to one another in the hallway, "I'll allow it."

If Kathy was fascinated by Judge Greenspan, she was repulsed by Charles Peruto. It wasn't just that he was representing Nick Pinero, although that played a part. In the beginning, she thought the trial would be a search for the truth about what had really happened to Eddie that night. But even before the jury was seated she sensed that, for Peruto at least, the truth was far less important than the game that began each day when he entered the courtroom.

Room 304 was divided by a center aisle, with spectators separated from the attorneys and the judge by a gated railing. Joe Casey sat on the right side facing the judge; the defense attorneys sat on the left. The Polecs and their friends and supporters from Fox Chase sat on the right in the first row of "pews" directly behind Casey. Every morning, all the other defense attorneys would walk down the center aisle, turn left, and take their seats at the defense table. Not Peruto. He came down the center aisle, turned right, and squeezed himself along the narrow space between the railing and the first row of pews, all the way to the far right side of the room, passing within inches of the Polecs and forcing them to pull in their legs to let him pass. Then he turned left and crossed the entire width of the room on the way to his seat.

At first Kathy thought the daily one-man parade was either eccentricity or arrogance, Peruto trying to make sure everyone knew he'd arrived. She changed her mind the day he stepped on her feet. "He's trying to make us mad," she'd told John. "He sees me as the weak link, and he wants me to react so that he can make us, and Eddie by extension, look like the kind of people who get into fights." She refused to give him the satisfaction, smiling sweetly and quickly pulling her feet back every time he pressed by.

Peruto seemed to be playing games with Joe Casey as well. When he questioned the jury pool, Peruto sometimes strolled over to the prosecution's side of the room, stood beside Casey's chair, and even put his hand on Joe's shoulder while he talked. Kathy was convinced he always glanced over at her during these moments, as if to say, "See? We're all colleagues and friends on this side of the railing, and you really have nothing to do with it." Casey finally reacted to the touching the same day that Peruto stepped on Kathy's feet. He got up from his seat, walked to the center of the chamber, and drew an imaginary line with a sweep of his arm.

"You see that, Chuck?" he said to Peruto. "That's your space on the other side of the line and this is my space over here. If you keep invading my space, then I'm going to have to ask Bill Danks there to shoot you."

He said it with a smile, but it was clear he meant it, and Peruto never ventured over the line again.

Casey had faced Peruto in five or six previous cases. He considered him a tough and able adversary who would stoop to any depth and play every angle in order to win. Peruto didn't disappoint.

Judge Greenspan had ordered the attorneys not to speak to reporters until after the jury was seated and sequestered. This was a high-profile case and she didn't want the potential jury pool poisoned by what they read in the papers or saw on TV. But she couldn't muzzle the attorneys in the courtroom.

Just before jury selection began and immediately after Kevin Convey announced his guilty plea in court, Peruto stood up and announced dramatically that his client would also like to cooperate with the prosecution. "It is the intention of Nicholas Pinero to plead guilty to certain charges," Peruto said. "He will plead guilty to voluntary manslaughter, which, I think, is his right, your honor. He would agree, as part of his plea, that he will commit no crimes in the future and he will cooperate truthfully . . ."

Joe Casey jumped to his feet, furious. "I don't agree that the defendant has the right to plead to voluntary manslaughter, or that the court can choose to accept it," he said. "I realize you can't gag the counsel in the courtroom. I could stand up and say all sorts of egregious things, I am capable of that . . . but I am biting my tongue. I request that all counsel restrain themselves a little bit until the jury is impaneled."

Judge Greenspan glared at Peruto. "This is very premature, very premature," she snapped. "It's not the time for this argument, by any stretch of the imagination."

Peruto knew that, of course, just as he knew that his announcement would be reported by the media. Sure enough, his "surprise offer" made headlines before the jury was picked. He managed to get the message out to prospective jurors that Nick Pinero was a reasonable person, willing to admit that what he did was wrong.

Kathy had watched the jury selection process with a mixture of boredom and disbelief. Almost immediately, Casey and the defense lawyers began to argue. Peruto accused the prosecutor of getting rid of black jurors. Casey responded by saying the defense apparently didn't want any whites.

"The record should reflect that the three defense strikes were all against Caucasians," said Casey.

"Your honor, we don't have any blacks because they have all been destroyed by the Commonwealth," countered Peruto.

Casey had called the process *voir dire*. When Kathy looked the phrase up in the dictionary, she couldn't get over the irony. It was French for "to speak the truth."

In truth, for all their posturing, both sides were looking for a similar type of juror. Casey wanted stable black women, middle-aged motherly types with strong family values and long-time community ties. He figured that they, of all people, would be offended at the idea of a bunch of affluent white punks invading a quiet neighborhood and beating an innocent victim to death. Peruto, too, wanted middle-aged black women, preferably mothers. He assumed they would not only sympathize with the victim's family, they'd feel for the defendants' families as well. These women, Peruto hoped, would be more familiar with crime and wouldn't have the heart to put a bunch of young kids in prison for life. Sure, they'd be disgusted by the murder itself, but they might also see it as a "youthful mistake."

In the end, the jury was mostly middle-aged and working-class, made up of nine women and three men. Five of the women were black, three were white, and one was Hispanic. Of the men, two were white and one was black. The alternates were an elderly black man and a young white woman.

By the time jury selection was completed, John and Kathy had fallen into a routine. They'd leave Fox Chase before 7:30 a.m. to beat the traffic on I-95 and the crowds at the Criminal Justice Center, where the trial was being held. One of the best-looking, worst-designed buildings in Philadelphia, the CJC featured an immense glass lobby and understated, oak-paneled courtrooms. Completed in 1995, it was intended to relieve City Hall of the burden of so many court cases. But the architects apparently never considered the volume of people that would go in and out of the building on a daily basis. By 9:00 a.m. every weekday, there was pedestrian gridlock inside the courthouse, a congestion so bad it sometimes took twenty minutes just to get from the metal detectors at the entrance to the few slow elevators fifty feet away.

To avoid the crowds, John and Kathy would squeeze past the long line of frustrated lawyers, cops, prospective jurors, and defendants and head for the cement stairwell. The stairway smelled like a bar the morning after, as every smoker in the building seemed to gather there under the NO SMOKING signs. Climbing to the third floor, they'd often run into Nick Pinero or Anthony Rienzi leaning against the wall and dragging on their cigarettes, looking like characters out of *Grease* with their slicked-back hair and dark suits.

"Don't go in the stairwell," John warned the kids from Fox Chase. "I'm not worried about you guys causing any trouble, I'm worried that they might accuse you of trying to start a fight, just to make you look bad." The same went for the third-floor men's room, where the defense attorneys often caucused with their clients during breaks. "Just go upstairs to the fourth floor," John told the kids. "It'll be safer that way."

During breaks in the proceedings, the Fox Chase crowd spent time in an unused conference room down the hall from Courtroom 304. The conference room became known as "Courtroom Bill," because Billy was forced to stay there while he waited for the day Joe Casey would call him to the stand. Courtroom Bill became an oasis for the Polecs—a place to talk privately, a place where Kathy could go and cry, where they both could pull themselves together after an emotionally difficult session. Courtroom decorum was so important to John that he had instructed the Fox Chase kids to dress up for the trial, telling the boys to wear coats and ties, the girls to tone down their makeup. "Yeah, right, Dad," Kristie laughed. "You're the perfect person to give us fashion tips."

John hadn't been to a barbershop for eighteen months, since he and Eddie had made their pool-table bet. He'd been trimming his hair himself, and he had to admit, it was looking pretty scraggly. "Okay, okay," he said sheepishly. The day before the trial started, he went in for a professional cut, then dug out a white shirt and tie and tried to practice what he preached.

Kathy closed her suitcase. Fourteen inches of snow were on the ground and there was no way to drive to Center City. They would have to take the train. Just getting out the front door was hard enough. The wind pushed them up against the house and the snow blew sideways into their faces. They slipped and slid down the steps and lugged their suitcases three-quarters of a mile to the Fox Chase train station, determined to make the 3:45 train.

When they got to the station, Kathy was amazed to find Mary Doherty, Terry Gara, Chris Regel, and more than a dozen other friends already waiting for them. Twenty people had promised to go with them to opening arguments no matter what the weather, and twenty people were standing on the platform in the middle of a blizzard.

Just as John set his suitcase down, an announcement came over the scratchy loudspeaker. "Attention, ladies and gentlemen, all trains on the SEPTA system have been canceled. Due to the weather, there will be no more service on any of the regional rail lines."

John stared in disbelief. "You can't stop the trains *now,*" he shouted at the loudspeaker.

Terry Gara dug her address book out of her purse. Mary Doherty began working her cell phone. The Southeastern Pennsylvania Transportation Authority operated a subway system, too, and it was still running. But the station was in Olney, an hour's walk from Fox Chase on a good day. As the icy wind whipped around them, Mary called everyone they knew who owned a four-wheel-drive vehicle. Within twenty minutes, Chris Regel's wife, Rose, Dick Stuber, and Bill Pace were at the train ferrying the group to the Fern Rock subway station. But even with four-wheel drive it was treacherous going. The trucks slid on the snow-packed roads and the wipers could barely keep the windshields clear. Each truck had to make at least two trips between Fox Chase and Olney. But at 5:00 p.m., frozen but triumphant, the entire Fox Chase contingent sat in an empty subway car headed for Center City. Kathy looked around at the ragtag band: Billy and Kristie huddled together, laughing and shivering; Mary Doherty pulling chunks of ice from her eyebrows; Chris Regel looking like a Christmas bulb with his red face and bald head.

Just when Kathy could feel her toes again, the train pulled into Race Street Station, where the snow in some places had drifted to ten feet. Philadelphia looked like a ghost town as they hauled their suitcases up Race Street toward the Clarion Hotel. Kathy led the pack. Head bent against the snow, she imagined she was in labor, trying to make it to the hospital on the day Eddie was born. "Push, push, push," she told herself. In her mind, she was struggling up the snow bank to the ambulance that would carry her to the hospital where her baby would come out bottom first. But no matter how fast or how far she walked, she couldn't turn back time.

"Yo, Kath," yelled John. "Where ya going?" She turned to see the Fox Chase crowd half a block behind her. She'd overshot the hotel.

The desk clerk stared at the snow-covered crew as they checked into the five rooms they'd reserved. Kathy was planning a long hot shower after she unpacked.

"Never mind," said John as he hung up the phone in their room. "I just talked to Joe. Court has been canceled because of the storm."

With no way home, they decided to spend the night at the hotel. They awoke the next morning to the sight of thirty inches of snow on the ground and a caravan of police jeeps, courtesy of Joe Casey and Bill Bergman, pulling up in front to take them all back to Fox Chase.

30

Three days later, Philadelphia's version of the Trial of the Century finally got under way.

Joe Casey and Bill Danks sat on one side of the courtroom, backed by the proverbial mountain of evidence. Six defense attorneys, headed by A. Charles Peruto, sat on the other, armed with the shadow of reasonable doubt and a race card lurking in the deck.

The Polec family and their closest friends occupied the first row of seats behind the prosecution team. Approximately one hundred people from Fox Chase—friends, neighbors, school chums of Ed's—filled the right side of the courtroom. A roughly equal number of defendants' supporters, mostly kids, sat on the left side behind the defense table, so that the courtroom was divided into rooting sections, like a high school gym on the day of a big game.

The media were on the Polecs' side, literally and figuratively. About two dozen reporters sat in the assigned press seats directly behind the family. Most of the reporters had covered the case from the beginning and had come to know the Polecs well enough to address them by their first names and to feel a strong affection for them. In a society that babbled incessantly about family values, they seemed to be the real thing.

The press had no such feeling for the defendants' families, partly because none of them had opened themselves up to reporters the way the Polecs had. From the start the Rienzis had bristled with hostility, hiding their faces from the cameras, shouting at reporters to leave them alone, one time even punctuating their feelings by flipping the bird. "I know my son is innocent because he told me so, and he knows if he ever lied to me I'd smack him in the mouth," Mr. Rienzi once said to a reporter in the hallway, causing another reporter to comment aloud, "That apple sure didn't fall far from the tree."

Still, the reporters knew there had to be heartbreak in the defendants' families. Mrs. Pinero seemed so sadly elegant it didn't seem possible she was the parent of such a brutal thug. Tom Crook's mother was clearly anguished for the Polec family, and just as anguished that her own sense of what was right had helped put her son in a position to spend the rest of his life in prison. Dewan Alexander's mother didn't come to court because she was on dialysis, dying of cancer. No one from Bou's Khathavong's family had shown up for any of his court appearances.

"Members of the jury," Judge Greenspan began, "you have been selected to perform one of the most important and solemn duties of citizenship. You are to sit in judgment upon criminal charges made by the Commonwealth against your fellow citizens."

The judge explained to the panel the nature of the legal proceeding they were about to observe, cautioning that "statements made by counsel do not constitute evidence. The questions that counsel put to witnesses are not themselves evidence. It is the witnesses' answers that provide evidence for you. Let me repeat, the opening statements, as with any other statements made by counsel, do not constitute evidence, and you are not to consider these opening statements as established facts."

When she was done, Casey faced the jury box and started in with the Commonwealth's case. "On November 11, 1994, at about 10:00 p.m., Eddie Polec was sixteen years old, a normal, healthy, active, and relatively typical teenager," he said. "Less than twelve hours later, Eddie Polec was dead. Why? Because he just happened to be there."

Turning to a map of Fox Chase that rested on an easel in the center of the room, Casey asked, rhetorically, "Where is 'there'?" and with a pointer he began to trace the boundaries of Eddie's world. " 'There' starts at the Fox Chase Recreation Center right here," he said, "and it forms an irregular, four-sided figure, which goes up to a 7-Eleven store just about at the Montgomery County line, comes down to Stoxy's Steaks, includes a Dunkin' Donuts, a McDonald's, a Pizza Hut, and goes back to the Fox Chase Rec. This area has everything that a teenager would want. It has fast food. It has junk food. It is a place to engage in athletics and in that Kabuki ritual of social graces, growing up."

Casey then took the jurors to the broader, more mobile world of the defendants, walking them through the chain of events that led up to the crime. He described how Diane Costanzo and her girl friend Jessica Simons had been verbally abused and harassed by a group of Fox Chase kids at McDonald's the previous Friday night. "But at no time will you hear that Eddie Polec was among the people involved in the incident," he said. He told how the story of the thrown soda had made the rounds at Abington High School and gradually grown into a dramatic tale of physical assault and even rape as Simons's ex-boyfriend, Bou Khathavong, talked up a road trip to Fox Chase the following weekend to avenge the girls' honor.

Casey went on to describe how "an invasive force" from Montgomery County descended on Fox Chase that fateful night, gathering force and fury over the course of four hours. He tracked the movements of five cars as they converged from half a dozen neighborhoods spread across three counties. He told how the occupants used cell phones and beepers to gather new recruits from shopping malls and convenience stores; how they stopped along the way to acquire baseball bats, beer, and marijuana; how the caravan ultimately careened into St. Cecilia's parking lot in hot pursuit of three kids they'd never seen before; and how twenty-four teenagers then either joined in, cheered on, or did nothing to stop, a gruesome killing.

Casey's opening statement ran more than an hour. It was comprehensive, painstakingly detailed, and oddly dispassionate, the work of a prosecutor convinced he had the facts on his side.

Charles Peruto didn't let the facts get in the way of a good defense. He knew he stood a snowball's chance in hell of winning an acquittal for his client. The police had statements from nine Abington witnesses who said they either saw Nick Pinero hit Eddie in the head with a bat or heard Pinero admit to it after the fact. And Pinero had admitted it in a psychiatric interview that Peruto submitted to the court two days before the trial and then withdrew.

Peruto planned to put on a "boys-will-be-boys" defense, arguing that there was bad behavior on both sides that night and things just got out of hand. Yes, there was a killing, but it was not first-degree murder.

Maybe the jurors had gotten the picture of "caravans of people coming to do harm," he said. Actually, he told them, "what you have are a few automobiles with young people, all in the sixteen to seventeen age bracket, coming down to an ambush that had been set up from a week before. There were sixty to a hundred Fox Chase kids at the Rec that night," he said. "Knowing that the kids from Abington were coming down for a 'rumble,' the usual crowd had recruited others.

"Neither those lying in ambush nor the kids that came down intended to do serious bodily harm or to kill anybody," Peruto said. But while they waited, the Fox Chase kids were drinking beer. And "Mr. Eddie Polec, who met this terrible tragedy, was not just somebody who happened along. He bought the keg of beer." The Fox Chase kids were "getting a little juiced up . . . getting ready for the ambush."

Listening to Peruto's parallax view, John Polec took notes so furiously his pen dug deep into the pad. My God, Kathy thought, he's saying Eddie caused his own death. She tried to calm herself by saying a Hail Mary.

Peruto continued to hammer his ambush theme, using the word over and over again. The scene described might have been lifted from an old Western—the part where an overwhelming force of wily Apache lures a hapless band of cavalry into a box canyon and then shoots them like fish in a barrel. In Peruto's script, the Fox Chase kids had initiated the hostilities by throwing rocks at the Abington cars. Then they slipped back through the hole that was "conveniently" cut in the fence behind McDonald's and waited in the darkness, leaving a few kids in sight so that "when these stupid jerks get out of their cars and come over are they going to be surprised." Between sixty and a hundred Fox Chase kids lay in wait. "And are they without weapons? They have stones, they have bottles, and when these kids came through from Abington, boy, they got exactly what was planned for them."

Using Casey's map, he traced the path of the Abington kids after the fight at McGarrity's—retreating back through the hole in the fence to their cars, fleeing the battlefield with their wounded, when suddenly they were attacked again.

"You come out of this street and there is St. Cecilia's, the parking lot, where the tragedy occurred. And what happens? There is Eddie Polec again, with his brother, with others, and stones again being thrown, and it is responded to again. It certainly wasn't planned for them to go there, but here again it is instigated with stones and they come out, and yes, Eddie Polec got terribly beaten in the excitement . . . It happened out of the passion of the moment, the terror of the moment, the stupidity of the moment. Yes, they were suckered into it, but that doesn't mean this should have happened."

John gripped the edge of his seat, trying to keep himself from leaping over the railing and grabbing Peruto by the throat. Couldn't anyone stop this? The man was lying, making up things that never happened! Was this legal? Why didn't Joe Casey jump up and shout "Objection!" and set the record straight?

But in the strange world of American jurisprudence, Peruto technically wasn't lying, just mischaracterizing the evidence to his client's best advantage. Among seventy-five witness statements taken by police, there was only one—from Kerri Medernach, a friend of Eddie's—that could be interpreted as suggesting rocks were thrown near the church. Peruto's staff had highlighted it for him in a memo: "Note: In her statement that night it says, 'Somebody threw a rock at the red car.' This is in the context of the area before the church, NOT at McDonald's." But the only red car mentioned by any witness was Diane Costanzo's Plymouth Duster, and all evidence showed that Costanzo had left Fox Chase well before the attack at the church. Not one Abington witness mentioned anything about rocks being thrown near the church. So in all likelihood, either Medernach had misspoken or the detective who took down her statement had misinterpreted what she said.

Before taking his seat, Peruto made one more statement that was false. "Now, who named Nicholas Pinero?" he asked the jury. Then he answered, "Nobody." Actually, the list was long, including Pinero himself. But Peruto could say that, because Judge Greenspan had told the jury not to consider his utterances as fact.

Dewan Alexander's attorney, Michael Wallace, followed Peruto. His client "hadn't a thing to do with Eddie Polec," Wallace said, and had been a hundred yards away fighting with someone else when the fatal beating occurred. Next, John McMahon told the jury that the evidence would show that "at no time" had his client, Anthony Rienzi, held a bat in his hand or held "this young Edward Polec up in the air while another individual or individuals struck him with baseball bats."

Janis Smarro began by quoting from the confession her client, Tom Crook, had made to the police: " 'I want to tell you the truth. I never intended to kill anyone. It was supposed to be just a fight.' " She told jurors that Crook admitted to hitting Eddie with a bat, though not on the head, and that he was sorry for what he'd done. Crook went to the police on his own, without a lawyer, with no warrant out for his arrest, no cops calling around to question him. There was "no carrot dangling," she said, no promise of leniency, no "We'll give you five years in jail" in return for testimony. And he made a full and truthful sixteen-page statement, for which he was rewarded with a first-degree murder charge. She contrasted that with the treatment of the prosecution's star witness, Kevin Convey, who had lied to police for weeks before admitting he was the one who brought Eddie down with a bat, and then was allowed to plead guilty to a third-degree murder charge.

She told Crook to rise and face the jurors. "I am not going to stand before you and tell you he wasn't there," she said. "And I am not going to stand before you and tell you that he didn't participate. But what I will stand here before you and tell you is that he never intended to kill Eddie Polec. He did not premeditate. He did not deliberate. He did not set out with a conscious intent and purpose to kill Eddie Polec. That was not his state of mind."

Oscar Gaskins, representing Carlo Johnson, put off his opening statement until after the prosecution presented its case. So it was left to

Bou Khathavong's attorney, Michael Applebaum, to introduce the race card.

In a way, Michael Applebaum had the best defense of them all. Not a single witness could place Khathavong among the group that beat Eddie. The sole basis for the first-degree murder charge against Khathavong was the undisputed fact that—driven by "a warped sense of chivalry," as Applebaum put it—Khathavong was the principal instigator of the foray into Fox Chase to avenge his ex-girlfriend's honor.

Applebaum first defined the Rec as "a group of kids who engage in fighting, harassment, and antagonizing many people who come into their neighborhood, their turf. In fact," he said, "it is common knowledge among the people of Abington and the surrounding communities that the Rec travels in numbers and they 'tune up' people who go through their neighborhood."

From there, he went to the incident at McDonald's the week before the crime. "What you are going to hear is that there were several young ladies from Abington who were in the Fox Chase area, trying to have a meal at McDonald's, when a few young men from the Rec, who knew that one young lady who was white had a baby with one of the defendants here, who is black, and because of that she was fair game, easy prey, an easy mark, a loose woman. They went up to her, they accosted her, they squeezed her breasts, pinched her rear end, and they made obscene gestures to her and thought that she should go to bed with them."

Applebaum was wrong. Neither of the white girls in question had borne a baby to either one of the black defendants, Dewan Alexander or Carlo Johnson.

He went on to describe what had happened at McDonald's. He told the jury they would hear that one of the young men there was Eddie Polec.

Heads snapped up around the courtroom. Reporters stopped taking notes. "What did he just say?" During all the pretrial hearings there'd been no mention of anything tying Eddie to the earlier incident on November 4. Joe Casey had told the jury in the morning that "at no time" would they hear that Eddie had been present at that initial altercation. But they just had. Was there a secret witness? Was somebody lying?

John and Kathy were apoplectic. They knew Eddie had been working at Boston Chicken that night, right up until closing time. Any number of people who worked with him could testify that he couldn't possibly have been at McDonald's.

The prosecution's first witness was Dr. Ian Hood, the deputy medical examiner. John thought he was prepared for Hood's testimony. He'd heard a version of it during the preliminary hearing, and he'd seen the real thing at the morgue. Moreover, the defense had convinced the judge to limit the number of autopsy photos Casey could show the jury and the amount of time they could be displayed. Three pictures of Eddie's body and one of his hand were to be projected on the screen for no more than two minutes total.

Eddie's head had been "free to move on its shoulders while he was being beaten," Hood said. "It was not on the ground being broken up like a pumpkin would be if you did the same thing to it." He went on: "The skull could be described as having an eggshell fracture, like taking an egg and hitting it with a spoon, you get radiating fractures that completely fragment."

Kathy dug her fingernails into John's arm and buried her head in his shoulder. The head shots were bad, but the picture of the hand was devastating. Casey included it to make a point. It showed a bruised and swollen fracture of the middle knuckle on Eddie's left hand. It was a classic defensive wound, Hood said, not the typical "boxer's fracture" you see from an offensive injury. Eddie had thrown no punches, just held up his hand to ward off the bat blows that were raining down on him.

John stared at his boy's hand. He had never noticed it in the overwhelming horror of the hospital room or the morgue. But now he could see that same hand, unmarked and unbroken, resting on the side of the pool table, steadying the cue for a shot.

In his cross-examination Peruto went right to the issue of whether Eddie was drunk the night of the beating. Eddie had survived twelve hours or so after the beating, he reminded Dr. Hood. Wasn't that enough time to dissipate the alcohol contained in twelve drinks of whiskey?

Hood had to answer yes to every question Peruto put to him. But John couldn't see why the issue was relevant. Even supposing Eddie had been falling-down drunk—for which there was absolutely no evidence—how could that mitigate what had been done to him?

After court adjourned for the day, Michael Applebaum told reporters, "The first impression was that Eddie Polec was polishing the brass on the altar at St. Cecilia's when he was just drug out and beaten on the steps. That's not the case at all."

In the car on the way home that evening, Kathy cried. "Eddie died over and over again in that courtroom today, John, and we were just as powerless to prevent it as we were that night in the parking lot."

Day two was no better. Casey's first witness was Dr. Lucy B. Rorke, a neuropathologist who'd examined Eddie's brain. Peruto and the other lawyers fought hard to keep her from taking the stand, on the grounds that the damage to Eddie's brain had already been described and would be "prejudicial" to the defendants, but the judge overruled them.

"Everything from the Commonwealth's perspective is prejudicial to your clients," she said testily. "That's the idea of proving their case."

After an unsuccessful attempt to cast aspersions on Rorke's credentials, Peruto went back to his favorite theme: "Alcohol and drugs alter the person's ability to think, reason, and determine, am I correct?" Casey objected, the judge sustained, and Peruto sat down.

Under direct questioning by Casey, Rorke told the court that Eddie's brain had been removed from his skull, preserved in formalin, and sent to her office, where she examined it in the company of a forensic pathologist and a number of her students. She weighed it and found it to be 30 percent heavier than normal because it was engorged with blood.

Among the damage she found were "diffuse axonal" injuries deep inside the brain, the result of the brain having rotated inside the skull. "That situation prevails if you have trauma exerted on the brain coming from various directions and where you get a rotation of the neck and the head like this or like this," she said, turning her head from side to side. "If you have rotating forces, you have the brain going at various angles and you are tearing the blood vessels and you are tearing the fibers."

In other words, Eddie's brain was practically ripped from its stem.

Dr. Rorke came armed with color slides to show the extent of damage. The defense had fought to keep them from being displayed, fearing not so much their content as their effect on the Polecs in full view of the jury. Judge Greenspan had ruled that only three photographs could be shown, for no more than two minutes each.

As Casey was preparing to project the slides, Janis Smarro asked for a sidebar conference with the judge. She was concerned about three of the jurors, whom she claimed were "focusing in on the Polecs" as Rorke testified. "Mrs. Polec is resting her head on Mr. Polec's shoulder and is being consoled by her daughter and someone who appears to be either a friend or from Victim's Assistance, I don't know, but they are continually concerned and handing her tissues." Kathy was "weeping and wiping her eyes continuously," she said.

Casey protested that Kathy had been "an absolute model of decorum," and the judge agreed. "Whether she is weeping or not, she is certainly doing whatever she is doing with absolutely no noise whatsoever, and she is resting her head on her husband's shoulder. He does have his arm around her, but that is to be expected." She saw no reason to remove them from the courtroom.

Peruto tried once more to keep the pictures from being shown, but the judge stood her ground.

So the photographs were shown, and the Polecs didn't fall apart. Kathy closed her eyes and prayed to St. Joseph while John stared at the sickening images in wonderment. He was looking at his son's brain, outside of his body, sitting on a steel table. That used to be Eddie's mind! The part of him that controlled his smile and his voice, that once held the answers to those bedeviling algebra problems and Latin translations, that stored all those memories of family trips to Hershey Park and summers at the shore. Now it was reduced to a bloody pulp, like some discarded slab of meat on a slaughterhouse floor.

"This is the undersurface of the brain," he heard Dr. Rorke saying, "and you can see the same kind of hemorrhage and tearing of the tissue. All of this irregular material is the torn tissue."

John marveled that he could sit there watching and listening and not be struck instantly insane and sent screaming into the street. Maybe that would be the sane reaction. So maybe he was already insane. Or maybe it would come over him suddenly sometime in the future, like the post-traumatic-stress thing that afflicted Vietnam vets.

As a final point, Rorke was prepared to testify that of the two thousand traumatized brains she'd examined in her career, this was the worst damage she'd ever seen. But Casey couldn't manage to get that into the record. Each time he tried to ask the question, the defense team popped up like jack-in-the-boxes: "Have you ever seen a brain that suffered more trauma?" "Objection!" "Could you quantify it from one to one thousand?" "Objection!" "Can you rank it within two thousand? "Objection!" "Of the two thousand you've observed, how many had had this severe trauma?" "Objection!" The judge sustained each objection, and Casey finally gave up, figuring the jury had gotten the message anyway.

During cross-examination, Peruto seemed to be laying the groundwork for a "diminished capacity" defense of Pinero. Over Casey's repeated objections, he peppered Rorke with questions about the effect of alcohol on the human brain. "Alcohol does alter behavior, does it not?" "It also impairs the ability to recall details, am I correct?" "It also interferes with a person's ability to control his actions, does it not?" "Alcohol on the brain has the effect to alter judgment and realization of the activities being performed, am I correct?" "You do not have one single iota of what stimuli were present in anyone who inflicted any damage in this case, am I correct?"

Then he moved on to the slides. "What do you think, if anything, that the jury would learn by seeing those gory pictures?" he asked. "Do you think you need a picture of a broken leg for a jury to understand what a broken leg is?"

Rorke was seething. "I don't *deal* with broken legs," she spat back contemptuously. "Legs are outside of the body and everyone knows what a leg looks like. But nobody's brain is sitting outside of their head, so they don't have the slightest idea in most cases what a brain looks like."

The prosecution's first non-expert witness was seventeen-year-old Billy Oehler, a friend of Eddie's from their days at St. Cecilia's. Oehler testified that he was at McDonald's on Friday night, November 4 and witnessed the harassment of Diane Costanzo and Jessica Simons. He even admitted that he was the one who had started the whole incident by challenging an Abington kid to a fight. But he didn't recall seeing Eddie there that night.

In his cross-examination, Peruto was alternately sarcastic, intimidating, and mocking. When Oehler said he didn't understand a question, Peruto made a show of seeming astounded, waving his arms and rolling his eyes in disbelief. "You really don't understand that?" he said. "You really don't?" Then he proceeded to talk to Oehler as if he were mentally slow. "Now, you took umbrage . . . maybe I better use a different word . . . It bothered you that. . . ."

Because Oehler hadn't testified on direct examination about the night Eddie was beaten, trial protocol prevented Peruto from questioning him about it. But that didn't stop him from trying. Each time, Casey objected and Greenspan sustained, leaving Peruto sputtering.

"Be on notice that we would like your subpoena to continue," he barked at the teenager. "Do you understand that?"

"Yes, sir."

"Because we will ask you what happened on the eleventh. Do you understand that?"

"Yes, sir."

"You were interviewed by the district attorney; you understand that, don't you? I would like to interview you, so will you wait for me during the break, please?"

"Yes."

Oehler maintained his composure on the witness stand, but he broke down in the hallway after it was over. He was being comforted by his father in Courtroom Bill during the afternoon break when Peruto barged in and demanded his interview right then and there. Oehler's father got up from his seat and started for Peruto. "I don't like the way you're talking to my son," he growled. "In case you've forgotten, he's a minor." Detective Danks stepped between the two men. Peruto regarded the senior Oehler for a moment, then shrugged. "Why pick a fight with me?" he said, turning and walking away. Danks restrained Mr. Oehler from going after him.

The incident prompted the judge to warn the defense to stop bullying the young witnesses. Oehler was never called by Peruto.

At the end of the second day of testimony, John and Kathy Polec faced reporters outside the courtroom. Asked about Michael Applebaum's allegation that Eddie had participated in the harassment of Diane Costanzo at McDonald's, John said calmly, "I think Mr. Applebaum has Ed mistaken for someone else."

"I'm glad they showed the pictures," said Kathy. "The jury has to see that, and the families of the kids who did this have to see, too. How can you take a bat to someone's head and not mean for them to die?" As for Peruto's comportment, she said, "I guess if you are trying to defend somebody, if you throw out enough smoke, someone will believe something."

Smoke practically billowed out of Peruto as he cross-examined a string of teenage witnesses. Eighteen-year-old Thomas Ruth testified that he was at the 7-Eleven store in Fox Chase around 9:30 the night Eddie was beaten, when all of a sudden four or five cars with music blasting "pulled up in all different parking positions and took over the whole parking lot." He identified Pinero, Crook, and Khathavong as being among the fifteen to twenty teenagers who demanded directions to McDonald's.

"I heard Bou Khathavong say, 'Come on, we have to do this. We have a job to get done. Let's do this before the police come.'

"He was loud and I guess it just seemed like he was kind of their leader . . . Everyone was looking up to him and looking at him when he was talking to them. When he was getting to his car, he was jumping up and down, and he said, 'I'm so psyched, I could kill someone.'"

Ruth had waited for months before telling police what he'd seen at the 7-Eleven that night, fearing retaliation from Bou Khathavong's pals in Abington. Only after long talks with his father and his minister had he come forward. And he was still frightened on the witness stand, gulping and hesitating when Joe Casey asked him to point out Bou in court. His testimony was potentially devastating, evidence that at least three of the defendants had joined in a conspiracy to commit murder well before the fatal attack. But it was a seemingly innocuous statement of Ruth's that Peruto went after at the start of his cross-examination. Asked by Casey how he knew Eddie, Ruth had responded, "I went to St. Cecilia's before I went to my new high school and I was on the soccer team and I was an altar boy with him in the sixth grade." Peruto wasn't going to let that altar-boy stuff stand.

"Mr. Ruth, you went through a preparation for your testimony, didn't you?" he began.

"Yes."

"Were you a close friend to Eddie Polec?"

"During high school years I barely saw him, but when I was in grade school I was, yes."

"You knew from your preparation that you would take the stand and be asked how you knew him, am I correct?"

"Yes."

"You went over the fact that you were to make the point that he had been an altar boy, am I correct?"

"No."

"How did that come up?"

"Objection."

"Sustained."

"You are talking about years and years before this incident, aren't you?" Peruto persisted.

"That's when I was closest with him."

"There were no beer parties back then, were there?" Peruto sneered, and Casey's objection was again sustained.

Outside the courtroom, Kathy Polec threw her arms around Ruth and cried. "He was badgered relentlessly, but he kept his composure," she told reporters. "He'd been so scared to get involved. I was so proud of him."

Ruth was followed to the witness stand by Terrance Nurse, a seventeen-year-old Abington dropout who testified on direct that he was among the mob that had chased Eddie into St. Cecilia's parking lot, that he saw Nick Pinero and Tom Crook hit Eddie in the head with baseball bats while Anthony Rienzi held him up "by the hip of his pants and his shirt collar," and that Dewan Alexander punched and kicked Eddie as he lay on the ground.

But Nurse brought a lot of baggage to court, starting with his appearance. In contrast to Tom Ruth's gray suit, white shirt, and tie, Nurse wore baggy black jeans low on his hips, scuffed sneakers, and an earring. He slouched in the witness chair and muttered many of his answers. And he came with a criminal record. He was on probation from a juvenile conviction for credit card fraud just four months earlier.

"Tell me," said Peruto, "did the police come to you or did you go to them?"

"They came to me."

"Didn't they tell you that you were a member of a conspiracy?"

"Yes."

"Didn't they tell you that all people involved in a conspiracy are equally guilty?"

"Yes."

"They told you that they were charging the people in the conspiracy with first-degree murder, didn't they?"

"I'm not sure. I don't remember."

"Did they tell you why you weren't going to be arrested even though you were part of the plan in going to McDonald's and fighting?"

"No."

"Was it suggested to you that if you give a statement involving these kids, you could escape being arrested?"

"No."

"Did you figure it was just an accident that they overlooked you?" Peruto pressed on. "Isn't it a fact that the reason you were not arrested is that you said you saw things that you really didn't see?"

"I know what I saw."

But there were problems for the prosecution in what Nurse claimed he did and didn't see. First of all, he said there were only three carloads of Abington kids at St. Cecilia's, as opposed to Casey's carefully established five. He said he saw Eddie trip and fall, then saw Pinero, Crook, Rienzi, and Alexander attack him at the same time that he himself was chasing and fighting with another kid somewhere else in the parking lot. And finally, he said he didn't see Kevin Convey with a bat anywhere near Eddie.

Peruto went right at the inconsistencies: "You don't even know who it was who had a bat in his hand, do you?"

"I do know," Nurse insisted.

"You *do* know? Well now, you tell me, which of them had bats, if any?"

"Nick Pinero and Tom Crook."

"Well, if it was Nick Pinero and Tom Crook, then Kevin Convey, who pleaded guilty to it, didn't have a bat. Is that what you are saying? Did Convey have a bat?"

"I don't know."

So it went for three hours as the defense team picked apart Nurse's testimony and his earlier statement to police. Nurse grew more sullen and evasive as the day wore on, answering questions with I-don't-knows or I-don't-remembers.

A typical exchange came when Anthony Rienzi's lawyer, John McMahon, questioned Nurse about his chase through the parking lot.

"Did you tell this jury that Rob Colefield was running alongside you?"

"Yes."

"You are positive about that, right?"

"From my knowledge of knowing, I am."

"I am asking what you saw. Did you see him running alongside you?"

"I guess he was right there. He is supposed to have been right there."

"Sir, did you see him alongside you?"

"No, I didn't see him alongside me."

If Nurse seemed less than reliable when McMahon finished his cross-examination, he seemed less than human when Dewan Alexander's lawyer, Michael Wallace, was done with him.

"How many times did you go near Mr. Polec's body?" Wallace asked.

"Once running up and again when I was coming back [to the car]."

"Did you or did you not walk right over him coming back?"

"Yes."

"You walked right over his body?"

"I didn't step *on* him; I stepped *over* him," Nurse said, as if that made all the difference.

In his questioning of Nurse, Oscar Gaskins, Carlo Johnson's attorney, made the surprising allegation that Bou Khathavong had been beaten up by some Fox Chase kids in front of his home several weeks before the incidents in question. Nurse acknowledged that he'd heard about it.

"Did you have any information that when Bou got beat up he was with Carlo at the time?" Gaskins asked.

"No."

"Did you know, or did you learn, that as a result of that Carlo, in fact, went to the hospital?"

"No."

"Did you know that these Fox Chase kids, when they beat up Bou, in fact also robbed them and had them at gunpoint with a shotgun?"

Joe Casey was out of his seat. "Objection, your honor, it's from left field, and that's the clearest objection I can make."

"Sustained," said Judge Greenspan, "and I will remind the jury that anything said by counsel is not evidence."

Gaskins was indignant. "I am prepared to demonstrate and prove everything I said."

"I hope so," said the judge, "but for now it is not evidence."

Nor would it ever be, because Gaskins would never present any evidence that the beating or shotgun robbery took place.

For reporters and spectators, it was a riveting day of testimony, filled with plot twists and dramatic outbursts, the stuff of great courtroom theater. But for John Polec it was depressing. The way he saw it, the defense was determined to make the jury believe that Eddie and his friends were a band of drunken armed robbers who got what they deserved. The truth didn't matter during a trial, only zealous advocacy. When reporters asked for his comments at the end of the day, John sounded uncharacteristically bitter.

"The Fox Chase kids were doing nothing different that night than kids in Fox Chase have done for thirty years," he told reporters. "If that's justification for them to murder him the way they did, then there is something really screwed up with the justice system. Five thousand people came to his funeral. That says more than the fact that he would sell some beer."

By the fourth day of testimony, Peruto's bad-cop act was wearing thin even with the other defense attorneys. Because he sat in the first chair at the defense table, he was always the first to cross-examine, so they sometimes had to wait hours for him to finish his exhaustive and often repetitive questioning. Several of them, particularly Janis Smarro, were visibly uncomfortable with his hounding of the young witnesses, and they began throwing out their own objections.

For his part, Joe Casey tried not to rise to his chief adversary's bait.

The Polecs were his model for dignity under fire and he didn't want to do anything that would embarrass them. But during Peruto's cross-examination of Fox Chase teenager Jack Cole, Casey finally lost it.

The teenager had started to answer one question about his police statement when Peruto interrupted him with another question. "Your Honor," Casey said, getting up from his chair, "he was going to reply in his own way and counsel cut him off."

"I'm sorry," Peruto said, caustically. "I couldn't read that like Mr. Casey, because he *rehearsed* him."

Rising to his full height, Casey bellowed, "If we are going to get into name calling, then I have a few chosen epithets for *that*, Counsel!"

Undaunted, Peruto continued to hammer away at Cole on one of his favorite themes. Cole had testified that he and Kerri Medernach were walking up Ridgeway Street minutes before Eddie was attacked when the Abington caravan passed them on the way to the church.

"You are aware, are you not, that around St. Cecilia's as you approached, there were rocks thrown in that area, too, weren't there?" Peruto asked.

"No."

"Was there a sudden exclamation from this girl about rock throwing?"

"No."

"Did you ever become aware of any utterances by her concerning rock throwing?"

"No."

Peruto even beat up on John Atkinson, the teenager who was nearly clubbed to death by the Abington mob shortly before they fell upon Eddie. Atkinson was in some ways the perfect prosecution witness. Six-foot-five and all-American handsome, he had a heartbreaking story to tell about dreams deferred and a difficult recovery from devastating injuries. And he remembered very little about the attack, which made him very tough to cross-examine.

Under gentle questioning by Casey, Atkinson testified that all he recalled was somehow ending up on his hands and knees in McGarrity's parking lot and seeing a light-skinned black kid standing over him with an aluminum bat raised above his head. "And I turned my head back around and felt myself get hit with the bat," he said, breaking into sobs. "I remember screaming and curling up into a ball to try to cover up."

Atkinson said that doctors at the hospital had told him that, judging by the number of lumps on his head, he'd been hit anywhere from eight to ten times. But it wasn't until weeks later that he realized how badly he'd been injured. He was Christmas shopping with his mother at a department store.

"The bill was $19.00 and I had a $10 bill and some ones," he said. "So I gave the lady the ten and tried to count out the ones, but I had to stop. I would get to three or four and have to start over again. And then she just told me to give her all the money I had in my hand and she just counted it out for me."

After that there were regular visits to a neurologist at the University of Pennsylvania, to a grief counselor at CORA, and to a "cognitive therapist" who helped him learn how to read again and retain information.

"It really put a halt to everything," he said. "I stopped going to school around March, the second semester, and I had to go on antidepressants, protriptyline. I would wake up in the morning and just be hysterical, crying, and there were times when I was not sure whether or not I wanted to be alive."

Peruto was relentless in his cross-examination. Every time the teenager answered a question with "I don't know" or "I don't remember," Peruto parroted it back—"You don't know? You don't remember?"—as if to suggest that he was feigning memory loss. At one point, Atkinson was trying to describe the person he saw standing over him with the bat when Peruto suddenly asked, "Were you ever shown photographs of a large number of kids to look at?"

Atkinson looked blank. "I don't understand what you mean."

"You don't understand what I mean when I said, 'Were you ever shown photographs?' "

"No."

"Are you telling me that you don't know what photographs are? Are you really, John? Come on!"

There was a murmur of disapproval throughout the courtroom. Kristie Polec sprang from her seat, but John grabbed her before she had a chance to say or do anything, and Mary Doherty quickly escorted her into the hallway to calm down.

Peruto pressed on, going so far as to suggest that Atkinson had faked his injuries to cover up his own complicity in the fight.

"While you were at the hospital, you called your friend and found out about Eddie, didn't you?"

"Yes, a couple of hours later."

"Now, did you ever make a complaint to the police that you had been assaulted?"

"I'm not sure. I gave a statement to the police."

"You mean when they came to your house?"

"Yes, sir."

"A couple of days later?"

"Yes."

"By then you knew about Eddie, didn't you?"

"Yes."

"Did it ever occur to you to tell the police these things that you saw and experienced?"

"Yes, I did tell them."

"You didn't tell them until they came to see you, though?"

"Yes."

"Did you think you could be helpful, knowing that your friend had met this unfortunate, terribly serious injury, resulting in his death? Didn't it occur to you to tell them right there in the hospital that you were in on it, knew something, could help the police with it?"

"There were no policemen at the hospital."

"These phone calls to your friends, et cetera, your conversations with your mother, did you ever suggest to them to let the police know how you had been innocently accosted?"

"I think so, yes."

"You think so?"

It was painful to listen to, ugly to watch. But it was the kind of performance prosecutors pray for—the chief defense counsel behaving like a complete asshole in front of the jury. Truth was, Joe Casey didn't really need John Atkinson to remember the details about what had happened in McGarrity's parking lot. For that he had nineteen-year-old Matt Malone, a lifelong friend of Eddie's and the son of a Philadelphia cop.

"I was standing at the top of McGarrity's hill and I heard a commotion," Malone testified. "I looked down the hill and I seen Katie Harrigan get struck by a bat and kicked twice by somebody with a white sweatshirt and with a hood on. She started to scream, and she kind of fell forward a bit, but caught herself with one of her hands, like her knees were bent, and she was leaning forward and she pushed herself up and ran up the hill past me. She was crying and she was kind of still screaming, and her facial expression was pretty terrified."

Katie Harrigan, a petite eighteen-year-old, was brought into the courtroom for identification. "Is that the young lady that you were referring to who was struck and kicked?" Casey asked.

"Yes, sir," Malone replied.

"Where was she at the time she was struck?"

"She was sitting on a little curb right outside the entrance to McGarrity's."

Casey directed the testimony back to Atkinson. "When you first saw John Atkinson, where in McGarrity's was he?"

"I seen him just to the right of where Katie Harrigan was sitting," Malone answered. "Coming from behind McGarrity's, all of a sudden he came into my view . . . he was being struck by a bat."

"About how many people were in the immediate area of Mr. Atkinson at that time?"

"Approximately six."

"How many of them had what could be described as a hitting weapon, a bat or a pole or something?"

"Approximately four."

"Go on, tell us what happened."

The story poured out of the teenager in a torrent, as if it had been pent up for too long. "He got hit one more time in the back of his head, and it echoed and it forced him to the ground . . . and I kept on seeing people hitting him. They were punching him. They were hitting him with bats. There was one pole. He was like on all fours and he was kind of rocking, like he was trying to get up, but he was rocking his weight back and was meeting the blows at the same time and it was pushing him forward."

Asked if he could identify any of the attackers, Malone pointed to Nick Pinero and Dewan Alexander. "Pinero had the bat; Alexander had the pole," he said.

"I decided to run down the hill and grab John," he continued. "At this time there was approximately two people hitting him. I ran down and grabbed him with my right arm and pulled him toward me to bring him out, and he got struck again on the back of the neck and this blow hit me on the left shoulder. John's head kind of dropped down, but my momentum made him run as a reaction and I didn't stop running until I got to the front of Fox Chase playground."

"Do you know who did the striking of that last blow?" Casey asked.

"Yes."

"Who?"

Malone's right arm shot straight out. "May the record reflect," Casey said, "the witness pointed at defendant Pinero."

Malone said that as he was running back up McGarrity's hill he saw Eddie standing on the train tracks, talking with Sean Roney. "I said, 'Ed, come on, let's go.' And he said, 'No, I'm not leaving; I have to wait for Billy.' That's his younger brother. And I said, 'Well, just make sure you take a different way home.' "

Malone described how he and three friends helped Atkinson through back yards to the safety of Stu Katuran's house several blocks away. "He couldn't walk . . . we had to literally pick him up over fences. Like, somebody would hop a fence and then they would hold his arms and two people would pick up his legs and put them over the fence, and then we would carry him, hold on to his arms so he wouldn't fall."

After a few minutes at Katuran's house, he walked back toward the Rec, Malone said.

"I got to St. Cecilia's and I seen Kerri on the ground right by Ed. She looked at me and I said, 'Who is that?' And she said, 'It's Ed.' And I looked over like this. I didn't really want to look that much, but I just glanced and glanced back, and I said, 'Are you sure that's Ed?' And she said, 'I'm sure.'

"She started crying and grabbing me and she said, 'I don't know, he doesn't look good,' and the police officer said he didn't know if he was going to make it."

"How did he look?" Casey asked quietly.

Malone started sobbing. "The left side of his head where his temple was had a dent, and the dent was maybe about a half-inch deep, and his one eye was closed and his other eye was going in circles. He was having trouble breathing. His nose was swollen. I started stepping back.

"As this was happening, they picked him up and put him on a stretcher and the back of his head just started pouring out blood, and the only thing I could say was 'How did this happen? How did this happen?'

"I saw a police officer and he grabbed me and said, 'Do you know what happened?' And I said, 'I don't know what happened here, but I know what happened earlier.' And he said, 'I want you to come with me and tell me what you know. Your friend needs you right now.' "

Malone buried his face in his hands and dissolved into tears. So did Kathy Polec and half a dozen other people in the courtroom. Judge Greenspan called a recess.

Charles Peruto's first question on cross-examination dripped with sarcasm. "Mr. Malone, would it be fair to say that none of the kids from Fox Chase did anything to anybody?"

At the close of the day, reporters descended on Peruto and peppered him with questions about his comportment. "If you are suggesting that I should change my tactics, I think I'm getting through to the jury," he said. "My client is charged with first-degree murder and aggravated assault. What am I supposed to do, not talk about it?"

Joe Casey was triumphant. "Matt Malone saved John Atkinson's life. Nick Pinero would have killed him if Matt Malone had not gone down there and dragged him out."

31

"The Commonwealth calls William Polec."

Billy took the stand shortly before noon on January 20. It was a Saturday. Judge Greenspan had ordered the unusual weekend session over the objections of defense counsel, Peruto in particular. The trial had been delayed for three days by snow and another two days by sick jurors. Fourteen people had been sequestered from their lives and their families for two weeks already, and she wasn't about to let this run on like the Simpson case. She was determined that the trial would continue without a break until the verdict was in.

As Billy swore to tell the whole truth, he knew he was about to drop a bombshell, and he wished he didn't have to do it.

He'd spoken to the police at St. Cecilia's the night Eddie was beaten and again at the hospital the morning Eddie died. But it wasn't until a month later that he gave an official, signed statement to Tom Perks. The detective had put off the interview for as long as he could, out of deference to the family. It was during their talk—in Billy's bedroom, out of earshot from the rest of the family—that Perks first learned what all the other Fox Chase kids were trying to cover up: Eddie had been running the keg that night. Billy just couldn't lie about it.

During the interview, Billy identified Nick Pinero as one of the people he saw hit John Atkinson with a bat and, later, as the same person who had chased him through St. Cecilia's parking lot with a bat in his hand. Billy recognized Pinero from his picture on the TV news, he said.

But in the ensuing months, Billy had become less sure. There was a lot of confusion that night, people shouting. He'd been terrified, running for his life, looking back over his shoulder. Had he really seen Pinero, or just another kid who looked a lot like him? Over and over again, as he lay in bed at night, he tried to conjure up the face of his pursuer. But he couldn't recall the precise features, only a general image. He confessed his growing doubt to Joe Casey the week before his testimony. It wasn't something Casey wanted to hear—his most believable witness backing off on a solid identification. But there it was, and Casey couldn't hide it.

With Billy on the witness stand, Casey went right to it. "Today, how sure are you that's the person you saw?" he asked.

"I'm not 100 percent sure," Billy responded.

"Has there been a change in your degree of certainty between then and now?"

"Yes, sir. The first time that I saw him on the news, I thought I was positive. But after further thinking—although I believe it was him—I could not be 100 percent certain of it."

"That is what you are here today to say?"

"Correct."

It would have been so easy for Billy to hold to his earlier statement. No one could have busted him for it; no one would ever have known. He knew from all the other evidence that Pinero surely was one of his brother's killers. But he felt that to tell less than the truth would be a betrayal. Eddie wasn't a liar.

Judge Greenspan called for a lunch recess after Billy's direct testimony. John was in the third-floor men's room when Chuck Peruto walked in. It was only the two of them.

"Mr. Polec, I just want you to know how sorry I am about what happened to your son and your family," the attorney said. "I had a son who died recently, so I know something of how you feel." John nodded and said, "Thank you."

Back in the courtroom, it seemed like a different Charles Peruto who cross-examined Billy. Gone was the belittling, condescending attitude. The blustering, sarcastic bully was transformed into a kindly old man just asking questions for clarification. John wondered if it was Peruto's humanity finally breaking through or a canny lawyer's calculation that the jury might react badly to him beating up on the victim's little brother.

Billy's performance on the witness stand was remarkable. Sitting erect, with his hands folded in front of him, the fifteen-year-old answered questions in a strong voice. "That is correct, sir . . . I have no recollection of that, sir . . . I believe so, sir . . . No, sir, I never said that." His face reddened, his eyes welled up at times, and he gulped what seemed like gallons of water, but he never lost his composure, not even when his description of the scene in front of St. Cecilia's that night reduced many in the courtroom to tears.

"When I first walked up and I saw the cops around, I knew that something had happened," he said. "And one of my friends, Brian Watson, grabbed me and just told me to stay with him. So I started getting real worried and upset, and he was grabbing me, hugging me, holding me away.

"I looked over and saw a kid laying with his head in a girl's lap, and when I looked over again I realized that it was my brother. And I just, I just stopped. I just froze for a long time, I don't remember how long, but I walked over and the guys made me walk away, the cops did, because they didn't want too many people around. And they let the girl hold his head in her lap, and there was blood all over the ground."

Billy held himself together until after he left the witness stand. Back in Courtroom Bill, he started shaking and put his head on the table and sobbed.

"You saw the real Billy Polec today," John told reporters at the end of the day. "He was forty years old on the day he was born."

"I just hope it's finally over for him," Kathy said quietly. "He's been carrying this around for more than a year."

The next day, January 21, would have been Eddie's eighteenth birthday. The Polecs spent much of the day listening to the details of his death.

The witness was Jason Mascione. As he'd done at the preliminary hearing months before, the nineteen-year-old former Abington student testified that he was recruited to go to Fox Chase that night by Bou Khathavong. He said he saw Pinero and Rienzi hit Eddie over the head with bats, that Rienzi held Eddie up for Pinero to hit three or four more times, and that Dewan Alexander kicked Eddie with heavy boots as he lay "curled up in a ball" on the ground.

Casey got down on the floor and asked Mascione to pick up the bat and demonstrate how Rienzi had swung it at Eddie. Mascione complied.

"Indicating a golf-type swing, is that correct?" Judge Greenspan asked.

"Yes, ma'am," Mascione replied.

"What, if anything, did you hear when defendant Rienzi hit the person on the ground in the head with the bat, using the golf swing that you just described," Casey asked.

"I heard a cracking sound."

"What sound did you hear as Defendant Pinero hit the person who was held by Rienzi three to four times?"

"The same thing."

For all the chilling details he provided, Mascione was a less than stellar witness for the prosecution. For starters, he'd been arrested less than forty-eight hours before the night in question and charged with theft, receiving stolen property, unauthorized use of an automobile, possession of a controlled substance, driving under the influence, and driving with a suspended license. He was already on two years' probation on charges of receiving stolen property and conspiracy.

What's more, Mascione wasn't very convincing when the defense pounded him with questions about where he was and what he was doing while Eddie was being beaten. Mascione claimed that he and his two best friends, brothers Jeffrey and Jason Lang, were just standing there watching, not participating. But given that the Lang brothers were on probation on assault convictions at the time, the defense attorneys didn't buy it. Neither did John Polec.

It was during Mascione's testimony that John pieced together exactly who was in the caravan that ended up at St. Cecilia's. He wrote it all down in his notebook:

The lead car was driven by a kid named Paris Williams, with Dewan Alexander, Carlo Johnson, Bou Khathavong, and Nicholas Pinero riding along with him. This was the car that had spotted Eddie and the others walking up Ridgeway Street and led the pursuit. Williams drove the killers right into the parking lot but hadn't been charged with so much as running a red light.

Zach Dallas drove the second car, which contained Rob Colefield, Tom Crook, Antonio Mills, and Terrance Nurse. Only Crook was charged. Earlier that day, Dallas had tried to strike up a friendly conversation with Billy in the courthouse hallway.

The third car was driven by Joe Glenn, who was driving the Lang brothers and Mascione. No charges were filed against any of them.

Car number four was piloted by Maureen Yodzio, who transported her boyfriend Kevin Convey, Anthony Rienzi, Ed Rodgers, Leon Braithwaite, and Cem Onus. One of the bats belonged to Yodzio, who supposedly kept it in her car at all times for protection. But unlike Carlo Johnson, she wasn't charged with providing a murder weapon.

The final car belonged to Aubrey Williams, Paris Williams's girlfriend. With her were Michelle Bottone, Melissa Filaferro, and Victoria Sorrentino. Only Williams and Bottone were questioned by the police, and none of the girls were charged. They'd watched the murder on Friday night and the next day attended a party for a friend a couple of blocks from the church where Eddie's friends were mourning.

John counted seventeen teenagers who had watched Eddie get

beaten and hadn't intervened, and who were not on trial today. He'd seen some of them in the courtroom and hanging out in the hallways, laughing and joking.

What kind of kids are these? John wondered. How did they get this way?

John's spiral notebook was rapidly filling up as he jotted down testimony, comments of counsel, and his own impressions of what was going on. He couldn't understand why the jury was not allowed to take notes. How could they be expected to listen for days on end to confusing and conflicting testimony from scores of witnesses and then deliberate the facts from memory?

As he left the courtroom at the end of the day's testimony, John anticipated the group of reporters waiting outside on the steps of the CJC. Encountering them was a twice-a-day ritual the family neither dreaded nor enjoyed. They'd answer a few questions, then stroll to their car with photographers walking backwards in front of them, shooting away. He never understood why their editors absolutely had to have a shot of the family walking from the courthouse every day. But he and Kathy always tried to accommodate them, walking at a normal pace and trying to keep a conversation going between themselves.

But today the reporters were standing in the lobby, where cameras weren't allowed. And instead of bolting for the door to ask questions, they just said, "Good night."

John figured it was because they realized it was Eddie's birthday and they'd decided to let the family go in peace this one time. He and Kathy were no longer surprised by such things, but they were grateful for the consideration.

32

At 11:00 a.m. on January 23, Joe Casey called his star witness to the stand.

Kevin Convey, the nineteen-year-old grandson of a Philadelphia cop, was the prosecutor's last best chance at first-degree murder convictions for the six defendants. By his own admission, Convey had been in the eye of the storm that night, an active participant in the recruiting, the transportation to Fox Chase, the fight at McGarrity's, and the fatal attack at St. Cecilia's, where he admitted to being the one who had knocked Eddie to the ground and the first to hit him with a bat.

Looking like anything but a killer in a navy suit, white shirt, and tie, Convey told the court how he and five others first drove "into the city" in Maureen Yodzio's '89 Honda Civic to buy $100 worth of marijuana and four 40-ounce bottles of beer. Along the way, they were "flagged down" by Carlo Johnson and Bou Khathavong in Zach Dallas's car at a gas station on Broad Street.

"Carlo told me that they might be renting a U-Haul truck . . . to take everybody down to Fox Chase," Convey said. Carlo also told him "they were going to buy angel dust," or PCP, Convey said, and he "talked about curbing somebody."

What was "curbing?" Casey asked.

"If somebody was laying down on their stomach, he would open their mouths up over at the corner of the curb and kick down on the back of their head," Convey replied.

Casey bent down and put his mouth on the edge of the table. "You mean like this?"

"Yes."

Before his group reached Fox Chase, Convey said, they'd consumed all the beer, along with five or six fat marijuana "blunts." But Carlo never scored any angel dust, he said. How did he know that? "Because we would have smoked it."

Convey's description of what had happened next was in stark contrast to Peruto's "ambush" scenario. In McGarrity's parking lot, there were two separate fights, he said, in which Abington kids outnumbered Fox Chase kids thirteen to two. He went on to fill in the last few gut-wrenching details of what had happened to Eddie in front of St. Cecilia's. "I grabbed the baseball bat out of Maureen's car, and I was the first one out, chasing them," he said. "It was me and Leon Braithwaite in front; Anthony Rienzi, Cem Onus, and Ed Rodgers were right behind. We pulled up to the kids. There was three of them. I raised the bat above my head and I swung it sideways, and the boy arched his back and then he stumbled."

"After he stumbled, what happened?" Casey asked.

"He flipped over because he knew I had the bat, and he turned around and tried to defend himself with his feet."

"You said he flipped?"

"He rolled over onto his back."

"You told us he arched his back; did he continue to run or did something happen to him?"

"He took about one more step and then he fell."

"What part of his body did you see him fall on?"

"On his knees, I believe."

"Then what happened?"

"He rolled over onto his back, and then he put his legs up to defend himself from the baseball bat, and I hit him once or twice."

"Where did you hit him?"

"In the legs."

"What part of his body were you closest to?"

"The feet."

"What was he doing with his feet?"

"He was trying to kick at the bat."

"Go on and tell us what happened after that."

"Anthony Rienzi, Cem Onus, Ed Rodgers were the next to catch up with him, and then they kicked him."

"Who next came on the scene?"

"Jeffrey Lang, Jason Lang, Jason Mascione."

"What did they do?"

"They were kicking him."

"What were you doing with the bat?"

"By that time, he kind of moved away from me, just from, like, everything that was going on, and I was just standing there, watching."

"As you were standing there watching, what, if anything, did you see?"

"I was just watching them kick him."

"What happened to the bat that you had?"

"Thomas Crook came up and asked me for it . . . I gave it to him."

"What if anything did you hear the boy who died say as Thomas Crook hit him?"

"I heard him say that he didn't do anything."

"In what tone of voice?"

"He was kind of screaming, crying," Convey said, fighting back tears himself.

The only other sound in the courtroom was Kathy Polec's sobbing.

Convey proved to be Casey's most powerful witness. He had admitted to participating in an act of medieval brutality, but his words had the ring of truth about them. Unlike Terrance Nurse and Jason Mascione before him, he was believable. But his testimony also exposed the Achilles' heel of the prosecution's case, the fact that so many kids were involved. The D.A.'s office had decided to try only the most culpable in order to keep the trial manageable, but that left many in the courtroom, including the jury, wondering along with John Polec, "Where are the others?"

When it came time for his cross-examination, Charles Peruto quickly showed why he was the most sought-after and highest-paid criminal lawyer in town.

"Did they tell you what possible sentence you could get if you went to trial?" he asked Convey.

"My attorney did."

"And what did he tell you?"

"If I get found guilty of first-degree murder, I could get life in prison."

"Did he also tell you that the law says life in prison means life, not parole?"

"Yes."

"How old were you when he said that?"

"I was eighteen years old."

"That was very frightening to you to spend another maybe seventy or eighty years in prison, wasn't it?"

"Yes, it was."

"Did he tell you that first-degree murder is a willful, deliberate, and premeditated killing?"

"Yes, he did."

"Did you willfully premeditate the killing of anyone?"

"No, I did not."

"You also pleaded guilty to conspiracy to murder, didn't you?"

"Yes, I did."

"Did you ever conspire with anyone to kill?"

"No, but I conspired to fight."

"Who did you conspire with?"

"Everybody that went down there with me that night."

"Did you conspire with Zachary Dallas?"

"Yes, I did."

"Was he arrested?"

"No, he was not."

"Maureen Yodzio, is she in jail?"

"No, she is not."

"Did you go down there with her?"

"Yes, I did."

"She was present for all of your conversations, wasn't she?"

"Yes, she was."

"Same as Ed Rodgers?"

"Yes."

"Cem Onus?"

"Yes."

"Leon Braithwaite?"

"Yes."

"Did you have an agreement with Tom Crook to beat Edward Polec?"

"No, I did not."

"Bou?"

"No."

"Pinero?"

"No."

"Johnson?"

"No."

"Rienzi?"

"No."

"Alexander?"

"No."

"You didn't do that, did you, conspire with them to beat Edward Polec?"

"No, I did not."

"You were told, weren't you, that you had to plead guilty to that to get your deal?"

"Yes, I did have to."

"You pleaded guilty to that conspiracy, am I correct?"

"I pleaded guilty to criminal conspiracy."

"You knew that if you didn't plead guilty to that, you wouldn't get your deal, didn't you?"

"Yes, I did."

"Now, did you have explained to you that there was also a degree of homicide known as manslaughter?"

"Yes."

"Was it explained to you that manslaughter can be an intentional killing, but in the heat of passion, no time to cool and hot-blooded, that sort of thing?"

"I didn't know it could be intentional, no."

It was a textbook example of the old courtroom adage: "If you can't argue the facts, argue the law." For the next five hours, Peruto's team-mates on the defense argued the law, pounding Convey with questions about his two previous untruthful statements to the police, about inconsistencies between his testimony and that of other prosecution witnesses, about his claim that he never hit Eddie in the head with the bat. Convey stuck to his story; never wavered, never broke. It was an impressive performance, John Polec thought. But he worried that the damage was already done, that the jury was still pondering Peruto's points about the apparent inequity in who was charged and who was not, about why the prosecution had made a deal with Convey after he lied for months, and not with Crook, who had confessed from the start.

But it was during Janis Smarro's cross-examination of Convey that Peruto produced one of the trial's ugliest moments.

"You hit him with C-4, which is that brown wooden baseball bat, correct?" Smarro asked.

"Yes."

"You were hitting him at that point because he was kicking at you?"

"No."

"Why were you hitting him?"

"Just to hit him."

"Why?"

"I don't know."

"Would you step off the stand," Smarro instructed. "Would you pick up C-4 and would you show us how you were hitting him, how you were swinging the bat?"

As Convey stepped down, Joe Casey rose from his seat. "I would be delighted to represent Eddie Polec," he said. "Tell me how to position myself."

"Imagine that Mr. Casey is now Mr. Polec," Smarro said to Convey, "and you are chasing after him with your baseball bat; his back is to you."

"I was running after him and I swung, and he looked over his shoulder," Convey said.

"Take the bat and show us what you did with it while this kid was glancing over his shoulder trying to get away from you."

"Then I swung—"

"Swing it," Smarro urged.

All eyes and ears were riveted on the re-enactment. Then, just as Convey started to swing at Casey's fleeing Eddie, Peruto wisecracked, "Two-to-one, he arches his back."

There was an audible gasp, as if the entire room had been punched in the stomach. As Smarro wrapped up the demonstration and Casey and Convey returned to their seats, Oscar Gaskins matched Peruto for boorishness by applauding their performance. John and Kathy Polec got up and walked out of the courtroom, seething.

The next day, Casey called Kathy Polec to the stand. He led her quickly through the events of November 11 and 12, from dropping Eddie off at a friend's house on Friday night to his death at the hospital the next morning. Her testimony lasted less than ten minutes and no one cross-examined her.

"Mrs. Polec, may I say I am very, very sorry," Peruto said as she stepped down from the witness stand, "and I hope God will give you strength."

She smiled thinly. "Thank you, sir."

John followed her to the stand. He answered six questions about identifying Eddie's body, then stepped down. His testimony lasted five minutes.

With that, the prosecution rested.

33

For the next two days, the defendants' Dream Team of attorneys seemed almost defenseless. After all the dramatic, detailed testimony presented by the prosecution, the defense case played like an afterthought, just so much housekeeping duty. One newspaper reporter characterized it as "listless."

Peruto's first witness was eighteen-year-old Keith Flannigan, who was involved in the fracas at McGarrity's and, shortly thereafter, fled across St. Cecilia's parking lot with Billy and Eddie. Flannigan had been subpoenaed, but not called, by Casey, and his appearance as a defense witness apparently was intended to show that not all Fox Chase kids were angels. But his testimony backfired on Peruto.

Peruto elicited the fact that Flannigan had a weapon with him that night, a small "bindery ring" used to cut boxes at a bakery. Then he asked the teenager what he'd done with the box cutter at McGarrity's.

"Carlo Johnson had Rich Stuber up in the air," Flannigan replied. "He was holding him over his body, up in the air, and he body-slammed him on the rocks. He was then on top of him, striking him in the face. His shirt was coming up. So I ran over. I cut him with it and pushed him off and grabbed Rich and we ran up the hill."

"Did you tell that to the police?"

"Yes."

"Where was that ring when you were talking to the police?"

"On the table, next to my couch."

"In your own home?" Peruto responded, feigning shock and disbelief.

"Yes."

"Was it confiscated?"

"No."

"Were you arrested?"

"No. I used it to help my friend who was getting beat up real bad. He got bones broken."

During cross-examination, Casey managed to bring out that Flannigan was given the box cutter by his grandmother, for his own protection, after he "was jumped in the park up the street from me," an attack that resulted in a kick in the eye and a broken nose.

Peruto repeatedly popped up with objections during Casey's questioning, trying to keep that information from the jury. Finally Judge Greenspan rebuked him. "Please, Mr. Peruto," she snapped, "he's cross-examining *your* witness."

"Not *my* witness," Peruto retorted. "A person I had to call because he *wouldn't*."

"Do you want to make speeches now?" Casey shouted.

"Mr. Peruto," the judge said sternly, "the next time you do that, you will be held in contempt."

On redirect, Peruto fell back on sarcasm, asking Flannigan whether Casey had told him what a "hero" he was.

Flannigan drew a blank. "Excuse me?"

"Forget it," Peruto said, turning his back and walking away.

More illuminating than Flannigan's testimony was what occurred during a recess shortly afterward. On his way out of the courtroom, Flannigan's father, Patrick, bumped shoulders with Carlo Johnson in the hallway. "Excuse me," said Patrick Flannigan, and kept on walking. Incredibly, Johnson wheeled around and went after him, with eyes bulging and fists clenched. "What are you pushing into me for?" he shouted. "Let's settle this like men. Let's take it out into the parking lot. I'm ready for you."

"You wanna hit me with a bat?" Flannigan shouted back.

A police detective standing nearby grabbed Johnson and pressed him against the courtroom door. "C'mon, Carlo, you don't need this." But Johnson raged at him, "Why are you messing with me? It's them."

Fortunately for the defense, the jury didn't see the incident, which was duly recorded by Philadelphia *Daily News* reporter Marisol Bello, who was standing several feet away.

"They're animals," Patrick Flannigan told Bello as Johnson was hustled away by his father. "This just shows what they are. This reinforces my belief that these kids, all of them, wanted to prove how bad they were."

Peruto's next witness was seventeen-year-old Michelle Bottone, who'd been in Aubrey Williams's car with the other girls when the attack on Eddie occurred. She testified that the first person who jumped out of the cars chased Eddie and hit him in the back of the head with a bat.

"When that person struck Eddie Polec in the back of the head, what happened?" Peruto asked.

"Eddie slid face-first on the ground."

In less than five minutes, Peruto had all he wanted from Bottone. Her testimony suggested that Kevin Convey, who'd admitted to being the first person out of the car, hadn't missed when he'd swung at Eddie, as he claimed. Rather, he'd knocked Eddie to the ground with a bat blow to the head. And if that was true, then Casey's star witness was at least as guilty as the six defendants.

"Cross-examine," Peruto said, taking his seat at the defense table.

The abruptness took Casey by surprise. "There is no further questioning from that side?" he asked.

"I put a witness on and I said cross-examine," Peruto snarled.

During a testy cross-examination, with Peruto objecting to his every question, Casey managed to pull a different story from Bottone. In her statement to police she'd said she thought it was Pinero who struck that first blow.

"Right," Bottone told Casey, launching into breathless teenage-ese, "but then after Aubrey had said, 'No, it is Kevin,' and he could have passed for Kevin, too, I glanced and I just thought it was him [Pinero]. And after she said, 'No, it's Kevin,' I was, like, 'Oh, it's Kevin,' I thought."

"Today, as you sit there, you are not sure if that was Kevin or Nick, is that correct?"

"I don't know who it was," Bottone replied.

"Thank you," said Casey.

Peruto's final eyewitness to the attack was seventeen-year-old Theresa Wech, whose hysterical call to 911 as Eddie lay bleeding had elicited the responses that so enraged the public when the tapes came out. Wech and Sharon Donahue were walking through St. Cecilia's parking lot just as the attack began, and their screams eventually frightened the mob away. But Wech's recollection of those few terrifying, confusing moments seemed to contradict Convey's version of events. She, too, testified that the first person to catch up with Eddie hit him with a bat.

"He hit him around here," she said, pointing to the back of her head.

"When he hit Eddie Polec, what happened to Eddie Polec?" Peruto asked.

"He fell down."

"Did that person stop hitting him or continue to hit him?"

"He kept hitting him."

Wech also testified that she saw only three people gathered around Eddie, one hitting and two holding him.

Through gentle questioning, Casey tried to get Wech to say that she was hysterical and crying as the attack occurred. But she held firm, saying she didn't get upset until the mob had fled and she and Donahue ran up to Eddie.

"We rolled him over," she said. "I was upset because it was Ed, and I told her to stay here or whatever and I was, like, 'I am going down to the phone.'"

"What did you see when you rolled him over?"

She struggled to maintain her composure. "He was bleeding and choking."

After Theresa Wech, the defense tried to tie up loose ends. Oscar Gaskins put Diane Costanzo on the stand for five minutes merely to establish that she'd never had a romantic relationship with his client, Carlo Johnson, though no one but Gaskins seemed to think that had any significance.

It was the first time John and Kathy had seen Costanzo, and it was hard for them to look at her. This was the girl whose exaggerated tale of assault had set everything in motion, the girl whose honor the six defendants killed Eddie to defend. And she still didn't get it. Like her friend Michelle Bottone, she seemed put out that she had to answer all these questions in court.

Casey, too, was put off by Costanzo's demeanor. For the first time in the trial he got nasty with a witness. When she told him she had left Fox Chase around 10:00 p.m. that night and driven to Germantown, he asked if it was "to buy weed," as Jessica Simons had told investigators.

Both Peruto and Gaskins objected, Greenspan sustained, and when Casey finished his cross-examination, Peruto demanded a sidebar with the judge, fuming about "prosecutorial misconduct."

Finally, Peruto called his client's parents, Eleanor and Carlos Pinero. Not surprisingly, they testified that Nick had never been known to be violent and had a "very good" reputation.

Oscar Gaskins then put on a string of eight character witnesses, including Carlo Johnson's father. All of them testified that Carlo was a fine, churchgoing, choir-singing young man. During his questioning of Johnson's father, Gaskins tried to introduce into evidence a photograph that Detective Tom Perks had brought to the Johnson home the first time the police interviewed Carlo. It showed Carlo with a girl named Erin Kennedy, who'd borne him a child out of wedlock. Kennedy was white.

Casey objected to the photograph, knowing Gaskins was trying to suggest to the jury that the police arrested Carlo because they didn't like the fact that he was dating a white girl, and in a sidebar conference with the defense team he accused them of trying to play the race card again, just as Michael Applebaum had in his opening statement.

"Let's move on," said the judge, so Gaskins moved on to Vincent Minnetti. The sixteen-year-old testified that on the afternoon of November 11, Terrance Nurse had approached him at Abington High School and asked him to go with him to Fox Chase "to point out where everyone hung out." He said Nurse told him "they were going to get a truck to go down there, a U-haul truck."

"And do what?"

"Beat up whoever they saw."

"Do you know another young man named Antonio Mills?" Gaskins asked.

"I know who he is."

"Can you describe him to the jury?"

"About five eight or five nine, kind of stocky, and he has burns on his face."

It seemed like idle questioning, since Mills's name had barely been mentioned throughout the trial. But soon it became clear what Gaskins was getting at.

Joe Casey called Sharon Donahue as a rebuttal witness to Theresa Wech. Donahue contradicted her friend by saying there were ten to twelve kids surrounding Eddie, and three or four had bats.

"Do you know the race of any of those persons?" Casey asked.

"I seen one black kid," she said.

When Peruto cross-examined, he zeroed in on that "one black kid."

"Would it be fair to say you saw a face among these people in the vicinity of Eddie Polec that you described in detail to the police?" he asked Donahue.

"Yes."

"Was that description a kid with U-shaped stitches from the top, around the center of his left eye, around to the bottom of the eye, and a black male?"

"Yes."

"He is the one that hit Polec with the bat, right?"

"Yes."

"Would you please look at the defendants here very closely and tell me if any of them have the sort of stitches that you described."

"No, they don't."

Oscar Gaskins had one final witness, Stacy Martin, whom he'd subpoenaed that very morning. She testified that she'd gone to high school with Antonio Mills.

"Are there any distinguishing marks on his face?" Gaskins asked.

"Yes," Martin said. "He has scars around his eye. They go around his whole eye."

"On the right side?"

"Yes."

"What is his race?"

"Black, African American."

And there it was, slipped in at the eleventh-and-a-half hour: the suggestion that someone the prosecution hadn't charged and the jury hadn't seen might have been one of the people who beat Eddie to death with bats.

On that note, the defense rested. After four weeks and forty-nine witnesses—twenty-seven for the prosecution and twenty-two for the defense—it was time for the lawyers to present their closing arguments.

Because the state always gets the last word in a trial, the defense went first, starting with Janis Smarro. She sounded the themes that all the others would echo, beginning with the one Charles Peruto laid out the day they learned Convey had made a deal.

"Ladies and gentlemen of the jury," Smarro began, "imagine, if you would, your outrage if you were to pick up a newspaper, turn on a radio or television, and hear or read the headline 'District Attorney gives five years to a self-admitted liar who chased a sixteen-year-old boy in a darkened church parking lot and hit him, brought him to the ground, and proceeded to beat him with a baseball bat.'

"Imagine what you would think. Imagine what your reaction would be. Imagine the questions that you would have."

"Is there any one of you who isn't sitting here saying, 'If it weren't for Kevin Convey, would we be here? If it weren't for Kevin Convey jumping out of a moving vehicle in a church parking lot and racing after Polec and swinging his bat, would we be here?' Is there any one of you who has any doubt about how the injury, the first blow to the head, was inflicted? Is there any one of you who believes that that bat didn't make contact with Eddie Polec's head?

"And yet they gave Kevin Convey a reward, a reward of five years. The man who set the wheels in motion, the cause of you being here, and Tom Crook being here.

"Kevin Convey is a liar," she said. "If the police really believed what Kevin Convey was selling, wouldn't they also have to believe that Jason Mascione took part in the death of Eddie Polec? If they believe Kevin Convey, why is it that they never arrested the Lang brothers?"

Michael Wallace picked up the "doubt" issue right where Smarro had left off. "Is there any doubt in your mind that Billy Oehler was the one who started this incident? If there is, you don't have to go any further than Mr. Oehler's answer to my question: 'There is no question, I started the incident.' And the incident we're talking about is the November 4 incident, when the entire fiasco, which ultimately leads to Mr. Polec's death, starts."

Of Dewan Alexander, Wallace said, "For an hour of his life, he has been sitting in jail for sixteen months because Jason Mascione and Terry Nurse say that he kicked somebody in the stomach.

"There are five or six witnesses to take him out of St. Cecilia's, and they are all witnesses that come from Fox Chase. We have just two people who put him at St. Cecilia's, both Abington witnesses who have records for lying."

Michael Applebaum stated the obvious at the outset, noting that his client, Bou Khathavong, "is not going to be poster boy for Teenager of the Year; there's no question about that." But all the prosecution had proved, he said, was that Khathavong "did nothing more than have a big mouth."

His client also "had a look that Detective Santiago didn't like," Applebaum continued. "He had sloppy jeans, a white hoody sweatshirt, a white baseball cap tilted backwards. He wore earrings and had a hip-hop kind of style. Detective Santiago didn't like that, so he was charged. He was in the same clothes he wore that night. He didn't know any of those police officers. Nobody in his family is a cop. He had nobody to turn to. He went with them voluntarily, and he has never been home since, because he doesn't have the bail money. This could be any one of our children . . . Those detectives beat at him for hours and hours . . . "

"Objection," Casey shouted. "There is no testimony of that. That is outrageous—They beat at him. Gimme a break!"

"The jury will remember the testimony," Judge Greenspan soothed.

Applebaum went so far as to claim that Khathavong's personal style actually helped prove his innocence. "When your persona is as a hip-hop, cool kind of guy, you don't jump up and down and say, 'I'm so excited, I could kill somebody.'"

In conclusion, Applebaum said, "My grandparents came to this country to escape that kind of prosecution, selective prosecution. And many of your ancestors came to this country unwillingly, but had to endure, under the guise of the law, under the guise of authority, a police decision which is selective as to who they are going to put at the defense table. That is what is happening here . . . He doesn't belong here. He shouldn't be here."

After a rambling preamble that referenced the Star Chamber trials of the fifteenth century, the Salem witch trials of the seventeenth century, and the lynch mobs of the nineteenth century, John McMahon said that the only evidence that Anthony Rienzi hit Eddie or held him for others to hit came from "scripted testimony" from Mascione, Convey, and Nurse.

"Did you hear one detail from any of these witnesses who claim to have identified Rienzi doing something that never happened? One detail as to what kind of clothes he was wearing? One detail as to whether he was wearing a hat? One detail at all that the witnesses were truly in position to see and observe? No. The record is devoid of one single detail as to Anthony Rienzi, period."

But that was not the case with Antonio Mills, he pointed out. "Yes, there was a big mistake made," he said, "because Antonio Mills, identified by Sharon Donahue in terms of description, in terms of being the person beating Eddie Polec with a bat, was not arrested. I will tell you what happened, right here and now, as to Anthony Rienzi. I submit to you that the police made a wrong turn early in this investigation. They made a wrong turn, and instead of going down the street to pursue and build the theory of their case against Antonio Mills, they made a wrong turn toward Anthony Rienzi. Antonio, Anthony; Antonio, Anthony. They made a wrong turn. And once the steamroller got going, it was hard to turn back."

In his closing, Oscar Gaskins finally made the point he'd wanted so badly to emphasize with the photograph of Carlo Johnson and Erin Kennedy.

"When I have a black defendant and a white complainant . . . I usually find a problem with race in those kinds of situations," he said.

"When I talk about race, it's because a short time after this whole incident took place the police were obviously of the impression that my client was one of the initiators because they had the testimony of another person. They were of the impression that this whole thing started because my client was related in some fashion to the young lady who had the confrontation on the fourth, that my client was directly involved with Diane Costanzo, that she was his girlfriend."

He cast Costanzo as a kind of crusader for racial equality, as opposed to the apparently bigoted kids of Fox Chase. "Miss Costanzo has this bad habit of driving black males around in her automobile in certain neighborhoods," he said, "which produces rocks being thrown at her car when that takes place, and that is what she was doing on the fourth and that is what she was doing on the eleventh. But in none of those instances was she with my client."

Gaskins saw bigotry in the descriptions the Fox Chase kids initially gave to police. "I suggest to you that it is not unusual for people to see two blacks and say, 'Suddenly we are being inundated by black people.'

"All of the witnesses from the other side said, uniformly, that a horde of blacks and Puerto Ricans came up that hill. Read the names and tell me whether or not there are any Puerto Ricans on the list: Zachary Dallas, Rob Colefield, Thomas Crook, Antonio Mills, Terrance Nurse, Paris Williams . . . Is there a Puerto Rican in that bunch? No. But they saw hordes of Puerto Ricans and blacks coming up the hill."

And he saw bigotry in who was charged and who was not. "These people, Aubrey Williams and the people in her car, what were they?

Scouts, scouts. They came back and told them, 'The boys are at such-and-such a place.' They didn't lock Aubrey Williams up, and the rest of the people in her car. And you know they are neither black nor Puerto Rican—Sorrentino, Filaferro, and Bottone, with an *e* on the end of it.

"Now, whether I have proved it or not, use your common sense. You know they are not black, and they didn't get arrested."

For all those who admired his caustic wit and courtroom theatrics, Charles Peruto did not disappoint. He kicked off his closing argument with a folksy anecdote from his childhood.

"Billy Celinder lived across the street from me growing up," he said. "What an unlucky kid. He was an only child. The Taylors had twelve kids. My family had five kids. You could always blame it on the other guy: not me, not me! That is a natural tendency. But poor Billy was all alone. He didn't have any brothers and sisters.

"What do we have here, essentially?" he asked. "Teenagers, still with that schoolish kind of thought."

He then proceeded to lampoon the teenage witnesses from Fox Chase as inept liars intent on making their peer group seem both innocent and brave, at Casey's prompting. "What did he say about Flannigan? Flannigan's a hero? Flannigan's grandmother taught him well. 'Hey, kid, take this with you. It's a ring that you can use to slash with.' There is no decent purpose for such a thing unless you are a box cutter on the job.

"Now picture the scene. He has to rescue a kid. This kid is being set upon. Now, one guy has his back to him, so he slashes that. With that kind of a weapon, if you punch a guy in the face, you blind him. You can slash him all up for life. That's our kid, Flannigan, the hero. Why wasn't he arrested for that? He told the police. They didn't even bother to take the ring off him, did they?"

Referring to John Atkinson, Peruto observed, "The kid couldn't count to nineteen. I don't mean to demean that. Yes, he got whacked; he probably had a concussion. But I can't let go of the pun that most of our high school kids today can't count to nineteen anyhow.

"Then there's the nicest kid I've seen in years, Billy Polec, fourteen years old. 'Yes, I went and bought the cups,' like it's an ordinary thing to do. What the hell are we coming to?

"You'll be happy to know," Peruto told the jurors, "during your sequestration, they passed a bill with much money in it and Philadelphia is supposed to get 116 more cops. You just can't police this kind of thing, these regular beer parties and everything else. It's a sad commentary."

Then Peruto did what he apparently had learned growing up across the street from Billy Celinder: he blamed it all on the other guy. Convey lied about seeing Nick Pinero hit Eddie with a bat, he said. It was Convey, not Pinero, whom Billy Polec saw hitting Atkinson with a bat at McGarrity's. It was Convey, not Pinero, who chased Billy across the parking lot with a bat in his hand. And it was Convey, not Pinero, who struck the first crushing blow to Eddie's head and knocked him to the ground.

"Remember, even the Abington kids who knew Pinero confused him with Convey, thought that they were looking at Nick when it was Kevin. Nick's mistake, ladies and gentlemen, his big mistake, is that he was born looking like Kevin Convey."

Finally, Peruto launched an attack on Joe Casey's bargain with his star witness.

"Read the book by Donald Trump, *The Art of the Deal,*" he said. "I would be the most famous defense lawyer in the history of America if I could make deals with people the way they make deals with people, to get them to say what I want them to say.

"Before Convey made his third statement to police," Peruto continued, "he read all of the statements of all the other people. He knows who says what. He knows what their positions are. He knows what their testimony should be. So what does he do on that third statement? 'Hey, bing, bing, bing. Here you go, Mr. Casey.'

"And Mr. Casey goes, 'Well, you are now telling us this and you are now telling us that, and I like it.' Total, bing, deal." In other words, Peruto said, Convey "follows the script, the mathematical equation: Crook plus Rienzi plus Pinero equals the deal of the century. The guy comes up with the violin playing, telling the right story, and he gets the deal. This guy is glib. This guy is clever. We all know that. It was demonstrated by Mr. Casey right on the floor, that the *wind* knocked Eddie Polec down. Imagine!

"This guy is the one that you have to believe beyond a reasonable doubt, and I am telling you that you can't believe him if he tells you today is today.

"If it weren't for Kevin Convey, Eddie Polec would have made it to safety with his brother, Billy. He is the one who brings him down—either by wind, by fright, by arched back, or by caving in of the skull. If it weren't for Kevin Convey, Eddie Polec would have been with Billy, in safety. And this is the guy you're being fed."

As for the six defendants, he summed up by saying, "They are not guilty; they were never guilty. No more, no less guilty of doing anything than any of these other people did, and the fifty to seventy, or the twenty or the seventeen kids from Fox Chase, except Kevin Convey. He made his deal; that is put to rest. But first-degree murder for these kids. Forget it.

"Return your verdict in accordance with your conscience, in accordance with reasonable doubt. Not guilty."

Joe Casey stood to face the jury with fire in his eyes. "In every criminal case, defense attorneys do one of two things," he said. "They put everyone else on trial but their clients, and for a very good reason. If you are not looking at these defendants, if you are thinking about everything but them, then they have done their job. . . . If you are looking over there to see what a horrible prosecutor I am, or what a horrible office I work for, how I suborn perjury, what a sleazy guy I am, then you are not going to be looking at these defendants or at the testimony you saw under searing cross-examination . . . by a group of six defense attorneys. . . .

"A second tactic that the defense always uses is to kind of confuse things, create cloud and smoke," he continued, matching Peruto's folksy anecdote with one of his own, about an old World War I veteran he knew, Morris Hunter, who'd told him how in trench warfare the enemy carried out "all sorts of nefarious activity under massive smoke-screens." But Morris had told him, "We had a secret weapon; we had giant fans to blow away the smoke."

"Let me be the giant fan to blow away the smoke screen that has been laid down," Casey told the jurors, "so that you can clearly see what occurred in McGarrity's auto lot and at St. Cecilia's parking lot."

But before he got into the specifics of the evidence, Casey had a few things he wanted to get off his chest. The first had to do with Michael Applebaum's allegation in his opening statement that Eddie was present during the harassment of Diane Costanzo at McDonald's.

"That is absolutely, categorically untrue," he said. "Why was that said, and why am I upset? I do not say, 'Speak no ill of the dead.' But I do say that if you speak ill of the dead, then speak the truth. That was said early on because he wanted to tarnish Eddie Polec a little in your mind, and dirty him up. He's really not all that good a kid, is he? Speak the truth. Eddie Polec wasn't there."

For a similar reason, he said, Peruto had made a comment "about this being such an important case, with aerial photographs and all that." The idea, Casey explained to the jury, was "to make you resent, in a way, the special treatment given to this kid."

"Let me tell you something; let me tell you something," he hissed. "In twenty-three years—in twenty-three years—nobody gets special treatment. There are no special lives. Every life in Philadelphia, *every* life in Philadelphia, is the same—the same—to every prosecutor that I know, and to me. I didn't make any special efforts in this case. I give 100 percent to every case. I don't care if it's a five-year-old kid shot down in a store in South Philadelphia. I don't care if it's a twenty-seven-year-old emaciated young man nobody cares about who is addicted to crack and gets shot because he didn't have $120 to pay his drug dealer. *Every* life is precious.

"So there is nothing special about Eddie Polec's life that is not special about every other life that is ever lost, and there is no special treatment. There was a prostitute dumped in New Jersey sometime ago and

I had aerial photographs for that. I will prepare 100 percent for every case that I have, and if I do not, then the taxpayers should get a new guy."

Casey's face was red, the veins in his neck were bulging, sweat was beading on his forehead.

"Let's go to Fox Chase now, and Friday night, November 11, 1994. It is not unusual for kids to gather at the Rec, and it is not unusual for them to drink beer. The attorney for defendant Khathavong said that if they watched their children a bit better, it would not have happened, but he would not dwell on that."

Again, Casey's eyes flashed with anger and his voice rose. "How dare he suggest to these parents that they are responsible for the death of Eddie Polec. How dare he suggest that!

"Why did he say it? He is covering the activity in the trenches. Blow it away. Get rid of that smoke."

Then Casey took the jurors through the evidence step by step, and defended his witnesses point by point. Gone was the dispassionate prosecutor whose opening arguments had nearly put people to sleep. Now he spoke with the fevered zeal of a Southern preacher at Sunday-morning services.

"There is a curious dichotomy or schizophrenia that the defense attorneys exhibited when talking about Kevin Convey. On the one hand, they *want* you to believe him when he says that Bou Khathavong was not around the crew that beat Eddie Polec to death. But they *don't want* you to believe him when he says that Anthony Rienzi *was*. They *want* you to believe him, and suggest that he is telling the truth, when he says that he *didn't* see Carlo Johnson in the group that beat Eddie Polec to death, but they *don't want* you to believe him when he says that Thomas Crook *was*. They *want* you to believe him when he says he *didn't* see Dewan Alexander around the crew that was beating Eddie to death, but they *don't want* you to believe him when he says that Pinero *was* beating him. They *want* you to believe Convey when he says that he was down buying drugs and beer, but they *don't want* you to believe him when he says Carlo Johnson said *he* wanted to buy angel dust. You can't have it both ways.

"The attorney for defendant Khathavong wants you to believe that the police told Tom Ruth to say that Bou was jumping up and down saying, 'I'm so psyched, I could kill someone.' Well, of course, he has to have an explanation for that, so it has to be those dirty lying cops.

"Where is the evidence of that? It is gossamer fantasy; it is part of the Big Lie. It is part of the Big Lie. It was perfected by Hitler and Goebbels: Throw enough mud at the wall, say it loudly and long enough, and somebody will believe it. It is the Big Lie. They want you to believe these cops would do anything.

"Much has been made of the fact that there were no charges brought against Keith Flannigan for what he did to Carlo Johnson. First of all, in order for a criminal charge to proceed, you need a complainant. I can't call a spirit to that stand and say, 'Describe what happened to you, sir.' If Carlo Johnson had come forward and said, 'I want Keith Flannigan locked up,' don't you think that he would have been asked questions?"

Casey took the jurors from McGarrity's, up Ridgeway Street, and into the church parking lot. "The defendants weren't sitting there neatly attired, as they are now. . . . They weren't calm, sitting with their heads down as they are now, being docile and attendant." They were a "blood-lusting crew" that night, when "what is really inside of them came out.

"What then occurs is what brings us all here. Jason Mascione tells us that Eddie Polec is on the ground, covering his head, kind of wiggling around. If he had been hit by that bat blow in the head by Kevin Convey [as the defense claimed], he would not have been protecting himself, or wiggling around. He would have been just lying there, vegetable-like.

"The injury on the right side of the head fits in with his being on the left side, does it not? He is curling, like this, and an injury that wasn't talked about was that terrible, terrible fracture to Eddie Polec's hand which was probably administered at the same time that blow was administered. I say that because after that disabling blow was administered, Eddie Polec would have been unable to put his hands up. It also suggests that Convey was being truthful when he said Eddie was on the ground pleading for his life. Otherwise, he would not have had that defensive injury. He would have just been lying there.

"Put all the testimony together, and it fits. Blow away the smoke. Is it clear now?

"Dr. Hood described all those injuries on the left side of his face. What is there about those injuries that we know? They are within a six-inch-square area. What is the significance of that? Well, if you've ever used a baseball bat, or have ever taught kids how to play ball, the hardest thing to teach them is to keep their eye on the ball, just as I asked you to keep yours. It's hard; it's hard to hit an object consistently in that small an area. . . .

"The significance of that is that they didn't accidentally hit Eddie Polec in the head with the bat. Rather, they had to take aim. . . .

"First-degree murder is a killing with malice, a specific intent to kill. What is malice? It is hardness of heart, wickedness of disposition, cruelty of mind. Close your eyes and picture Eddie Polec being beaten to death. . . . You can open a dictionary to 'malice' and see a picture of that. So keep that in mind. Keep those injuries in mind.

"Let me say something about the nature of a baseball bat," he said, picking up exhibit C-4 from the prosecution table, "something that is different from other deadly weapons. If you were to go over here with a gun and shoot that gun at someone, maybe you would hit them, depending on how good a shot you are; maybe you wouldn't. But . . . they are way back there. There is an impersonal quality to killing with a gun.

"But what is there about a baseball bat?" he asked, holding C-4's taped handle in his right hand while tapping its blunt end on his left palm. "You can't very well stand here and kill somebody over there with a baseball bat. You can throw it, and if you are lucky, it will hit somebody. But I would not even attempt to argue that you have intent to kill if it were thrown. It is fortuitous where it would land. I would argue that is third-degree murder. But with a baseball bat, with a baseball bat . . ."

Lightning-quick, he raised the bat high over his head and brought it down with all his might on a cardboard evidence box sitting on the table. The sound was deafening, jolting a number of people out of their seats, causing them to cry out in surprise. Juror No. 8 started weeping.

"There is something about a baseball bat that just personifies malice and the intent to kill," he went on. "You can't do it from a distance. You have to be up close. Remember, I talked about that six-inch square? You have to look exactly at what you are doing when you are raining blow after blow. That is a very personal act. It is not one time. It is two times; it is three times; it is four times; it is five times; it is six times; it is seven times; it is eight times, to the head. What other intent could an individual have? If you hit someone in the head repeatedly, it is a rhetorical question I ask: What other intent could you have?

"When you go back into the jury room to deliberate from the evidence, I am urging you that we have established the defendants' guilt beyond reasonable doubt. That Nicholas Pinero is a first-degree murderer because he hit Eddie Polec in the head with a bat. He took that over-the-head shot. He used a deadly weapon on a vital part of Eddie Polec's body . . .

"What sound did Mascione talk about? What sound did he talk about? What kind of people would do that? Them!" he said, gesturing toward the defendants. "That kind of person! That is who would do that!"

He stood in front of the defense table and pointed at Pinero with the bat. "You, sir, from the evidence, are guilty of first-degree murder and conspiracy.

"Thomas Crook, you took the bat from Kevin Convey. Your fingerprint is on here. We have been told that by Jason Mascione; we have been told that by Kevin Convey; we have been told that by Terrance Nurse. We have been told by all of them that you hit Eddie Polec in the head with this bat. You are guilty of murder in the first degree and conspiracy under the evidence in this case.

"Anthony Rienzi is the other beater. Anthony Rienzi also held him while Nick Pinero beat him. Murder in the first degree.

"Bou Khathavong, the man who proclaimed his intent to kill. 'I'm so psyched I could kill someone.' Murder in the first degree, from the evidence, as well.

"Carlo Johnson supplied two bats. Murder in the first degree.

"Finally, Dewan Alexander, the man who kicked Eddie Polec, either in the head, as one witness said, or in the chest and stomach, as the other witness said."

Suddenly Casey softened. Turning to the jury box, he said that if they found that Alexander, Johnson, and Khathavong had not formed a specific intent to kill that night, only the intent to do serious bodily harm, then the law permitted them to find them guilty of murder in the third degree.

"But as to those who wielded bats—Pinero, Rienzi, and Crook—the evidence permits no verdict but murder in the first degree. The evidence permits no other verdict. Thank you for your attention," he said, and took his seat.

The minute the jury was excused, all six defense attorneys stood up and demanded a mistrial. They cried foul because Casey had referred to Hitler and Goebbels, because he'd called the defendants predators, because he'd referred to them as a blood-lusting crew, because he'd inflamed the jury by banging the box with the bat. Greenspan denied the motions. Then all six moved for a directed verdict of acquittal on the first-degree murder charges. Denied again.

As the courtroom emptied, Peruto was left whining about the length of Casey's closing argument. "It was sixty-seven minutes longer than mine," he complained to the judge. "I calculated it to the minute."

Poor Billy Celinder.

34

The jury deliberated for six days. For the Polecs, the wait was interminable. They were told to go home. Both the court crier and Joe Casey promised that when the jury came back with the verdict, there would be enough time for them to get to the courtroom.

But John wasn't taking any chances. What if it snowed again? And having just endured five weeks in an environment where the victim seemed to have no rights, he doubted the criminal justice system would wait one second for the victim's family. So the Polecs stayed at the courthouse, in Courtroom Bill, during the entire deliberation.

In a way, John dreaded the moment when the verdict would be announced. For fifteen months he'd been asking Fox Chase kids to believe in the system, to do the right thing, because the system of laws in this country was better than the alternative, anarchy. Taking the law into one's own hands was the wrong way to pursue justice. After all, Eddie was dead because a group of thugs had chosen to avenge a perceived wrong. And for fifteen months, there had been peace in the neighborhood, no retaliation, no further blood spilled avenging Eddie's death.

But what if the system failed? What in God's name would happen if the killers were not convicted?

On the sixth day of deliberations, Monday, February 5, at least one hundred people from Fox Chase showed up in Courtroom Bill to wait with the family. They figured this was the day, and they were right. The jury reached a verdict at 4:00 p.m., and it would be announced at 5:30.

It was wall-to-wall in room 304. The tension was palpable. A contingent of twenty deputy sheriffs ringed the room and prowled the hallway and aisles, ready to quell any disturbance that might break out in reaction to the verdict. Detective Tom Perks sat next to Kathy; Detective Dominic Mangone was stationed beside Billy and Kristie.

As the jury filed into the jury box, the only sound in the courtroom was muffled weeping coming from the defendants' side of the room.

"Your Honor, all parties are present," said the court crier. "May the verdicts be taken?"

"They may," said Judge Greenspan.

"Will the foreperson please rise," said the crier. "Mr. Pinero, please rise. Madame Foreperson, with regard to Mr. Pinero, have the jurors reached verdicts in this case?"

"Yes, we have."

"Have all twelve members agreed upon those verdicts?"

"Yes, we have agreed."

"With regard to criminal homicide, please read your verdict in full."

John sucked in his breath and held it.

"Murder in the third degree," said the foreperson.

John exhaled sharply, as if he'd been punched in the solar plexus.

"With regard to aggravated assault, victim Atkinson, how say you: guilty or not guilty?"

"Not guilty."

John struggled for air while his mind raced. Third degree? That meant Pinero would be free someday, probably when he was still a young man. And if it was third degree for the worst of them, then the jury had probably acquitted Khathavong, Alexander, and Johnson.

But it didn't turn out that way. The jury found the three bat-wielders—Pinero, Rienzi, and Crook—guilty of third-degree murder and conspiracy, Khathavong and Johnson guilty of conspiracy, and Alexander guilty of voluntary manslaughter and conspiracy. As with Pinero, Alexander and Johnson were acquitted of assault charges in the beating of John Atkinson.

As the jury foreperson finished, Bill Danks looked over at Kathy. Her eyes were filled with tears. There was weeping on both sides of the room, but no one moved. Joe Casey's head dropped to his chest and he whispered softly, but just loud enough for Kathy to hear, "Eddie Polec is dead, and so is justice in the city of Philadelphia."

Outside on the steps of the Criminal Justice Center, an army of reporters and photographers waited for the family and the prosecutor to appear. Casey begged off. He wasn't up to talking to the press, he told John. "I'm afraid I'll say something careless that would detract from the strength Eddie's family and friends have shown all these months. You talk to them for me." Then he went to his office, sat down at his desk, and cried.

Outside, John faced the sea of cameras and microphones. He was devastated by what had happened, but he didn't want to say anything that would cause anyone to react badly. He didn't want any other kid to die that night, or any night thereafter.

"We accept this verdict," he told the crowd. "We may not understand it, but we accept it."

Kathy declined to comment, so the cameras and microphone swung around to the kids. "It seems like all they are getting is a slap on the wrist," said Kristie. "Just fifteen years in jail? We have to accept it, but it just doesn't seem right, from what Eddie had to go through."

Then it was Billy's turn. John's heart was in his throat. Billy had shunned the media for fifteen months, never wanting his face on TV or his picture in the paper, always keeping his grief inside. As the verdicts were being read, John had seen on his face the look he'd had the night he ran up to them in St. Cecilia's parking lot, like the worst thing in the world had just happened.

But he needn't have worried. When Billy finally opened his mouth to speak, he gave the media, and everyone else who heard, a statement to remember.

"My brother was the most forgiving person you will ever meet in your life," he said. "And I wouldn't be surprised if he had a hand in saying to the jury, 'These kids are sixteen. Why don't you make them think about what they did, but one day let them go back to their families.' That's just the way Ed was."

35

As he took his seat next to Joe Casey the morning of March 19, St. Joseph's Day, Bill Danks tried to imagine the day ahead for the Polec family. After all he had been through with his daughter's death, he knew it would be impossible for him to describe to anyone else what it meant to lose her. He'd never been able to find words that came close to conveying the pain, the deep ache he got in his arms ten, maybe twenty times a day, when he felt like hugging his little girl but couldn't.

But that was exactly what the Polecs were expected to do today. This was the day Judge Greenspan would sentence the six defendants. And before she did that, all four of the Polecs would stand in court and deliver what are called, in the bloodless language of the law, "victim impact statements."

In a judicial system geared toward protecting the rights of the accused, such statements are a relatively new part of the sentencing process, and the only time that a victim or victim's family is given a direct role in a trial.

From what Danks had seen, it was rarely a satisfying experience, and always a heart-wrenching one. He'd watched so many people struggle to articulate their grief in court. It was a task that would bring poets to their knees, and yet ordinary folks were somehow expected to find the right words, strike the right tone, make clear their loss. Mostly they couldn't. Sometimes only the rage came through, as a family member disintegrated into screaming invectives at a defendant. More often, there were just tears. Danks had seen mothers, wives, and sisters cry so hard they lost their ability to speak altogether. In the end it was usually the body language, the person bent double with the weight of the loss, that said to the killer: "See what you have done!" But most often the killer wasn't even looking.

Before the Polecs delivered their statements, the defense attorneys had one last chance to make a pitch for leniency. In addition, attorney Michael Applebaum was asking to have Khathavong sentenced as a juvenile. "This oughta be good," Danks whispered to Casey as Applebaum stood to address the court.

The attorney had his work cut out for him. Judge Greenspan had in her hands a report from the sheriff's department on Khathavong's behavior during his sixteen months in custody. It wasn't good. Deputies said he constantly mouthed off to them and argued with other prisoners during the daily bus ride from jail to court. In the holding area adjacent to the courtroom itself, he swore and swaggered around as if he was hanging out at the mall, not standing trial for murder.

"He was being a real little jerk," Applebaum admitted to the judge.

"Or maybe," Casey cut in, "he was acting true to his nature."

Applebaum called Bou's nineteen-year-old brother as a character witness. Sean Khathavong told the judge he was sure that Bou could change. It had already started to happen, he said.

"I never saw my brother cry until the day I told him my grandmother passed away, and I had to tell him in jail, so he couldn't see her. That's when he cried. I just never seen him cry before. That's when I knew the wall was down," Sean said, breaking down himself.

"Your Honor," Casey interrupted, "may the record reflect that the witness is crying but the defendant is not?"

Sean told the judge that, like Bou, he'd once been a delinquent, too. But he'd straightened out his life and was now an assistant manager at a retail store, thanks to his experience at a school for wayward boys called George Junior Republic. Applebaum was hoping to convince Greenspan to sentence his client to a stay in his brother's alma mater rather than a prison. He waved around a piece of paper and indicated that Bou's acceptance into the school was assured.

Next, Applebaum called Dr. Stanley Rosner as a witness. The psychologist told the court the sad story of Bou's young life: his birth in a refugee camp in Thailand; the family's move to the United States when Bou was a toddler, the immigrant parents so poor they were forced to work almost around the clock and had little time for their children; the father who felt the only way to get his boys under control was to whip them with extension cords. The beatings were so severe that school officials tried to intervene, Rosner said. But nothing ever came of it, because Bou and Sean denied there was a problem "out of loyalty to the family and the wish not to cast a bad light on their parents."

Joe Casey was ready for Applebaum. He produced school records, court documents, psychological reports, and even Bou's own probation officer to paint a picture of a teenager who'd been given every opportunity to turn his life around and hadn't. In the space of a little more than three years, Bou had been placed in the Montgomery County Youth Center, in Lakeside School for Boys, in New Life Boys' Ranch and the Vision Quest, Outward Bound, and Home Quest programs. But none of those made any long-term difference.

Then Casey produced a surprise witness, Barbara Luberski, an administrator at George Junior Republic. She was in Philadelphia visiting Bou's probation officer, Dene Harris, and had been invited by Harris to attend the trial for the day as a spectator. When Casey learned of Luberski's presence in the courtroom, he'd decided to call her to the witness stand. She testified that the school had never been told about Bou's background and had no program that would be appropriate for him, since he had already received his high school equivalency certificate. "Therefore," she said, "we would not accept him."

Nor would Judge Greenspan accept the notion that Bou should be sentenced as a juvenile. Concluding he was "not amenable to treatment," she refused to decertify him as an adult. Asked if he had anything to say, Bou stood and addressed the court for the first time: "I would like to say to Eddie Polec's family that I am sorry for my involvement, for the whole incident."

Charles Peruto was the only other defense attorney to put on a witness at the hearing. Through Dr. Elliot Atkins, a psychologist, he hoped to explain to the court how a kid who had never been in serious trouble before could have taken such a violent detour. Reporters leaned forward to hear Atkins's testimony, eager for anything that would shed some light on Nick Pinero, the most enigmatic of the defendants.

Part of Nick's problem, said the doctor, was that he had no real identity, no sense of himself outside of his peer group. "If something were to happen to someone in the peer group, it would be no different than an insult or slight or assault on himself."

Atkins attributed Nick's excessive reliance on his peer group to the fact that he had a learning disability that had begun in kindergarten. Over the years, he had such a hard time keeping up in school that his mother started doing his homework. "Nick had a very strong reaction as a young adolescent to coming home and having his mom do his work, so he rebelled and tried to do it on his own, and couldn't."

The way the doctor told it, the more Nick failed, the more his mom did his work, the angrier he became and the more he needed to prove himself with his friends.

There were snickers coming from the press seats. "Oh, it's the old I-killed-him-because-my-mother-did-my-homework defense," whispered one wag. The snickers turned to outright guffaws when Atkins told the court that Nick, who initially said he was "deeply involved in Christianity," had expressed a sudden desire to become a Muslim. "So now it's Muhammad Pinero?" laughed one correspondent.

Dr. Atkins plowed on, describing how Nick had built up anger at his mother for being too close and rage at his father for not being close enough. But despite that anger and rage, the doctor concluded, Nick was "not a violent young man."

What definition of "violent" was he using, wondered John Polec.

When the defense was done, Joe Casey called for the victim impact statements.

Father James Olson told the court that Eddie's funeral "was the hardest thing I have ever done, and I never want to do anything like that again." He remembered his favorite altar boy as "the kind of person you would want to have living next door to you. You would want your daughter to take him to the prom. He was the type of person you'd want as your own son."

Colleen McGovern, the girl Kathy had always hoped Eddie would take to the prom, spoke for all of his friends. His death "tore our lives apart," she said, her voice cracking. "We never expected anything like this to happen to anybody, to any of our friends. It was never thought of, and then one day it all just happened, and he wasn't there anymore." Racked with sobbing, she couldn't go on. She was helped off the witness stand and back to her seat.

Then came the family. Each of them had agonized for hours about what they wanted to tell the court, the defendants, and the world about Eddie's death. But they had not discussed their statements with one another, so none of them knew what the others would say.

Kristie went first. "If I tried to count the ways Eddie's death has affected our lives," she said, "I would be here for another five hours. The most fond memory that I have of my brother is when he was fourteen years old, and he pestered me and pestered me to get him a job where I worked, at a restaurant. So I finally went to the manager and they agreed to hire him at the age of fourteen, and he was such a hard worker he got them in trouble with the Department of Labor, because he worked too many hours for a fourteen-year-old.

"Eventually, when he turned sixteen, the company was expanding, and they sent me out to other stores to train new employees. So, of course, I asked if my little brother could come along with me, and he did." She told how they'd gone to the Boston Chicken in Flourtown and the one in Abington, and how everyone there had treated them with respect. "Everyone liked Ed, because Ed got along with everyone." There'd been no long-standing Abington–Fox Chase feud. She and Ed had worked with lots of kids from Abington Senior High School, but "not one sits in this room. They were people with class and dignity and respect. They were the people that came to Eddie's funeral, and they were friends with my brother."

She indicated the defendants. "These people sitting before you right now are the rare exceptions. . . . They talked about this fight all week. Their lawyers would like you to believe that Fox Chase kids were up at McDonald's planning and getting ready for this big huge fight, when really . . . they were doing the same thing that had been done for years and years. The same thing I did when I was in high school. There were kids up at the Rec that night because there were kids up there every night. Maybe we shouldn't have been there. Maybe we should have been somewhere organized. But we were not there causing problems; we were just being kids. . . .

"He was a great kid, my brother, and I miss him. Every single day, when I wake up, I miss him. I can't count the number of times that I think of him during the day. I can't count all the times I find myself jumping in the car, and just driving to get out of the house and get out of the depression, and just drive around, and no matter how close Billy and myself are, there is always something missing, and that's Ed.

"Finally," she said, turning back to Judge Greenspan, "for hours we listened to Mr. Peruto's opening statement, and time and time again he said, 'There are no saints in this room, there are no sinners; there's just today's kids.'

"Well, Your Honor, if the six sitting before you, who are responsible for my brother's murder, are today's kids, then I certainly am scared to death to see what tomorrow's kids will be."

Until that moment, Billy hadn't been sure if he wanted to speak. But when Kristie sat down his legs seemed to push him to a standing position and propel him to the witness stand.

"While sitting here this morning, I listened to Bou Khathavong's brother, Sean, talk about how once a week he goes to visit his brother in jail and how hard it is on him," he said. "I'd like him to take a second and realize that at least once a week I, too, go to visit my brother. And I'd like him to imagine what it would be like for him not to be able to talk to his brother on the phone, or through bars, but to have to picture his brother in his mind, because his brother is now six feet underneath the ground.

"I can't tell you the pain and suffering that these six, and the rest of the perpetrators who came down that night, have caused me. Each one of them in their own special way led to my brother's death. Each one of them, even though they didn't pick up a baseball bat and hit him, murdered my brother. I wake up in the morning and realize that without these young men sitting before you, I would still have my brother. I would never be in this courtroom."

He glared at the defendants. "My brother never hurt any one of you, not once. He didn't know who you were. He didn't know your names. I would just like to ask you, if any of you would like to answer me, what did my brother do to provoke what you did to him?. . .

"Forever in my mind will be the memory, not the memory of what Eddie Polec was after you beat him at Saint Cecilia's Church, but what Eddie Polec was before November 11, on November 10, and the sixteen years of his life before this event happened. The smiling eyes, the smile that just said more than any word ever could. You will never understand.

"All of the apologies, the I'm-sorrys or anything that anyone can ever say to me will never make up for the loss that I feel, thanks to you.

"I have nothing else to say. Thank you, Your Honor."

John had jotted down his thoughts in the notebook he had used during the trial. But when he took the witness stand, his hands were shaking so badly he couldn't read what he'd written. To help with the shaking, he asked the judge if he could stand as he spoke to the defendants. Judge Greenspan said he could. He looked down at the six, but none of them looked back.

"I have sat here quietly and tried to keep the peace for sixteen months," he told them. "Sixteen months of watching you in this courtroom. My son lived sixteen years. His future was ahead of him. My son had more time ahead of him than he had lived, and when you killed him, you robbed him and stole from his future. He can't do anything that he likes to do anymore; my son can't do any of those things that one day you will do again. He can't drive a car. You will get married someday, maybe. He will never get married. He will never have kids. You stole from him. You put him in a grave six feet under dirt, for absolutely no reason."

He told them that four thousand people had come to the funeral home to see Eddie's body and pay their respects. "They stood in line for hours. That's what Eddie Polec was. That is what you stole from me. That is what you stole from Kathy and Kristie and Billy.

"The following day, it was a horrible day. It rained a cold, driving rain. But fifteen hundred people packed the church, and five hundred more stood outside in the rain, just to be there. God, I think about the impact he had! No publicity and all of these people show up. And you murdered him.

"I sit at night and think: What could he have been? I hear about how you can be rehabilitated and I think, *He* didn't need to be rehabilitated. He was good to start with. And what could he have done with his life? I will never know what his future was because of what you did, because you did not leave him alone, because you wouldn't let him go home on November 11."

He reconstructed the moments leading up to the attack. "I think about Ed running through the parking lot, and he hears people screaming and cursing behind him. And he turns to look. And when he turned around, he lost his balance and stumbled, and he skidded on the ground and stopped at the church steps. And I think about how you and your murderous friends gathered around him. What was it, ten to one, by Convey's testimony? There are only six of you here, but you outnumbered him ten to one. He is on the ground, he is defenseless, he is unarmed, and you beat him and you kicked him and you punched him.

"He lay on that ground, and Convey says that he screamed, 'I didn't do anything.' He couldn't have done anything to you, because he didn't know who you were, damn it! You beat him and punched him, and then all that helplessness ended when you saw Rienzi grab the bat, and you took the bat and smashed the back of his head, didn't you? And the blood gushed out, and fractures went through his head, that we saw in the pictures, and a little piece of bone jammed into his head, because of what you did.

"He is on the ground, and I know my son. When he got hit on the head, he shook. When he fell off his bike, he shook. He must have been shaking so bad that Pinero and Crook couldn't get a good shot at him, so you held him, you picked him up and you held him, so that Crook and Pinero could whale away at him, time after time.

"And then you sat in this courtroom for all of these months and never said a word one time, or I'm sorry. You said that you weren't guilty, and then the jury found you guilty, and in the time that you sat here, it was always quiet. You let other people talk for you. You let other people tell the jurors your side of the story. And when you were letting other people do it, a lot of times, whether accidentally or on purpose, they seemed to kind of get the facts a little messed up, and not once did any of you stand up and say, 'Wait a minute; that's not the way it was.'

"You sat quietly. You sat quietly and you let misstatements go along. You let other people say things that you knew weren't true because you wanted to be free. You wanted to escape punishment. You wanted to go home, the very thing you kept my son from doing on November 11 . . .

"I realize you are all going to have a chance to stand up and talk to the judge, and a chance to say 'I'm sorry.' But I will say to you all, do not turn around and look back at that row. Don't look at me! Don't look at Kathy, Kris, or Bill! Don't bother. I've heard you deny everything for all these months. I've heard you allow others to lie on your behalf. If you get up and say that you are sorry, there is no way that I am going to believe you, nor is anyone else in Ed's family. So don't waste your time.

"Don't turn around when you ask for mercy from this court. Don't look at me when you denied my Ed mercy in that parking lot."

He turned to the defense attorneys. "Miss Smarro, Mr. McMahon, Mr. Wallace, I have no bone to pick with any of you. I didn't like what you did an awful lot of times, or the way you argued the law, but when we were in here, I realized that the three of you were doing your jobs. That was your job to do, to argue the facts.

"But, Mr. Applebaum, Mr. Gaskins, and Mr. Peruto, what you did in this courtroom I found to be disgusting at times, because you came in trying to convince the jurors that my son and his friends were the same as your clients. . . . You told the jury in the very beginning, in the opening arguments, how everyone knew that the Fox Chase kids 'tuned up' anyone that came into Fox Chase. And you insinuated to the jurors how Fox Chase kids toted shotguns with them while they robbed and pillaged out in Roslyn. Check the record.

"Mr. Peruto, you tried to conjure up this image at McGarrity's that the Fox Chase kids lured your clients into an ambush, and I sat here and couldn't believe that you were attacking my son and his friends to save your clients. That was unbelievable to me. I couldn't understand how you could tell the jury that your clients and their friends and my dead son were the same. Because it is the difference of night and day. It is opposite ends of the spectrum. Here are murderers, and here are Ed and his friends. They are not even close . . .

"And then, when you closed your arguments, what did you tell the jury? That we wouldn't be here if the parents had done their job! You repeated that comment on television! You insulted me and my wife to defend your clients, and when you closed you said Philadelphia has to hire 116 police officers to crack down on the crime wave in Fox Chase. Sarcasm! It's not right; it's not right at all.

"But that is not what we are here for, and I apologize," he continued. "We are here because today you have to sentence them, Your Honor, and all I can ask you . . . is to do it as fairly as possible . . . " He looked straight at Pinero. "The tests say that you are not violent," he said. "Well, I'm sorry, but my Ed, from his grave, thinks that you are violent. I need to know that the six of you are sentenced to every possible day in jail that the law allows, because while you are in jail, while you are behind bars, you can't kill anybody again. You can't take a baseball bat when you are in jail and kill an innocent kid in a parking lot . . .

"No matter what the courts do to you, it doesn't bring Eddie back. It doesn't take him out of the ground and put him back at the kitchen table. There is no satisfaction for Ed's dad here. But for Kris and Bill, and for all of the other kids, and for all of the people that wrote saying they would support the court if the sentence was imposed correctly, it is very important that you go to jail for as many seconds as the law possibly allows, that you spend every possible moment locked behind bars.

"And then, when all this is said and done, when you are sentenced, no matter what the sentence is . . . I want every one of you to understand this right now: I will be there every time that somebody has to decide whether you come up for work release, when you come up for furloughs, when you come up for parole. I will be there to remind the decision maker of what you did to Ed, how you beat him over and over again with those bats.

"I will spend the rest of my life, if I have to, making sure society is protected from you killing again. And when I die, I am going to be the first spirit each of you will run into in the next world. And I will be there to make sure that in the next life, when you are judged for your actions here, it is with real punishment. Because the Lord can seek revenge, and I want to be there when he does it, for what you did to Ed, and what you did in this courtroom, and what you did to my family. I will be there to make sure that he punishes you the way it can't be done here on earth.

"I will never forget, for all eternity, how you slaughtered Eddie Polec."

There was silence when he finished, as if every person in the courtroom was conjuring the image of him hounding Eddie's killers into the hereafter.

It was Peruto who finally broke the quiet, to dispute John's account of his gibe about the 116 extra police officers. Then Oscar Gaskins attempted to defend his depiction of criminal behavior by Fox Chase kids. Applebaum followed suit.

Bill Danks watched in disbelief. He had never seen defense attorneys put on the defensive like this. It was as if John had become the moral equivalent of judge and jury, and the attorneys were trying to justify themselves to him.

Before the trial, the largest audience Kathy Polec had ever addressed was a kids' soccer team. And two months earlier she'd sat at the witness stand looking and sounding like a scared little girl, her voice barely rising above a whisper. But it seemed to be a very different woman who took that seat now and addressed the defendants, who sat with their heads bowed.

"In the months that have passed since you murdered Eddie," she began, "not only have I seen the strength and love that kept our family and our community so united, I have also seen the searing pain, the inconsolable grief, of Eddie's loss. I look at the faces of his friends and his peers, and I am met by eyes that reflect a sorrow and a pain that go well beyond their years.

"On November 12, Eddie died. You not only murdered their friend, you murdered their innocence, and you stole their childhood. In these sixteen months, they have seen and lived more of life's experiences than some people ever will, and they have responded with dignity, maturity, and responsibility, in the face of a horrific tragedy and under the scrutiny of the mass media. They have shown what today's kids are, and they have shown you for the anomaly that you are."

Kathy had typed her speech, but quickly found that her thoughts ran faster than the written words. So she glanced at the papers only occasionally to make sure she didn't leave anything out.

"I look at the faces of my friends and I see how delicately and intricately our lives have been interwoven through these years . . . I watch my other two children. I see Billy. I know that he has not only lost his brother, he's lost his best friend, someone who taught him to be at ease with who he was, to see beauty and joy, and to love life. I talk to Kristie and I hear how her life is shattered by a veil of pain and sorrow. Even the happiest of moments is not as bright or joyous as it once was.

"I watch John. I see the pain and the frustration of not wanting Eddie's death to be in vain. I watch him come home from work every night, his face drawn and colorless when he passes that pool table where he and Eddie played. And I know that we are all haunted by the same echoes of past conversations, of everyday life, which we shared so freely and openly in our home, and the plans for a future that will never be.

"Each member of a family not only has a place or a station, he also brings to the family a special gift and quality. Eddie had a unique gift to see and feel your spirit, your soul. When you were with him, when you felt his smile, you saw his eyes with such light and joy shine on you, it lifted your own spirit. That is what you destroyed. To have been graced with such a special person and have him so violently and senselessly torn from us causes such torment that it is indescribable.

"There is so much that I would like to say to you, because I will never again meet you in my lifetime, at least I pray that I don't. Like musicians in an orchestra, we can stand alone and we can produce a work of beauty. But together, in harmony, we can accomplish a masterpiece. You have taken that delicate and complex balance of harmony that, as a family, we so lovingly and painstakingly forged, and you crushed it, just as surely as you crushed Eddie's skull.

"You sentenced Eddie to death, and you sentenced us to a lifetime of drifting in an ocean of pain . . . The night that you murdered Eddie will haunt me forever. You left St. Cecilia's and you laughed, and you high-fived each other. We are left with the memory of a child in a hospital bed. I begin to shake when I think of him. My muscles constrict in spasms of agony and torment when I think of him alone, surrounded by you, crying out for his life. I become paralyzed, with a dizzying sensation, when I think of him being held and beaten repeatedly, savagely, over his head, the sounds of the bats crashing onto his skull . . .

"I will forever see the tubes and that ventilator, and the blood seeping from his mouth and his nostrils, and ingrained in my mind will be the sound of those monitors, as his blood and his brain swelled, and his heart failed from the stress of everything.

"When you went home, and you were safe and in your parents' arms, this is what you left us with. And it is not tragic enough that we lost Eddie because you murdered him, you've also subjected us to your attempt to murder, to brutalize his name, his spirit. And for this I don't even need these papers."

She placed the pages on the railing in front of her and glared at the defendants, her voice suddenly going hard and cold. "You have chosen lawyers to represent you who, in some instances, have been representative of the evil that you have tried to mask. You made a sport of hunting and murdering Eddie, just as some of your lawyers made a sport of laying down the odds and then clapping at the re-enactment of your savagery. You clubbed an innocent child mercilessly, just as some of your representatives clubbed innocent witnesses with sarcasm and innuendo. You murdered Eddie on holy ground in the presence of God, just as your attorneys brutalized Eddie with lies in this courtroom, witnessed by the eyes of justice.

"Your hands will forever be stained and covered with Eddie's blood, as will the thirty pieces of silver you paid those who represented you so well. You caused us to lose our son. You destroyed all the hopes and dreams for his future. But Eddie will always be remembered because, at the tender age of sixteen, he realized what was important in life, that it wasn't the notoriety or the wealth obtained; it was respect and love for others, and the time you take to share that.

"And no matter where you go, no matter what happens, each and every one of you will always be remembered as Eddie Polec's murderers."

As Kathy walked back to her seat beside John, the judge fought to maintain her composure, and veteran reporters wept openly.

And then it was all over, except for filling in the numbers.

No one was sure which way Judge Greenspan would go. Throughout the trial, both sides had tried to read her. Each was sure she favored the other. The defense team complained bitterly that her rulings were overtly pro-prosecution; Casey and Danks felt she'd bent over backward "in an abundance of caution," allowing the defense more latitude than they deserved.

Casey hoped she would send the kind of message the jury had failed to send. "It is very clear that Eddie Polec is dead," he told her. "Nothing you can do will bring him back. It is also very clear that because of the nature of this case, the sentence you impose can say, not only to the defendants, but also to everyone in the courtroom, and . . . outside this courtroom . . . that while Eddie Polec is dead, justice in Philadelphia is alive."

But Judge Greenspan needed no prodding.

"I have received thousands of signatures and, even more extraordinarily, thousands of letters from individuals asking for the maximum penalty in this case. I will say to the Polecs that the outpouring of community sentiment on their behalf is a beautiful tribute to them, and that they have met their loss with extreme grace, courage really, in the face of unbearable pain, and I recognize that. That goes as well for their outstanding children, Kristie and Billy, who have in their own strength been an inspiration to us and a tribute to their brother, a great tribute to their brother.

"However, the defendants should be aware, and this record must reflect, that I need no encouragement from the community, for the sentences that I impose today must not be a vote of the community, and it is not. In my view, the jury in this case has shown all the sympathy and mercy that these defendants deserve."

Judge Greenspan then asked each defendant if he had something to say before sentencing. Only Tom Crook chose to speak. As he had on the day of his arrest, Crook wept openly as he spoke. "I planned to apologize to the Polec family," he said. "But under the request of Mr. Polec, when he said he didn't want to hear it, I will not; I will respect that. But I would like to apologize to the court and I would like to apologize to my family. I want to thank them for being here for me, for these last few months in jail. It is a scary place. I want to say that I am sorry for my little brothers and sisters. For messing up real bad, and not being able to be there for them the way I used to be there for them.

"I am sorry to my mom because I love you so much. Again, I miss you. I hope that my wrongdoing and punishment can somehow help the next generation see what is right and what is wrong and not come to jail, because it is not a place to be. And I am at your mercy, Your Honor."

In the end, Crook was the only one who got any mercy from the court. Judge Greenspan shaved six months off his maximum sentence of fifteen to thirty years. Pennsylvania law requires that inmates serve at least their minimum sentence, so if Crook proved to be a model prisoner, he would serve at least fourteen and a half years behind bars.

The judge gave the other defendants every second the law allowed. Anthony Rienzi got fifteen to thirty years for being one of the principal beaters, Dewan Alexander got eight to twenty for kicking Eddie, and Bou Khathavong and Carlo Johnson got five to ten for conspiracy.

Just before Judge Greenspan handed down her sentence on Pinero, Charles Peruto made one last pitch for mercy. "If we are going to send a message, then what kind of message are we sending?" he asked. "If you are a rat fink and a big liar and are willing to do the Commonwealth's bidding, then you are going to get a sweetheart deal? Is that the message? Because that is what we are saying about Convey."

Judge Greenspan had run out of patience. "No," she said sharply, "the message that I am sending today is the fact that your client beat another individual, a perfectly innocent individual, to death with a baseball bat, and he will receive a just sentence for that."

She stared down at Pinero. Under the law she couldn't give him any more time than she had Rienzi. So she gave him a piece of her mind.

"I am most troubled by your role in this event, Mr. Pinero," she said. "And I do think if there is anyone totally responsible for the fact that Mr. Polec died, it is you. There is no reason, as far as I can see— and I will say it again—to show mercy with regard to this sentence. There is nothing in your record that convinces me that you are deserving of mercy. You have a background here that is well explained by Dr. Atkins, and it is troublesome to me that it has produced in you the ability to do what you did that night. But it only explains your behavior, it does not excuse it.

"So for all those reasons and, most specifically, for your role in this crime, I sentence you to ten to twenty years for murder and a consecutive five to ten years for conspiracy."

That meant Pinero would become eligible for parole in the year 2010. John added the numbers in his head: Nick could walk out of prison at the age of thirty-two, sixteen years after murdering Eddie, who only got to live sixteen years. Such was the symmetry of justice.

After the sound bites were recorded for the nightly news, the Polecs drove to Cardinal Dougherty High School, where they sat in the principal's office and recorded a videotape that would be shown to the faculty and student body the next day. They explained the decision, said they accepted it, and thanked the students for their support and for their "impeccable behavior when human emotions screamed so loudly for retribution."

From Cardinal Dougherty, they went to St. Cecilia's, where they delivered the same message to a gathering of two hundred young people and their parents. The hardest part was explaining the jury's decision to acquit the defendants in the beating of John Atkinson. How could that act, and those terrible injuries, deserve no punishment at all?

Through all the questions, John and Kathy kept their anguish to themselves. They were determined to display no displeasure with the decision, to ensure that not one more drop of blood was shed, not another life was lost, not another child was harmed in Eddie's name.

It was past 9:00 p.m. when they got home. Kathy flipped on the lights in the living room, turned up the heat, and put on a kettle for tea. Now what? she thought. What was she supposed to do with the rest of her life?

Throughout the trial they'd all been so focused on Eddie. He was *the* topic of conversation, in court and out. She'd felt connected to him every moment, as if she were somehow rushing toward him. "We've all worked so hard," she told Mary Doherty, "and now that it's all over, I feel like he should come home."

Kristie stood in the doorway. "I'm leaving," she announced. "I gotta get back to school." She leaned down and gave Kathy a long, hard hug.

Kathy looked at her family. Somehow they all had to get back to their lives. She would return to her corner tomorrow, John would go back to work, Billy would go back to Cardinal Dougherty, and they would all have to find their own ways to be close to Eddie.

"I love you," Kathy called as Kristie headed out the door. "Be careful."

36

In the weeks after the sentencing, John received two unexpected letters. Neither was welcome. The first was from a priest in Arizona, blasting him for his speech to the defendants. Who was he to insist on being present when it came time for God to render judgment? The very idea was blasphemous!

The second was addressed to "the Polec family." It was an anonymous note from Graterford Prison outside Philadelphia, saying that Eddie's killers were "at the mercy of the other inmates and being attacked on a regular basis."

John was upset. He wanted them in prison, of course, but it didn't seem right that they were being raped or terrorized. He immediately called Father Olson, who contacted the chaplain at Graterford. The chaplain listened and promised to keep an eye on things. A few days later he called back and said to forget the letter, it was an old prison ploy. According to the chaplain, it was possible that one of Ed's killers, or a friend of theirs, had sent the letter in hopes that the family would feel sorry for him when it came time for parole.

With the trial over, John found he still could not rest. There were too many battles left to fight in Eddie's name: laws to change, lawyers to sanction, more kids to be charged, and, of course, a 911 system still to be fixed.

In April 1996, he launched an all-out assault. He began lobbying legislators to change the laws governing first-degree murder. Under the Pennsylvania penal code, if a person sets out to commit a robbery and happens to kill someone in the process, the punishment is an automatic life sentence. But if a person sets out to beat someone within an inch of his life and kills the victim instead, the punishment is not an automatic life sentence. In that case, the prosecutor has to prove the perpetrator formed a specific "intent to kill," that he had murder in mind. And that, John believed, put juries in the shrink business.

"A trained psychologist would not speculate on a person's state of mind, would not dare judge whether someone had an intent to kill, without ever talking to them," John told lawmakers. "And yet we are asking juries to be clairvoyant, to conclude beyond a reasonable doubt the state of mind of people they have never met, never talked to, never even heard speak. It's absurd."

John argued that the law should be based on "intent to harm." If a planned act of violence ends in a death, he reasoned, then the perpetrator should be just as accountable as the person who plans a robbery that ends in death. As it stood now, the state was valuing property over human life. "If those kids had picked Eddie's pocket, then they would have been put away for life," he said. "But because they simply beat him to death and then stepped over his body, it's somehow not as bad?"

The legislators listened politely but seemed to write him off as a harmless, bereaved nut trying to change the world. No one proposed legislation to change the law.

John went after the defense attorneys, too. He believed that Applebaum, Peruto, and Gaskins had knowingly lied to the jury and should be disciplined for it. He had no specific punishment in mind and no real expectation that they'd be disbarred. He just wanted someone to tell the world that what these attorneys had done was wrong.

He began a furious letter-writing campaign to the disciplinary board of the Supreme Court of Pennsylvania. He fired off dozens of letters backed by hundreds of pages of carefully annotated testimony, pointing out in painstaking detail each instance in which he thought one of the attorneys had made a false statement to the court. Chief among these were Oscar Gaskins's claim that Bou Khathavong and Carlo Johnson had been held up with a sawed-off shotgun by some kids from Fox Chase; Peruto's uncorroborated claim that rocks were thrown near the church; and Michael Applebaum's disparaging comments about Eddie during his opening statement. Applebaum held a special place in John's pantheon of lying lawyers because he'd tried to make his son look bad.

"Mr. Applebaum lied to the judge and the jury when he said my son arrived at McDonald's in the back of a jeep and took some kid's hat. He further lied when he said my son and others had sexually molested a young lady who was a friend of the kid whose hat was taken." How could he say that and get away with it? John raged.

But the disciplinary board rejected each of his arguments, saying it saw no evidence that any of the attorneys had acted "in bad faith." The board acknowledged that misleading statements were made to the jury, but said those statements were merely the result of the attorneys either relying on confidential information from their clients and other witnesses or simply becoming confused about the facts in the heat of the moment. As such, nothing that was said during the trial constituted a "violation of any existing rules governing legal ethics."

John concluded that the board was in the shrink business, too. Unless he could prove that the lawyers had *intended* to lie, he had no case against Peruto et al. The board's deputy chief sent him a consoling letter saying that the rules were ambiguous and sometimes "more emphasis is placed on a desire to ensure that individuals will have zealous advocacy than on assuring that truth will remain paramount."

After two frustrating years of dealing with the disciplinary board, John thought he finally got some good news. The State Supreme Court ruled in another case that "any misstatement of fact" by an attorney in court, regardless of the reason, was a violation of the professional rules of conduct.

John was ecstatic. This was the language he'd been looking for. He began his efforts anew, writing near-legal briefs to the disciplinary board, begging its members to re-examine his claims. But the board refused to budge from its earlier decision.

The district attorney's office also let John down. Despite ample evidence that seventeen other teens shared some responsibility for Eddie's death, the D.A. closed the case in September 1996.

Joe Casey delivered the news in person, accompanied by Charlie Gallagher, Lynn Abraham's right-hand man. For two hours they sat with John at the kitchen table, explaining the realities. If a Philadelphia jury had gone so easy on the six most serious aggressors, it was extremely doubtful that they'd ever convict a Maureen Yodzio or a Paris Williams. "We could charge them, but we could not prevail in court," said Gallagher, who thought that if the same kids were tried before a less crime-hardened jury in Montgomery County, "they'd all be doing time."

John wanted to scream. Kids who were responsible for Eddie's death would not be brought to justice because they had had the good sense to kill him in the city rather than the suburbs? "Life is not fair," Gallagher sighed. As if John needed to be told.

Friends and supporters of the Polecs urged them to file a wrongful-death suit in civil court, citing the Goldman and Brown families' success in the O. J. Simpson case. John considered it for a moment, but came to the conclusion that it would only hurt the kids' parents. What would be the point of that?

John continued his campaign against teenage violence. Though still painfully shy, he became a much-sought-after public speaker, regularly addressing high school students, church groups, and anyone else who invited him. When John Polec talked, people listened. And "if they listen," he told Kathy, "then maybe something will lodge in their unconscious, and one day, when they're tempted to get even with a kid for spilling a soda, they'll think twice before grabbing a bat and clubbing the first person they find."

John signed on as a volunteer worker for a non-profit, anti-violence organization called Lost Dreams on Canvas. The organization commissions artists to paint portraits of children killed by violence and exhibits the paintings at schools, shopping malls, city halls, and federal buildings throughout the Northeast. John quickly became the organization's unofficial transportation committee. He bought a pickup truck to move the seventy to eighty paintings, Eddie's included, from one exhibit to the next.

John's most consuming battle, however, was the one to reform Philadelphia's 911 system. In May 1996, one year after the city had promised to begin a pilot project based on the laptop computer and cell-phone technology he'd figured out at his kitchen table, 60 police cars were finally fitted with MDTs. But 506 cars answered 911 calls. John hoped that after two months of testing, the police would be able to install the units at the rate of sixty a month, and that by June 1997—two and a half years after Eddie's death—every patrol car in the city would have the new technology.

At first, the problem was money. City officials told John only half a million dollars per year had been budgeted for the MDT project. At that rate, only eight or nine cars a month would get the new system, and the entire fleet wouldn't be outfitted until the year 2000. Too long, John thought. Too many nights of thousands of kids hanging out at McDonald's, too much risk of another incident. For him, it was as if Eddie were still out there, fooling around with his pals, oblivious, unprotected.

John tried to raise the money himself. He wrote to the Pew Charitable Trust, the W. W. Smith Foundation, the McLean Contributionship, and the William Penn Foundation. Each turned him down, with regrets. The more he wrote letters and called on the community to give money to fix the emergency system, the more he felt like a court jester. But he couldn't stop.

In June, John and Kathy met with Ed Rendell. The mayor was polite, but he seemed exasperated by the fact that the Polecs had been hounding him for more than a year and a half—in person, by mail, and through the media. In the middle of the meeting, Rendell placed a phone call to an attorney and asked what the Polecs would have to do in order to file a lawsuit against the city. John interpreted that as the mayor telling them, in effect, "Go ahead and sue," as if it would be easier for the city to deal with a $50 million lawsuit than to fix the 911 system.

Two weeks later Rendell wrote to the Polecs, outlining what he called a "host of 911 reforms." He pointed out that the city had improved the supervisor-to-dispatcher ratio, hired additional dispatchers, improved supervision, and created a more comprehensive training program. In addition, there were technological improvements, including software that now alerted supervisors if five or more calls came from the same area, and two new radio bands, which meant an increase in airtime capacity. All of the reforms were having a "real impact," said the mayor, citing the fact that response time had dropped from an average of 7 minutes and 27 seconds per call to 6 minutes and 53 seconds.

As for the MDTs, Rendell promised to accelerate the rollout of the new technology, but only after the pilot project proved beyond a doubt that they would reduce response time, and only if the police officers with the equipment were actually using it.

But in early September, when the pilot program was supposed to be completed, John was told that an independent evaluator, a graduate student at Temple University, needed to collect at least two more months' worth of data. And he also learned that no one had even talked to the police to see what they thought of the computers.

So John talked to them himself. He went down to the 18th District on a Saturday night and interviewed the cops who were using the MDTs. They told him they loved them, that the little computers had turned out to be more useful than they'd ever imagined and made them feel safer even when making routine traffic stops.

In two months it would be the second anniversary of Eddie's death. John had been told that the statute of limitations was up on that date and he would no longer be able to sue the city. So he figured he had to use whatever leverage he had right now. It was time to throw a tantrum.

The MDT committee had a meeting scheduled for September 11, and John planned to crash it. But when he arrived at the Municipal Services Building, Joe Martz informed him that he was "positively" not allowed to come in. John was prepared for that. He handed Martz a letter, containing the ultimatum he had never wanted to deliver.

"Enough is enough," the letter read. "We mistakenly believed that the spirit of cooperation would cause the city to correct the problems quickly; we had expected the necessary 911 reforms would be implemented without delay. Instead of battling Eddie's parents in the courts, we hoped that the city would spend the money it saved improving the system. We were wrong."

John demanded that the city certify the MDT pilot as a success within five days, approve MDTs for a citywide rollout, and put in writing a legally enforceable plan to equip sixty cars each month.

Otherwise, "we will contact the necessary legal professional to begin a lawsuit against the city and any and all officials responsible for the safety of its residents and visitors."

John made clear that the Polecs would use any proceeds from the lawsuit to finance the necessary citywide purchase of MDT equipment to solve the air-time problem. Any additional money would be donated to the Lost Dreams on Canvas project, he said.

Five days later, the city blinked. Joe Martz informed John that the administration had somehow found enough money, $8 million, to fund the entire MDT project. One week later, Martz faxed John a copy of a letter from Ed Rendell.

"I am pleased to tell you that the City is prepared to commit to a schedule for a deployment of Mobile Data Terminals to *all* our patrol districts," the mayor wrote. He called the completion of the project a "turning point in the history of the Philadelphia Police Department" and quoted a veteran police officer as saying the MDTs were the "best piece of crime-fighting equipment since the two-way radio."

The letter committed the city to the installation of a minimum of twenty-five MDTs per month, every month, beginning in February 1997, with the exception of summer. It was not all that John had hoped for. At the rate the city was promising, all the MDTs would not be in place until January 1999, more than four years after Eddie's murder. But he could live with it.

There was a catch, however. "In response to this program," wrote the mayor, "the Polec family has agreed that it will not file a lawsuit against the City or its officials and employees for any claim arising from the death of Eddie Polec. I urge you to agree to this deployment schedule," the mayor said in closing, "so we may begin to take the steps necessary to prevent any future tragedies from occurring." And there was a line for the Polecs' signatures.

The way John read it, the city was saying it would not implement a new emergency system to protect its citizens unless the Polecs first signed away their right to sue the city over Eddie's death. Just to be sure, he called a journalist whose opinion he trusted and read the letter. "What do you think?" he asked.

"Sounds to me like a weird form of extortion," said the journalist. "But it also sounds like you have them by the short hairs. What are you going to do?"

John didn't hesitate. "We're gonna sign it."

On September 24, Joe Martz called John to tell him that the formal copy of the mayor's letter was ready for his signature. But after he signed it, he was handed a separate letter from the mayor that read in its entirety:

> As I have said to you many times before, our agreement to move forward on the MDTs is in no way related to any possibility that you might sue the City for events that led to Eddie's death. I want to reiterate that as strongly as possible.
>
> As a result, I am uncomfortable with any reference to a lawsuit being in the letter I am sending you. However, I understand that because of the statute of limitations problem you have requested that it be included. Therefore, we will do so, but I want to reiterate that the course we are following here is in no way related to any potential lawsuit, and I want you to be absolutely clear about that.

It was absolutely clear to John that the city's proposal was, in fact, a direct response to his threatened lawsuit and that the mayor was just covering his butt.

The city began installing the MDT units at the agreed-upon rate of twenty-five per month in February 1997. A year later, John found out that the computers were still being installed at the minimum rate. He also learned that some of the computers were going into patrol cars that didn't answer 911 calls, and that many of the installed units weren't usable because a glitch in the system's software artificially limited to 400 the number of MDTs that could be operational at any one time. The city had 800 patrol cars.

John called everyone from the mayor to the new police commissioner, John F. Timoney, about the problems. Only the commissioner took his call, saying there was nothing they could do until the computer software glitch was fixed. In the meantime, the city was living up to the letter of its agreement, which promised only that the MDTs would be installed, not that they would be operational.

According to the city, the software problem has since been fixed.

In August 1998, *The Philadelphia Inquirer* ran a front-page story on the city's reconstituted 911 system, touting the $11 million spent on new facilities, better training, and 400 MDTs installed in patrol cars. The article quoted city officials hailing it as "a system geared to preventing another Polec." They invoked Eddie's name, but no one thanked his dad. And that was okay with John. "It's Ed who should be remembered," he said, "not me."

In September 1998, the city officially dedicated its brand-new "911 Emergency Communications Center." About one hundred people—City Council members, community activists, and telephone and computer company executives—toured the rebuilt radio room on the second floor of the Roundhouse. Said the *Inquirer:* "John and Kathy Polec have waged a noble and sometimes bitterly impatient campaign to improve 911 communications by installing laptop computers in patrol cars. Thanks largely to the Polecs' urging, those PCs are now in 459 of the department's 800 patrol cars, with 150 more soon to be installed." But John and Kathy Polec were not invited to the dedication of the new facilities.

Billy Polec kept it together for nearly two years after Eddie's death. With the exception of the weeks immediately after the murder, he went to school every day. During the trial, he took his books to the Criminal Justice Center and studied in Courtroom Bill while waiting to testify.

Attending Cardinal Dougherty on an academic scholarship, he made the honor roll every semester, carrying a full load of advance-placement courses. "My brilliant little brother," Eddie had always called him, "the brain of the family."

But by the beginning of his junior year, Bill was clearly depressed. He was having trouble concentrating on classes that once would have been a breeze for him. He was losing his drive, his motivation to do the best he could. What did it matter? he thought. What did anything matter? Look what happened to Eddie. Sitting watching TV with his dad one night, he suddenly blurted out, "The first fourteen years of my life might have been the best I'll ever have." John thought that was the saddest statement he could possibly hear from a kid who had the personality and intelligence to take the world by storm.

When the news came that the D.A.'s office had closed the case, Billy took it hardest of all. That night, after Charlie Gallagher and Joe Casey had gone, John and Billy sat for hours in the basement while Billy poured out his thoughts. He felt angry all the time, he said, utterly powerless, as if he was bouncing from one event to another while other people called the shots over his life. Strangers decided to end his brother's life; bureaucrats decided not to punish anyone else for Eddie's death. He was simply existing, in a world without sense. John knew the feeling.

Billy said he'd give just about anything to be anonymous again, for people to look at him the same way they did any other sixteen-year-old. But everywhere he went, people recognized him and knew about Eddie. He was proud to be Eddie's brother, but he hated the looks, the sympathy part. He just couldn't imagine continuing to live this way.

"What would you like to do to make your life more bearable?" John asked. Billy couldn't think of anything. All he knew was that the only time he felt any respite, the only time he felt in control and at peace, was when he was skiing. Billy had gone skiing twice in the past two years and his room was now filled with skiing magazines. There was something about being alone on the slopes, he said, with the cold wind in his face and the long, clean runs of snow out in front of him, that made him forget what had happened. It reminded him, if only for a few moments, that life could be joyful and free, as Eddie had taught him.

Just talking about skiing seemed to lift his spirits, and the conversation drifted to lighter topics, like what friends were planning to do for the holidays. Billy mentioned that Brian Carey was thinking about going to Montana in January to visit a neighbor who was attending college there. Brian was a former boyfriend of Kristie's who had become fast friends with Eddie when they all worked together at Boston Chicken. He was four years older than Eddie, but the two were kindred spirits. Since the murder, Brian had taken Billy under his wing, stopping by the house to see him whenever he came home from Penn State, treating him like his own kid brother. For Billy, Brian filled a part of the void left by Eddie's death.

"Why don't you see if you could go with Brian?" John asked. "You'd not only get away from here for a while, you'd get to ski the Rockies."

The words were out of his mouth before he realized what he was saying. John had always conferred with Kathy in advance on any decisions involving the kids. Plus, Billy was in the middle of his junior year in high school; he couldn't just skip out West on the spur of the moment. And what parent in their right mind would let a sixteen-year-old traipse off on a trip with a twenty-two-year-old?

He was relieved when Billy shrugged it off. "Nah," he said. "I'd never go. But thanks anyway."

The next morning Billy seemed like a different person. "Options, Dad," he explained. "Just knowing there's an option, even if I have no plans to take you up on it, makes today a lot easier to face than yesterday."

For weeks thereafter, he talked about Brian's trip and how interesting and exciting it all seemed. But he always ended the conversation by saying, "Don't worry, I'm not thinking of going."

After Christmas came and went, Billy's spirits sagged again. He was just going through the motions. His grades were good, but he got no satisfaction from them. He was just living for the day when he finished school and never had to go back.

This time it was Kathy who spoke: "Bill, why don't you go with Brian?" She couldn't believe what she was saying. She'd already lost one son, and now she was sending her youngest, the baby of the family, out into the world on his own. But as hard as it was for her to let him go, it was harder to watch him wither in place.

So Billy went. He left home on January 28, 1997, exactly sixteen years, six months, and three weeks from the day he was born—the same age exactly that Eddie had been when he left home for the last time.

Billy and Brian Carey traveled 23,000 miles in the winter and spring of 1997, driving as far north as Alaska and as far south as Los

Angeles. Much of the time they skied the mountains of Montana, where Bill fell in love with the Western sky and discovered how to be Eddie Polec's brother without anyone feeling sorry for him.

By the time he returned to Philadelphia, in May 1997, he was older than Eddie ever got to be. He never returned to Cardinal Dougherty High. Instead, with the help of the school's principal, Father Paul Kennedy, he took courses at St. Joseph's University and obtained his high school diploma in June 1998, on time. He's now majoring in forestry and he hopes to become a ranger with the National Park Service, somewhere in the Rockies.

Kristie went back to college in March 1996, determined not to sink into self-pity. Whenever she got down, she said to herself, "No matter how hard it is for me, it was harder for Eddie. He's the one who was taken; he's the one who suffered the most."

Unlike Billy, Kristie found solace in her classes. In a theology course she studied the Book of Job and began to formulate what would become her life's philosophy: "Every day every one of us is tested, and every day we make choices. I could be bitter or violent or say I'm never going to be the same again. But I'm choosing to go forward, to prove to everyone that even if you go through hell on earth you can still choose to be good."

Inspired by Joe Casey and Kathy Boyle, she changed her major from accounting to social work. In the fall of her senior year she returned to the Criminal Justice Center, where she worked for four months as an intern for Families of Murder Victims. Now it was her job to help grieving families navigate the justice system. She explained complicated courtroom procedures, told them what to expect each step of the way, and provided the tissues for their tears. She never told anyone who she was, but some figured it out anyway. A few tried to comfort her in the midst of their own grief. "No," she told them. "I'm here for you; you don't have to take care of me."

In May 1997, she graduated with honors, winning an award for achieving the highest grade point average in her major. "I want to prove that I can make something of myself," she told people, "because Ed always boasted about me and I don't want to let him down. I want him to be proud of me, and I want to be proud of myself."

After graduation, she went to computer programming school, and in December 1997, at age twenty-two, she took a full-time job as a software developer at a Philadelphia investment company. She hopes to attend law school someday.

Kristie and Bill still visit the cemetery, although they don't wrestle on Eddie's grave anymore. And during Pearl Jam's 1998 concert in Philadelphia, the two remaining Polec children jumped to their feet and sang together at the top of their lungs when the band played "Alive."

Ed's friends continue to visit John and Kathy often, filling them in on the big and little details of their lives. On the second anniversary of Ed's murder, his friends held a memorial service at St. Cecilia's. A thousand people attended, including Joe Casey, who sat alone in the last row of pews.

Colleen McGovern, Ellie Stefano, Lisa Mahoney, Maryann Redlinger, and Bernadette Dietrich presented John and Kathy with a small brass Celtic cross.

At the end of the service, a bagpipe player led a procession of young people to a grassy plot in front of the church, where they planted a large wooden cross ten feet from where Eddie was beaten. Crafted by John Anastasia, a neighborhood carpenter, the cross remains there today, dedicated to the kids of Fox Chase and inscribed with a line from the Beatitudes: *Blessed are the Peacemakers.*

After the trial and sentencing, Kathy returned to her job as a crossing guard. For a long time she drifted, but her friends kept pulling her back. Her corner often seemed like the set of *Cheers*. Clare McClosky brought coffee; Ron Carey provided lunch; Isabelle, who worked at the library, gave her a new book every week; Chris Regel came around just to talk. When she got home, if John or the kids weren't there, someone else was—Mary Ellen Douglass, Terry Gara, Linda Baraniewicz, Kathy Goodwin, Cass Spoerl, Jerry and Pat Esack. They were determined to keep her in the world of the living. And it worked.

In the summer she volunteered at the Eddie Polec Memorial Soccer Camp, headed by his former gym teacher from St. Cecilia's. Teenage counselors ran the camp, but she helped to get the kids water, took them to the bathroom, and generally made a fuss over them.

In the fall and spring she helped Matt McDonald with Fox Chase Champions, a soccer camp for physically and mentally handicapped children. She led the kids through their warm-ups, stretching along with them to a recording of "Mickey Mouse-ercise" and dancing the hokey-pokey. She taught some of her fancy footwork to three of the blind campers who played the game by following a beeping soccer ball.

While John fought the external battles, Kathy waged an internal war. She continued therapy, learned to meditate, and spent as many hours as possible in her garden, where she found ways to be with Eddie. It was no longer an agonizing journey; it was a source of deep pleasure. Watching the chipmunks scurrying around, she could see him as he had been on a long-ago October day, trying to save a mortally injured squirrel. Then she would sense him coming to stand beside her. At such times, she knew there was a part of her that would never lose him.

Kathy also connected with John again. In the months after the murder she was searching so hard for Eddie that she'd lost sight of him. But as she got stronger, she realized that it was John who had pulled them all through, who'd kept the family together. She was proud of how he kept fighting, not just for their family, but to make things right.

For three years they hadn't really talked to each other about what had happened. It was too painful. Neither wanted to cause the other discomfort; neither wanted to bring on the tears. But gradually the walls came down.

They took an impromptu vacation in the summer of 1998. They

headed up the New Jersey Turnpike with no particular destination in mind, wound up in Maine, and decided to visit Nova Scotia, just to see what it looked like. While they were there, they decided to take a white-water rafting trip. Actually, Kathy decided and John reluctantly went along. He'd never much liked water and wasn't a great swimmer. "I'll do it just to prove how much I love you," he joked.

For nearly two hours, a guide took them and a group of other vacationers on the ride of their lives. Seated in the bow with his feet hooked firmly in stirrups, John was thrilled as they rode the rapids, holding on for dear life, soaked to the skin. Looking back, he saw Kathy in the stern, laughing and shrieking like a kid on a roller coaster. He knew then that she was finally her old self again.

Moments later, the raft hit a dip and slammed head-on into a huge wall of water. From the back, Kathy saw John go over. Her heart froze, and she leaped from her seat and hurtled over the others to the front of the raft. John's feet were still in the stirrups, but the rest of him was submerged in the swirling water. He was face-up, and she could see his eyes, wide-open. The raft was bucking and pitching. She planted her feet and took a deep breath, then bent over the bow, grabbed him by the life vest, and hauled him back on board.

"Boy, you must love him a lot," one of the other women said. Partly to calm herself and partly to cover John's embarrassment, Kathy wise-cracked, "Nah, I couldn't let him go, because he's got the car keys."

They ate dinner at a Pizza Hut that night. Sitting across the table from John, laughing and talking, Kathy thought he looked the same as he had when they were high school sweethearts, kissing on the front porch. And she remembered that John was there first. Everything had started with him. And he was still there. They were all still there. Eddie, too.

ACKNOWLEDGMENTS

We wish to thank:

Alice Martell, our friend and agent-for-life, who believed in this book from the very beginning.

Becky Saletan, our patient editor at Farrar, Straus & Giroux, who helped shape it in the end.

Bryn's former colleagues at WTXF in Philadelphia—Roger LeMay and John Mussoni, who allowed her to cover the Polec trial from voir dire to verdict, and Cathie Abookire, who never tired of listening to her scripts.

"The J-Girls"—Lu Ann Cahn, Marisol Bello, Linda Lloyd, and Margie Smith—classy competitors who kept Bryn company on the beat, and later gave of their time whenever we needed a fact, a picture, or a memory.

Our buddy Jim Nolan of the Philadelphia *Daily News,* whose writing and reporting are always an inspiration and whose assistance was invaluable.

Tommy Gibbons of *The Philadelphia Inquirer.*

Garrett Feldman, our excellent assistant at USA Broadcasting and the first person to read the manuscript.

Peggy Callahan and Fred Farrar, Bryn's former bosses at Fox News

Channel, who let her work when she needed to and write when she had to.

Our dear friend Brian Ann Zoccola, who helped organize a mountain of notes and transcripts, and provided insightful feedback on the manuscript.

The guys in Two Squad—especially Tom Perks, Art Mee, and Bill Danks—who spent hours with us patiently recounting details of the investigation, and whose kindness, humor, and integrity give police officers everywhere a good name.

Defense attorneys Janis Smarro and A. Charles Peruto.

Eddie's friends—Ellie Stephano, Colleen McGovern, Lisa Mahoney, Bernadette Dietrich, and Nick DiCarli—who endured painful interviews to help us get him down just right.

The Polecs' friends and family—especially Pat and Jerry Esack, Mary Ellen Douglass, Kathy Goodwin, and Linda Baraniewicz—who shared their memories and their coffee.

The Polec family—John, Kathy, Kristie, and Billy—who trusted us with their story and inspired us with their humanity.

Eddie Polec, whom we never met but came to know and love.

And finally, our son, Colin, who waited patiently so many nights while Mommy and Daddy wrote "just one more page."